# THIRD EDITION

# HAIRDRESSING
## FOR NVQ 1 AND 2

### Bob Woodhouse

## Hodder & Stoughton
A MEMBER OF THE HODDER HEADLINE GROUP

The author and publishers would like to thank the following individuals and institutions for permission to reproduce copyright material.

West Kent College, Tonbridge, Kent and photographer David Guy for the following photographs: 4.2, 4.3, 4.4, 4.5, 4.6, 4.7, 4.8, 4.9, 4.10, 4.11, 4.12, 4.14, 5.1, 5.5, 5.35, 5.36, 5.37, 5.38, 5.39, 5.40, 5.41, 5.42, 5.49, 5.51, 5.74, 5.75, 5.76, 5.77, 5.83, 5.85, 6.2, 6.3, 6.4, 6.5, 6.6, 6.7, 6.8, 6.9, 6.10, 6.11, 6.12, 6.19, 6.20, 6.31, 6.32, 6.34, 6.36, 6.37, 6.38, 6.43, 6.68, 6.77, 6.82, 7.36, 7.37, 7.38, 7.39, 7.40, 7.41, 7.42, 7.43, 7.44, 7.45, 7.46, 8.11, 8.20, 8.21, 8.22, 8.23, 8.24, 8.25, 8.26, 8.30, 8.31, 8.32, 8.33, 8.34, 8.35, 8.38, 8.41, 9.1, 9.2, 12.2.

The following originally appeared in *Milady's Standard Textbook of Cosmetology*, © 1994 Milady Publishing Company (a division of Delmar Publishers Inc.) Photographers: Michael A Gallitelli, Steven Landis, Eric Von Lockhart, Gillette Research Institute, New Image's Salon System. Figures 3.1, 3.30, 3.31, 3.32, 3.33, 3.34, 3.35, 3.36, 3.37, 5.3, 5.4, 5.6, 5.8, 5.9, 5.10, 5.11, 5.14, 6.58, 6.59, 6.60, 6.61, 6.62, 7.2, 7.3, 7.4, 7.5, 7.10, 7.12, 7.14, 7.15, 7.16, 7.17, 7.20, 7.23, 7.25, 7.26, 7.27, 7.30, 7.31, 7.32, 7.33, 8.1, 8.13, 8.14, 8.15, 8.16, 8.17, 8.36, 8.39, 8.40, 8.43, 8.44, 8.47, 8.48, 8.49, 8.50, 8.51, 8.52, 10.5, 12.1, 13.11, 13.12, 13.13, 13.27.

Additional photographs - B.D.I. Images: 1.5, 2.1, 2.2, 2.3, 2.4, 10.1, 10.2, 10.3, 10.4, 11.1, 11.2, 11.3, 11.4, 12.3; David Sparrow: 5.2; Pat Dudley, Claude Hannaert, and staff and students from Kingston College: 5.7, 5.80, 5.81, 6.21-6.30, 7.47, 13.8; Prestige Medical: 1.4; Science Photo Library: 13.19; The National Medical Slide Bank/The Wellcome Trust: 13.16, 13.17, 13.18, 13.20, 13.26, 13.28.

Every effort has been made to obtain necessary permission with reference to copyright material. The publishers apologise if inadvertently any sources remain unacknowledged and will be glad to make the necessary arrangements at the earliest opportunity.

Orders: please contact Bookpoint Ltd, 130 Milton Park, Abingdon, Oxon OX14 4SB. Telephone: (44) 01235 827720. Fax: (44) 01235 400454. Lines are open from 9.00–6.00, Monday to Saturday, with a 24-hour message answering service. You can also order through our website www.hodderheadline.co.uk.

*British Library Cataloguing in Publication Data*
A catalogue record for this title is available from the British Library

ISBN 0 340 81494 2

Second Edition Published 2000
This Edition Published 2004
Impression number   10 9 8 7 6 5 4 3 2 1
Year                2007 2006 2005 2004 2003 2002 2001

Cover photo from Stone/Getty
Typeset by Fakenham Photosetting Limited, Fakenham, Norfolk
Printed in Italy for Hodder & Stoughton Educational, a division of Hodder Headline Plc, 338 Euston Road, London NW1 3BH

# Contents

# Introduction

## How to use this book

You may use this book either as a reference text, a self-study aid or a support for guided learning. If used as a reference book, the contents list and detailed index will support you in locating specific references or information that you seek. The book may be used as part of an integrated programme of professional development provided at your salon, college and/or training centre. The text within the book will provide you with guidance in competent performance and good practice. Illustrations provide support to your understanding and show clearly the practical tasks.

At the beginning of each chapter the relevant elements of the Level 1 and 2 Hairdressing and Barbering awards are stated. Within each chapter icons are used next to the main headings to direct you to the relevant text for the award for which you are studying. If you wish, you can read all of the text. However, you may wish to focus on only those areas that are especially relevant to you.

Text that is not connected to an icon is relevant to all of the awards. Text specifically for Hairdressing Level 1 is indicated by the icon, text for Hairdressing Level 2 by the icon and text for Barbering Level 2 by the icon.

Within each chapter of the book you are provided with guidance in activities that will further develop your skills and enhance your understanding. In some chapters there are Key Skill tasks. These are designed to help you to produce evidence to achieve relevant aspects of the Key Skills as part of your Modern Apprenticeship programme. The exact nature of what can be achieved will depend upon what activities you undertake as part of the task. You should discuss this with your assessor before you undertake any activity. Questions are provided to allow you to test your knowledge gained from the section, and model answers are included at the end of the book. Remember, you cheat only yourself if you review the answers before undertaking the self reviews.

Also towards the end of the book, the Glossary provides an alphabetical listing of useful words and their meanings.

## How to undertake assessment of skills

National Vocational Qualifications (NVQs) and Scottish Vocational Qualifications (SVQs) are achieved through the confirmation of your competence, knowledge and understanding across specified criteria and situations. They require evidence of competence that is generated mainly through real work activity. The most frequently used method of assessment for hairdressing skills is by the observation of these activities and their results as they occur in the salon. This is effective in confirming that the competence of the candidate is current and relevant to the part of the award being assessed.

Alternatively, evidence of your performance can be provided through the presentation to your assessor of evidence of your activities through:

◆ testimony from your work colleagues

◆ your personal statement

- your responses to questioning

- a case study

- previous qualifications, relevant experience and achievement.

There are guidelines on good and acceptable practice in assessment; the awarding body often prescribes what methods are particularly suitable for different parts of the award. Discuss this with your tutor, trainers and/or assessor.

As an NVQ or SVQ candidate, you will negotiate the assessment of your competence with your allocated assessor. Your assessor will have current relevant hairdressing skills and a recognised assessor qualification. You will be guided towards undertaking assessment when it is expected that you are competent.

Before undertaking assessment you will plan with your assessor how and when this will take place. The detail agreed will include:

- how evidence will be presented – most frequently by you undertaking a task that is observed by your assessor

- the task that will produce appropriate evidence

- the units and elements of the award against which you are to be assessed

- when the assessment will occur – this may be a single event or a number of events that occur over a period of time

- when progress or achievement will be reviewed.

It is important that you fully understand what you are expected to do before you undertake assessment.

During an observation of your performance your assessor will encourage you to undertake the task while s/he is unobtrusive but able to observe effectively. As soon as is practicable following the assessment your assessor will provide you with feedback, and confirm and record the outcome of the assessment.

In the unlikely event that you feel the assessment has been undertaken inappropriately or the assessment decision is unfair, you should discuss this with your assessor. Assessment centres have guidelines in how to make an appeal if you believe you have been unfairly treated within assessment.

## How to achieve the award

You will achieve the full NVQ or SVQ award when your assessor has confirmed your competence in all of the required units of the award and this has been quality assured through the process of internal verification. Internal verification includes sampling the assessment process, including the support that you have received, the appropriateness of the decisions made and the prompt processing of the records.

You may wish to gain recognition for only specific units of the award, in preference to the full award. A certificate of unit credit may be claimed for completed units.

# Further and complementary qualifications

There is a range of NVQs/SVQs that are relevant to the hairdressing industry and that can support your further development and recognise the achievement of competence. As your role within the salon develops, you will most probably find the Level 3 Hairdressing award is a natural progression. You may wish to consider their appropriateness for your continued development.

There are NVQs/SVQs that apply to roles often undertaken in close relationship to hairdressing, including Beauty Therapy. Appropriate awards that confirm competence and are not specific to hairdressing but applicable to a wide range of organisations include Customer Service, Management and Business Development. Achievement of the award is dependent upon you the candidate being able to present evidence of competent work-based performance, and therefore requires you to be in the job role or at least in a position to undertake that role.

If you aspire to a role but are not yet within that role, or do not have access to the role, you may consider alternative qualifications that are based upon achievement through examination of knowledge and simulated or non-work-based activity. The achievement of these qualifications can provide an indication of the potential for performance when placed into the job role.

# The roles of HTB and HABIA in developing and maintaining standards

The author recognises the contribution that the Hairdressing Training Board (HTB) has made in the identification and development associated with the national standards. The HTB is part of the National Training Organisation – the Hairdressing and Beauty Industry Authority (HABIA). This is the independent, employer-led sector organisation recognised by the Department for Education and Skills for working with the hairdressing and beauty therapy sectors and government across education and training throughout the whole of Great Britain. It is mainly concerned with:

◆ identifying shortages in skills and the training needs for beauty and hairdressing

◆ influencing the provision of education and careers guidance

◆ developing the occupational standards, including NVQs/SVQs

◆ advising on training arrangements and their provision

◆ communicating effectively with employers and key partners to implement their plans.

As national standards of competence and the qualifications they are based upon are reviewed to ensure that they continue to be relevant to the needs of the industry, the structure and content of National Vocational Qualifications and Scottish Vocational Qualifications may differ from the descriptions within this text. You are advised to seek clarification and confirmation from your assessor.

# Working safely

## WHAT THIS CHAPTER WILL PROVIDE

The information in this chapter affects all other areas in the book. An important part of the efficient running of the hairdressing salon is the timely provision of relevant equipment in a safe and hygienic way that will enable hairdressers and technicians to work effectively. This chapter helps you become aware of current legislation and people's responsibility for health and safety while at work in the salon. It also describes how to prepare for hairdressing services and the maintenance of the salon work areas. Guidance is given in how to undertake a review of your salon, including indicators of good salon practice as well as some of the health and safely hazards that may be present and the risk they present.

# The Health and Safety at Work Act 1974 (HASAWA)

This is a legal obligation placed on all people at work. Within the hairdressing salon this includes salon owners, managers, team leaders, stylists, technicians, trainees, receptionists and those undertaking work experience. In fact it includes all people who work in the salon, whether full or part time, employed, self-employed or volunteers. The Act states that:

♦ the employer has a duty of care to employees and others within the salon, or those affected by the work of the salon

♦ employees have a duty not to intentionally endanger the health, safety and welfare of themselves or others

♦ employees must not interfere with or misuse any items provided in the pursuance of health and safety.

# Health and safety

If managed effectively, the hairdressing salon should be a safe and enjoyable place within which to work. Most hairdressers enjoy a satisfying career that is relatively risk free. However, the maintenance of health and safety at work is the responsibility of everyone. Safety legislation requires that all employers should provide a safe working environment and as an employee you have a responsibility to work within the guidelines of safety for the salon. Currently, if your salon staff team has five or more people in it, there will be a written health and safety policy. This will give you guidance about:

◆ who is responsible within the salon for aspects of health and safety

◆ reporting accidents

◆ first aid procedures

◆ emergency procedures.

You may receive training about health and safety and the particular provisions and procedures for your salon. Some features of safe working may be common sense but may not be apparent to all.

Features for safe working practice within your salon include the following.

◆ Wet floors can be slippery: always mop up spillages of liquids immediately.

◆ Hair can make floor surfaces slippery; sweep up hair clippings and place in a covered bin.

◆ Equipment provided for use in an emergency can save lives: do not tamper with fire extinguishers or other safety items.

◆ Easy unobstructed access may be required at any time in the salon; do not block doorways, emergency exits or stairways. Do not leave items on a staircase. Remember that low-level obstructions may cause people to trip and hurt themselves.

◆ To reduce the risk of using incorrect products do not decant products into unmarked or incorrectly marked containers.

◆ If you are unaware of how to use products and equipment correctly, always seek advice or read the manufacturer's directions.

◆ Before using electrical equipment check for any obvious damage to the casing, flex or plug connections. Any identified damage to equipment should be reported to the responsible person and that item taken out of use until checked and repaired.

◆ Do not trail electrical cables across walkways in the salon as these are a hazard for people who could trip over them or need to pull equipment over them which, in turn, may cause injury.

◆ Take care when moving stock and equipment. Lift heavy items with your

◼ Figure 1.1 Always lift heavy items in the correct manner

◼ Figure 1.2 Do not over-extend yourself when handling stock above head height

back straight (see Figure 1.1), bending at the knees. Do not attempt to lift more than you can reasonably cope with; if in doubt, seek assistance. If stock must be obtained from shelves above eye level, stand on appropriate steps only; do not over-extend yourself, risking strain or a fall (see Figure 1.2).

### HEALTH & SAFETY

Some fluids may be poisonous; alcohol-based fluids may be flammable or produce flammable vapour.

◆ Only use products or equipment that produce toxic fumes in suitably ventilated areas. Some cleaning fluids and electrical massage machines produce varying levels of potentially toxic fumes. Disposal of some chemicals and products directly into waste pipes can result in contamination as well as a reaction causing rapid discharge back out of the pipes. Sharp implements that may be contaminated with bodily fluids should be disposed of within a 'sharps' box, which is then disposed of professionally.

◆ Always follow salon guidelines in working practices. These will have been tested and approved for use in the salon. Failure to follow these guidelines may result in injury to yourself or others, and may cause difficulty in providing a remedy if the exact nature of the cause of an injury is not known.

### Self review

In the diagram below there are a number of unsafe practices; can you find them? Answers are provided in the Model answers section on page 285.

# What you should know

◆ The identity of the people responsible for health and safety in your salon and how to contact them. This information may be provided during your induction or stated within your salon's health and safety guidelines.

◆ Any specific responsibilities that you have regarding health and safety. These may be stated in your terms and conditions of employment or your job description.

◆ Any policies and procedures which are relevant to you. These may include processes for reporting and recording hazards or injuries, or the use of protective gloves when handling hazardous products. More information is provided in the next section.

◆ Any aspects of your particular job which are hazardous to yourself and/or others. Follow guidance, provided during your training and induction, about correct and safe working practices. Hazardous working practices may include moving heavy or cumbersome objects around the salon, the use of electrical tools, the use of cutting equipment, and the use of hairdressing products.

■ Figure 1.3 Unsafe practices

◆ Any hazards within the salon which could harm you or others, for example staircases, blind corners, projecting furniture and inward-opening doors.

# REMEMBER!

*If you are in any doubt ask your manager or supervisor for guidance.*

# KEY WORDS

**Hazard** – *something with the potential to cause harm*
**Risk** – *the likelihood of a hazard's potential being realised*

# KEY SKILL TASK

*This task could produce evidence that supports C1.1, C1.3, N1.2, & N1.3. Produce a risk assessment for your salon. Everywhere we work there are hazards. The purposes of the assessment are to:*

◆ *identify as many hazards as possible*
◆ *measure the risk of someone getting hurt by these either through correct or incorrect behaviour or use*
◆ *where there is a high risk, look for ways of reducing the risk to an acceptable level or removing the hazard.*

1 *Within your salon identify as many hazards as possible. Hazards may include staircases, door and cupboard openings, low or narrow openings, projecting shelves, equipment, trailing leads, products and chemicals. You may wish to show the location of the hazards on a floor plan of the salon.*
2 *Consider each hazard and calculate the likelihood of someone being hurt by it, both in correct use and incorrect use. Award each hazard a score or rating, for example 1 = very low risk, 2 = medium risk, and 3 = high risk.*
3 *For those hazards with a score or rating of 3, state how the risk can be reduced. This may be by using warning signs, producing guidance in correct and safe working, or by removing or modifying the hazard.*
*Before undertaking these tasks discuss your plans with your manager or supervisor.*

## Your salon's policies and procedures

Some salons have written policies and procedures about working practice and emergency procedures. These are often included in a staff handbook or posted on the staff noticeboard. Most salons will also have policies and procedures that are unwritten but communicated verbally. Some salons have a combination of both. While verbal communication is often more effective, having written guidelines can be useful when you wish to refer to them at a later date. If you are in any doubt about policies and procedures in your salon discuss this with your supervisor or manager. It is very likely your salon will have policies and procedures for the following areas.

1   Safe working methods, regarding the salon's preferred methods of providing services to clients and using equipment.

2   Handling, using and storing products including perm lotion, hydrogen peroxide, cleaning products, etc. Some products should only be handled using protective gloves. Persistent unprotected handling can cause adverse skin conditions, for example dermatitis (see Chapter 13). Some products should not be stored next to each other as they can react dangerously when in contact.

3   Storing and eating food and drink; rules and guidelines relating to smoking, consuming and working under the influence of alcohol and/or drugs.

4   A dress code – either a uniform or overall with the same or similar style being worn by everyone. As a member of the salon team you can project an image that infers to clients what style of hairdressing is provided. There may be guidance in acceptable hairstyles, levels of make-up and jewellery to be worn.

5   What to do in an emergency. Emergencies should be reported to your manager as quickly as possible. Emergencies may include any of the following.

   i   **Fire.** Your salon may have a fire alarm system, which should be sounded. A minor fire may be dealt with using the correct fire extinguisher. All fires should be reported promptly to the responsible person in the business. If in any doubt, the salon should be evacuated and the emergency fire service called.

 *HEALTH & SAFETY*

If you discover a fire and are in any doubt, call the emergency fire service.

   ii   **Flood.** Report to a designated person, who will turn off the water supply at the mains, and using dry hands turn off any electrical appliances that may be wet. If water has flooded through the ceiling, electrical circuits may have been affected, so turn off the electricity supply at the mains.

   iii   **Bomb alert.** Report any notification directly to your manager or supervisor. This could result in the evacuation of the premises and the authorities being informed.

   iv   **Gas leak.** Report to a designated person, who will turn off the gas supply, both at the appliance and at the mains (by the meter). Open windows, vacate the salon and report the leak to the local gas suppliers using their emergency number. Take care not to use a telephone (including mobile phones) in the affected area. Do not look for the gas leak using a naked light, nor turn on electric switches or use electrical machines, as this may cause a spark which could ignite the gas.

   v   **Suspicious persons and packages.** Any person acting suspiciously should be reported to the salon manager or your supervisor. It may not always be wise to approach a person acting in a suspicious manner; depending on the circumstances, it may be necessary to call the police or a security guard for assistance. This will normally be a management decision. Suspicious packages should always be reported to your manager.

The extent of your actions will depend upon your own personal level of responsibility which may be defined in the salon's health and safety policy statement. Advice should be sought from your manager.

## KEY SKILL TASK

*This task could produce evidence that supports C1.3, N1.2, & N1.3.*
*Produce a floor plan (using a simple scale) of your salon, showing the location of*
*emergency fire equipment, first aid boxes and exits.*

# Keeping the salon ready for hairdressing services

## Daily preparation

Each hairdressing salon has its own requirements when preparing for the working day. Your supervisor will provide you with guidance in this and you will become accustomed to the preferences and specific working patterns of each stylist. The cleaning of your salon may be undertaken by specialist cleaners or by the staff team. A level of cleaning and removal of hair waste, etc. will occur throughout the working day. Guidance in good hygiene and cleaning practice is provided later in this chapter.

Generally, at the end or beginning of the working day, salons replenish all consumable items. It may also be necessary to replenish at stages throughout the day. Do not allow supplies to run out as this can cause unnecessary delays for the client. Check levels of consumable supplies throughout the day and top up as required. Obtain your supervisor's permission to do this. Consumables will include:

◆ towels and gowns or capes (for hygiene, towels should be laundered between each use)

◆ tissues and cotton wool

◆ shampoos, restocking of dispensers and other at-the-basin products

◆ dressing table/work-station supplies, such as sterilising liquids, hair fixing sprays and styling products

◆ retail products.

Obtain permission before removing items from the stock room as these may be monitored.

## Products and tools

For any task to be undertaken effectively the requisite products and tools should be made available at the right time and in the correct sequence. A stylist may guide you in what s/he will require for each task. With time you should be able to prepare most items based upon your knowledge and experience from previous similar tasks.

The salon's appointment schedule will provide a useful reference in determining what is likely to be required for the day.

## Useful hints

1    If a client has previously received a treatment at the salon there will be a record of this. This can be very useful when preparing for a follow-on treatment and for the stylist during the consultation with the client. Most salons keep records of the chemical processes they provide their clients. Some very efficient salons keep records of all of the services they provide their clients, as well as any retail sales that are made. These records may be located within a card index or on computer. Any records held about people, whether on a card index or computer, are subject to the Data Protection Act (see below). You may need permission to access these records. Take care not to leave them lying around for others to read or to become misplaced.

> ## REMEMBER!
>
> *Your salon will have guidelines in how client information is used and what can be disclosed to others. If in any doubt ask your supervisor for guidance.*

2    Do not prepare products solely based upon the previous treatment record as the consultation may change the requirements.

3    Do not mix products too early, for example tint, as it may lose its strength before it is used.

4    Check the condition of the tools that you prepare, for example perm curler rubbers.

5    Have sufficient materials ready so that there is no delay during the delivery of the service.

6    Ensure that all equipment is stored away clean, ready for its next use.

### Useful Task

Make a chart of the services that your salon provides and for which you prepare. Within the chart list the range and quantity of equipment and products usually required. Check your findings with your supervisor.

# Data Protection Act 1998

This Act requires all organisations that hold data (personal information about living people) to register with the Information Commissioner.

The Act requires that data held by organisations should be:

◆    fairly and lawfully processed

◆    processed for limited purposes

◆    adequate, relevant and not excessive

◆    accurate

◆    not kept longer than necessary

◆    processed in accordance with the data subject's rights

◆ secure

◆ not transferred to other countries, without adequate protection.

Within the salon, data may be held about clients, staff and potential staff (job applicants). This data, whether stored electronically or in paper files, must be stored securely and its contents only communicated to authorised people. The salon determines who is authorised and will include this information in its registration with the Commissioner. The Commission provides guidelines in acceptable practice.

Those providing data must give their consent for its intended use. Each salon should have a person responsible (a compliance manager) for overseeing the collection, storage and processing of data, and ensuring that all staff are aware of their responsibilities for this.

# Salon hygiene

A hairdressing salon, due to the warm, moist atmosphere and the numbers of people who pass through the doors each day, is an ideal place for the spread of infection and contagious disorders. Section 77 of the Public Health Act 1961 empowers local authorities to make bye-laws for the registration of premises, and health and hygiene within them. These bye-laws may differ slightly between authorities, but they are all legally enforceable.

◆ Hygiene within the salon is not only a legal requirement; it is highly desirable from everybody's point of view. Your clients visiting the salon will wish to feel safe from the risk of infection. As someone employed in the salon, and therefore spending much of your time in this environment, you too will wish to feel safe, and the salon owner will view hygiene as an essential aspect for successful business.

◆ It is not always satisfactory just to be hygienic: your clients must see that this is the case. This will be reflected by the hygienic behaviour of all staff in the salon, and the high profile given to hygiene. There are three aspects to cleanliness and hygiene in the salon:

➤ premises and provisions for hygiene

➤ tools and equipment

➤ those employed or working in the salon.

## Premises and provisions for hygiene

All surfaces should be easy to clean. This includes work surfaces, basins, walls and floors. Hair clippings can be difficult to remove from textured surfaces. Floors should be swept daily and cleaned at least once a week. Spillages should be cleaned away immediately. Take care to dispose of contaminated cleaning items correctly. If in doubt, seek advice.

---

# REMEMBER!

*If your job is to clean surfaces and to empty bins, look on this as part of the team's work to maintain the correct environment for your clients. Remember, your clients will not be impressed by floors that are littered with hair or bins which are full to overflowing.*

There should be covered bins for hair clippings and other waste materials, and these should be emptied once full, and at least once a day.

# REMEMBER!

*When cleaning work surfaces using cleaning products, always follow the manufacturer's directions, including the use of protective clothing if required. Products used for cleaning and sterilising surfaces are sometimes flammable.*

## Tools and equipment

Gowns and towels used on your clients should be freshly washed before use. Tools should be washed and sterilised between use on your clients. In the salon you will find a range of methods used to sterilise tools. These include autoclaves, ultra-violet light cabinets and sterilising fluids.

### The autoclave

This produces steam at high pressure, allowing high temperatures to be achieved (see Figure 1.4). Due to the high temperatures used, the autoclave is only suitable for use on tools which are not damaged by heat. It is therefore not suitable for use on vulcanite or plastic combs, scissors with plastic inserts or for hairbrushes.

Take care when using an autoclave. Always follow the manufacturer's directions for safe use. The outer casing will usually become hot, and you should always allow adequate time for the pressure within to drop, and the temperature to drop, before opening to remove tools.

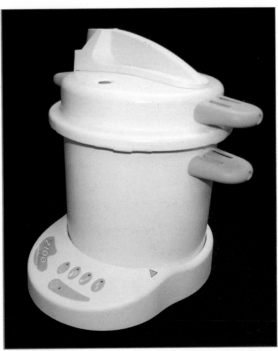

◼ Figure 1.4 An autoclave, used to sterilise tools in a salon

# KEY WORDS

**Disinfecting** – *making free of infections and removing bacteria*
**Sterilising** – *making totally free of living germs*

### Ultra-violet cabinet

This cabinet uses ultra-violet light to sterilise those surfaces that the light rays touch (see Figure 1.5). As a result it is only effective for tools that can be totally exposed to the light on all surfaces; it may be necessary to turn tools to ensure full coverage. To sterilise effectively, tools must be clean and dry when placed in these cabinets. You should not expose yourself to this light.

### Sterilising fluids

These are possibly the most widely used means for sterilising tools in the hairdressing salon. Tools should be cleaned before being immersed in the fluids. Fluids should be changed regularly as they:

◆ rapidly lose their strength; some have colour detectors to indicate their strength

◆ lose their efficiency when the fluid becomes dirty.

Some fluids attack the surface of metallic tools and may make cutting tools blunt. Aerosol sterilising fluids are available which are particularly useful with cutting tools. You should note that some fluids are disinfectants and not sterilisers.

Figure 1.5 UV cabinet, used to sterilise tools in a salon

 _HEALTH & SAFETY_

Follow the manufacturer's directions in the correct and safe use of sterilising equipment and products.

 REMEMBER!

_Before sterilising tools, always wash and dry them, as the presence of dirt, dust and moisture may impede the effects of the sterilising process._

## Those employed or working in the salon

Appropriate dress in the salon varies from high fashion to more protective wear. Your salon will have a dress code. It is anticipated that hairdressers will be dressed appropriately. Overalls or protective clothing should be washable and kept hygienic for use at work.

The Personal Protective Equipment at Work Regulations 1992 (PPE) requires that suitable protective equipment is provided for employees who may be exposed to risk while at work within the hairdressing salon. This usually means the provision of protective gloves for your use when handling perm lotion, hydrogen peroxide, tints and any other product where the manufacturer's directions indicate this. Protective goggles may also be required in certain circumstances.

 _HEALTH & SAFETY_

As an employee, you should report to your employer any loss or damage to personal protective equipment.

# The Control of Substances Hazardous to Health Regulations 2002 (COSHH)

Employers are required to consider potential hazards to people exposed to substances within the salon. The law requires all employers to review the potential risks for people from exposure to substances used in the salon. This includes assessing all substances for hazards, and for those that are hazardous either considering the use of alternative less hazardous substances, or setting up safe working procedures for use.

## Useful Tasks

1   Find out where the salon's first aid box is and if there is a trained first aider.

2   Find out what the procedures are for the safe evacuation of the salon in an emergency.

3   Produce a list of daily salon preparation tasks that could be used when introducing a new trainee to your salon.

## Self review

1.  Which method of sterilising in the salon uses moist heat at high pressure?

2.  How often should floor surfaces be swept?

3.  How should tools be prepared before being placed in an ultra-violet sterilising cabinet?

4.  How does the Data Protection Act impact on your salon's client records?

5.  What is the definition of a hazard?

6.  What is the definition of a risk?

7.  Do employees within the hairdressing salon have any responsibility towards health and safety?

8.  For what is a 'sharps' box used?

9.  How could you find out about your salon's health and safety procedures?

10. List three types of emergency that can occur within the salon.

## Useful contacts

BBC Health, Safety and Security Net        www.bbc.org.uk/ohss
HABIA                                      www.habia.org.uk
Hairdressing Beauty Suppliers Association  www.hbsa.uk.com
Health & Safety Executive                  www.hse.gov.uk
Information Commissioner                    www.dataprotection.gov.uk

CHAPTER 2

# Creating a positive image

## CHAPTER CONTENTS

**Unit G5**  Give clients a positive impression of yourself and
your organisation

### WHAT THIS CHAPTER WILL PROVIDE

This chapter will provide you with guidance in good practice in developing and maintaining positive
impressions of yourself and your salon to clients. Your client continues to visit the salon not only
because her or his hair is maintained but also because the experience is positive and enjoyable. Part of
the role of the hairdresser and everyone working within the salon is to project the appropriate image
to the client.

The impression you give of yourself will influence the client's perceptions of the salon and the service
it provides.

# Effective relationships with your clients

Your salon will project an image that is appropriate to the clients it targets. This image is conveyed
through the general look of the salon, its furniture, decoration, advertising and the appearance of its
staff. For example:

KEY SKILLS

- salons that target clients who are very avant-garde in their fashion choice will often have modern
  or futuristic furniture, the colours used in decoration will be strong and very fashionable,
  advertising will be placed in avant-garde publications or in places where fashion-conscious people are likely to
  visit, and staff will often project an avant-garde image themselves through clothes, make-up and hairstyles (see
  Figure 2.1 opposite)

- salons that target clients who are cost-conscious and want good value for money will often have functional but
  modern furniture, the colours used in decoration will often be neutral but well presented, they will advertise in
  ways that attract a wide range of types and styles of client, and staff will often project a neutral but fashionable
  appearance (see Figure 2.2 opposite).

12

Figure 2.1 An example of an avant-garde salon

Figure 2.2 An example of a functional, modern salon

When you first join the salon team find out if the salon has preferred:

◆ styles of staff dress or uniform – some salons provide a protective overall or uniform, others have themes of clothing, for example all black; often a uniform provides a level of protection for staff from chemicals and processes undertaken; some local authorities require that protective clothing be worn in the salon, not only to provide protection to staff members but also to provide levels of hygiene to protect clients

◆ hairstyles – some salons require staff to have their hair styled within the salon, acting as a living 'style book' as well as advertising the salon's work; often styling will include a relevant chemical process, hair colour or perm, and this can support the promotion of these services by demonstrating their impact

◆ make-up and jewellery – styles and amount of make-up may be guided by the salon and its image; some salons have guidelines regarding the wearing of excessive jewellery, others promote the wearing as a fashion statement

◆ accepted standards of behaviour and language – when you first join the salon take time to find out if there are preferred ways for staff to approach clients as well as colleagues; your supervisor is possibly most suited to provide you with this guidance; most salons wish clients to be greeted by name, some may prefer last names to be used rather than first names, in others the reverse may apply and in others the hairdresser's role is to determine and use the client's favoured approach to her or his name.

# Responding to your client

## Effective communication

It can be risky to assume that there has been effective communication between yourself and your client. Be aware that some clients may have sensory limitations. These may be hearing or sight disadvantages and, although such disadvantages may not be immediately apparent, they can be a barrier to effective communication. Some clients will inform you on arrival that they have special communications requirements; others may not consider this is relevant or may actively strive to hide this. You, as the hairdresser, need to ensure effective communication in a sensitive manner. You must understand your client's requirements and s/he must be aware of what you propose to do in relation to them.

 REMEMBER!

*Communication can be enhanced by mirroring language styles and using the client's preferred style of language.*

Language can form a barrier to effective communication. Your client may have English as a second language and may think and respond in a different language. This can inhibit or slow down communication. Some clients may not understand the English language so care must be taken to ensure that you and your client understand each other. Dialect from different parts of the country can also create a communication barrier, as can the use of technical or hairdressing-specific jargon. When identifying potential contra-indications to treatments, care must be taken to ensure your client understands what is being asked of her or him and that their response is an important part of the consultation process. Be prepared to rephrase your questions and to provide examples of possible symptoms or situations that can confirm the presence of these contra-indications.

*REMEMBER!*

*When experiencing communication difficulties raising your voice is not always the answer. Ensure you are facing the client; speak clearly and slowly, use non-technical language, visual images and check for signs of understanding.*

 Figure 2.3 Using visual images for effective communication

Visual images can often support verbal communication, and the use of style books, illustrations and colleagues' hairstyles can be used to overcome barriers to effective communication.

You may notice that when clients have understood your communication they will often:

◆ ask further questions

◆ smile

◆ relax

◆ nod their head.

# Information about services and products

The initial point of information to clients is through the salon's reception. More information on this is provided in Chapter 10.

During the initial consultation with your client take time to find out exactly what s/he wishes to have done. Be prepared to make suggestions based upon your professional knowledge. More information on client consulation is provided in Chapter 3. Always summarise your agreements with clients; by doing this you ensure that you have understood each other. Take care to always use non-technical language and avoid jargon. If providing a service for the first time to a client, or when changing a service provided, always summarise:

◆ what the service will involve

◆ the time taken

◆ the costs

◆ any follow-on services required to achieve or maintain the desired look.

When informing clients why their expectations cannot be met, be honest but tactful. Do not make undertakings you cannot realistically achieve. Always give your reasons and, wherever possible, offer alternatives for the client to select from. Giving your client choices allows them to feel they have made the decision and that it is not a compromise.

# REMEMBER!

*Your salon may have policies about undertaking services or using certain products on clients. Consult with your supervisor if you are not certain of what can be done and what is not in line with the salon's requirements.*

While working with your client be observant and responsive to her or his needs. In the early stages of a service you should identify whether or not your client wishes to talk or remain silent, other than responding to questions relevant to the service being provided.

Throughout her or his visit to the salon be observant of a client's body language, whether during the service or when making a retail sale.

# REMEMBER!

*Always acknowledge the presence of a client even when busy working with another. If you are unable to respond immediately to a client's questions, confirm to her or him that you will respond as soon as is practicable. Do not forget to fulfil your undertakings for clients.*

Look for signs of discomfort (for example fidgeting) as this may indicate physical discomfort with the service being provided, or emotional discomfort being caused through concerns about the service time or the suitability of the product being used or sold.

If you identify a situation where your client is at risk this should be dealt with immediately. If this is outside of your responsibility, then immediately but tactfully refer this to your supervisor.

Guidance in responding to clients who are angry is provided in Chapter 10.

# Feedback

## Individual

Throughout your service to the client obtain feedback, gathering information from your client about how they perceive the service provision. This feedback can provide you with guidance on the quality of the service and whether it is meeting your client's expectations. You will be able to use this information, if required, to adjust your service delivery to better meet your client's wishes (see Figure 2.4).

### Positive feedback

This confirms that the service is meeting the client's expectations and will often be demonstrated through:

◆ client's body language – willingness to make eye contact, relaxed stature, smiling

◆ positive comments – confirmation that what is being achieved fits the expectation, discussion about things other than the hairdressing task in hand.

### Negative feedback

This confirms that the service is not meeting the client's expectations and will often be demonstrated through:

◆ client's body language – fidgeting, frowning, arms firmly crossed

◆ negative comments – frequent questions about how the hair will turn out and requests for confirmation that it is turning out as planned, requests for confirmation from colleagues.

Always receive feedback positively; it can be used to help you improve the service you provide to your clients and colleagues.

■ Figure 2.4 Obtaining feedback from your client

## Salon

As well as obtaining feedback regarding your own service delivery your salon may have a policy and procedure for obtaining feedback that is centrally led and used to guide your salon as a whole to improve the service provided to clients. Informal questioning can be used to obtain feedback. Questionnaires may be used to provide a volume of feedback which can be used to evaluate the service provided. This will ensure a range of people are asked to respond to the same prompts and therefore provide quality data for review. When creating a questionnaire consider first what you want to find out. Design questions which will search those areas and that are easy and quick to respond to. This usually points towards a range of predetermined response options (multiple-choice questions). Providing a limited number of response options makes analysis of results more straightforward.

All areas of service provision can be evaluated from client feedback, including:

◆ quality of service

◆ cost of service/value for money

◆ speed of service provision

◆ quality of salon environment

◆ range of services available.

A culture of using feedback in a positive manner to improve the quality of service provided is good business practice. Individual members of the team should be encouraged to obtain feedback to check on client comfort and satisfaction, and to receive and use negative feedback positively. Feedback received should be passed on to the responsible person as soon as is practicable.

Salon managers often cascade customer feedback to the staff team and use this as a focus for celebrating success and achievements as well as areas for further development. Positive feedback from clients is often shared with other clients and can have a promotional effect.

# KEY SKILL TASK

*This task could produce evidence that supports C1.1, C1.3, N1.1, N1.2, & N1.3.*

*Undertake a survey of your clients' perceptions and experiences when they have visited your salon. Design a questionnaire that you can use to gather feedback from your clients about the quality of service you and your salon provide. Consider what you want to find out, which might include:*

◆ *why s/he chose to visit this salon in preference to others*
◆ *frequency of her or his salon visits*
◆ *the most enjoyable part of the service*
◆ *the least enjoyable part of the service*
◆ *acceptability of the time taken to provide the service*
◆ *value for money*
◆ *why s/he returned to the salon*
◆ *additional services s/he would like the salon to offer.*

*Design 20 questions with four alternative answers for each (multiple-choice). Test the questions with a colleague to confirm they understand the questions and how they should respond. If your colleague finds it difficult to understand or answer, your client is likely to as well.*

*When you have 20 multiple-choice questions that you feel will provide you with useful data to confirm what you and your salon are doing well and areas for improvement, use the questionnaires with a range of your clients over a four-week period. Following or during a treatment explain to your client the purpose of the questionnaire and with her or his consent ask the questions and note the answers.*

*At the end of your survey period process the data. This will include compiling the total number of responses to each question. You should be able to state this as a:*

◆ *number, for example from 200 completed questionnaires for question 1, 40 stated choice (a), 60 (b), 20 (c) and 80 (d)*
◆ *percentage, for example from 200 completed questionnaires for question 1, 20% stated (a), 30% (b), 10% (c) and 40% (d)*
◆ *chart, for example a pie chart, each segment representing a proportion of the total number of responses.*

**Question 1**

*From the responses, consider key actions that satisfy your clients and encourage them to return to your salon. Also consider what displeases your clients and what could be done to reduce this negative impact. Present the findings to your supervisor. Remember, before undertaking this task discuss the activity with your supervisor.*

# Complaints about services

Clients who return to the salon with a complaint about a service should be treated politely. Avoid appearing irritated, and respond calmly and with empathy but without acknowledging any responsibility. Once you have established that the client has a complaint, either deal with it promptly or, if the complaint is outside of your area of responsibility, ask them to take a seat in the customer waiting area and promptly refer to the person in the salon who is responsible for dealing with complaints. In the first place this may be the stylist; subsequently this may be the manager or proprietor. Complaints are best discussed in private, without an audience, either in an office or an area private from other clients.

The exact nature of the complaint should be established by talking with and questioning the client. Do this in a seated position as this helps to diffuse a heated or stressful situation. Establish all the facts and confirm these by checking salon records; for example, the date of appointment, treatment records, the person responsible, and charges made. Undertake all of this in a calm, non-judgemental manner. Remember, at this time you are gathering information – not making judgements. However the problem is resolved, the salon will wish to keep the client as a loyal customer. It is essential that throughout the complaints process the client is treated with respect and understanding so they feel able to continue their relationship with the salon.

## REMEMBER!

*Many salons have professional indemnity insurance to provide financial compensation in cases where damage has occurred and where the salon can be proven to be at fault. Remember that insurance companies providing this type of insurance have strict procedures with which to comply when handling complaints that subsequently lead to a claim. You should never admit liability without guidance from your insurance company.*

Once the nature of the complaint has been determined, the person responsible must decide what action is to be taken. When a complaint is unfounded an explanation of the problem and its causes can often be sufficient, separating and dealing with each aspect of the complaint in turn. It is important for the client to accept the outcome. When a complaint is justified a judgement may be made to provide remedial action without accepting liability.

In all cases detailed records should be kept, noting the conversation, statement, claims and subsequent agreements made with clients.

## Self review

1. State two potential barriers to effective communication with your client.

2. How should you respond to a client arriving while you are working with another?

3. Suggest two indicators that you are communicating effectively with a client.

4. Suggest one feature of body language that indicates client discomfort.

5. What is positive feedback?

6. How should you use feedback?

7. Who should you refer a complaint to when it exceeds your area of responsibility?

8. Should you automatically accept fault for a client's complaint?

9. In what area of the salon is it best to discuss a client complaint?

10. Suggest three aspects of service that may be monitored through a client questionnaire.

## Useful contacts

HABIA                                 www.habia.org.uk
Institute of Customer Service         www.instituteofcustomerservice.com

# CHAPTER 3

# Consulting with your clients

## CHAPTER CONTENTS

**Unit G7**   Advise and consult with clients

## WHAT THIS CHAPTER WILL PROVIDE

This chapter provides the essential knowledge to help you understand the skills used in client care. It will help you understand the need for consultation and negotiation in satisfying your clients' requirements.

## Client consultation

Consultation with your client will enable you to identify any factors that may limit or affect the services and products that you use. This is the opportunity to determine the most suitable techniques, products and equipment to enable you to create the agreed effect, and that both hair and scalp are suitable for these intended treatments.

Effective communication between you and your client is essential before beginning the hairdressing process, to ensure that your client's wishes are met. The use of style books, photographs, fashion magazines, computerised style viewers and wigs can aid in understanding proposed outcomes. Your consultation will normally

take place when both you and your client are seated, facing each other, discussing her or his wishes with regard to their chosen hairstyle. As the hairstylist, you will consider the suitability of the requested treatment and hairstyle for the client. Here is a list of critical influencing questions to ask yourself.

◆   What is your client's lifestyle?

◆   Does the hairstyle fit the client's employment requirements?

◆   Does the client's face and head shape suit the requested hairstyle?

■ Figure 3.1 Consulting with your client

21

◆　Does the client's haircut suit the requested hairstyle?

◆　Does the texture and length of the hair suit the requested hairstyle?

◆　Are there any hair growth patterns that may adversely affect the required hairstyle?

◆　Are there any previous chemical treatments remaining in the hair?

There may be occasions when the style/treatment requested by your client is not, in your opinion, achievable on, or suitable for, the client. Your negotiation skills will be required to counsel and guide your client towards a more suitable choice. You will need to be honest, sincere and objective to justify your statements to your client.

Records of previous consultations and services given to your client should be viewed, enabling you to check on previous products used and their outcomes. Many salons maintain a written record of clients' consultations/treatments. This will usually take the form of alphabetically indexed cards containing information about the products used on the client, the dates of use and the outcomes of these services. There are computerised customer information systems available, offering the same facility as the written record, but often making retrieval of the information much easier and more rapid. Maintaining these client records will provide a reference should a customer complain at a later stage. It will also help to ensure continuity when a previous treatment is to be repeated. The information contained in client records should be considered confidential (see Data Protection Act 1998 in Chapter 1). Many salons have a policy that your client may not have access to this information. Check with your supervisor or manager for advice on this before giving out any information.

Always consider additional services that will enhance the finished look and make maintenance of that look easier and more realistic for your client. Your client will look to you, as their hairstylist, for advice and guidance about their look and about which additional services, such as colour or permanent wave, may enhance this look. Hair colour may be used to improve the overall look of the hair, or to accentuate features of a particular hairstyle. The use of permanent waves or straighteners may help in the style retention and enable certain fashion effects to be achieved. Your client may not fully appreciate the effect that these additions to the service may have, so suggestions from hairstylists are an important part of their responsibility towards clients. While these additional services may cost the client more, they will be justified provided they add to client satisfaction and enhance appearance. Be aware that your professional ability will be reflected in the finished look and its ease of maintenance.

After-care products for home use may be suggested at this stage. You should explain their features and benefits to your client, and give guidance on particular products and how they should be used. These products will include basic haircare products such as shampoos and conditioners, styling and finishing products, and hair ornamentation and personal haircare tools including heated tongs, brushes, etc. As a professional you will need to guide your client towards the appropriate items for particular needs. To be able to do this you must be fully conversant with all retail products available from your salon, and their features and benefits (see Chapter 11 for more information).

Having completed your pre-service consultation, confirm the decisions with your client, clearly explain to them what the process will be, and give an indication of the time that this will take and the actual cost to your client of this treatment.

Keep a record of products used on your clients and those that your clients purchase for after-care. This will provide you with guidance on future visits. Some salons record these details on 'treatment plans' – a copy of which is given to your client and a copy retained by the salon.

Consultation is a continuous process while working with the client. Throughout the hairdressing process you should consult the client about their wishes. Watch the client for signs of discomfort or agitation which may indicate dissatisfaction with the process. If this becomes apparent, discuss it with the client. In order for you to deal with a problem you must first be fully aware of what the problem is. Should your client express a concern that is beyond your responsibility, excuse yourself from the client, and discreetly inform your supervisor of the situation. The client may require confirmation of the progress towards completion, s/he may require reassurance that the requested result can be achieved, s/he may have changed their mind about the required outcome or may be experiencing physical discomfort. It is important to solve these problems as soon as possible to prevent them becoming barriers to communication. For complex problems, deal with each aspect of the problem individually rather than attempting to deal with it all at once.

# Hair analysis

Much of your time as a hairdresser is taken up with servicing and styling clients' hair. For this reason, you should be able to recognise the condition and types of hair and be able to analyse them.

# Condition of the hair

Knowledge of hair and skill in determining its condition can be acquired by constant observation using the senses available to you: sight, touch, hearing and smell.

◆ **Sight.** Observing the hair will immediately give you some knowledge about its condition. Being able to look at hair is a major factor in its analysis, and touching the hair is the final determining factor.

◆ **Touch.** Hairdressers are guided by the touch or feel of the hair when making a professional hair analysis. When the sense of touch is fully developed, fewer mistakes will be made in judging the hair.

◆ **Hearing.** Listen to what your clients tell you about their hair, and any health problems, reactions to cosmetics and medication they might be taking. You will be in a better position to analyse the condition more accurately.

◆ **Smell.** Unclean hair and certain scalp disorders create an odour. If your client is generally healthy, you might suggest regular shampooing and proper rinsing.

# Qualities of the hair

The qualities by which human hair is analysed are *texture*, *porosity* and *elasticity*.

## Texture

Hair texture refers to the degree of coarseness or fineness of the hair (thick or thin), which can vary on different parts of the head. Variations in hair texture are due to:

◆ **diameter of the hair**, whether coarse, medium, fine or very fine; coarse hair has the greatest diameter; very fine hair has the smallest

◆ **feel of the hair**, whether harsh, soft or wiry – usually determined by the condition of its outer layer.

*Medium hair* is the normal type most commonly seen in the salon. This type of hair does not present any special problem. *Fine* or *very fine hair* requires special care. Its microscopic structure usually reveals that only two layers, the cortex and cuticle, are present. *Wiry hair*, whether coarse, medium or fine, has a hard, glassy finish caused by the cuticle scales lying flat against the hair shaft. It takes longer for chemicals such as permanent wave solutions, tints or lighteners to penetrate this type of hair.

## Porosity

*Hair porosity* is the ability of all types of hair to absorb moisture (*hygroscopic quality*). Hair has *high porosity* when the cuticle layer is raised from the hair shaft and easily absorbs moisture and chemicals. *Medium porosity* (normal hair) is most often seen in the salon. Usually hair with moderate porosity presents no problem when receiving hair services, whether permanent waving, hair tinting or lightening. *Low porosity* (resistant hair) exists when the cuticle layer is lying close to the hair shaft and absorbs the least amount of moisture. *Uneven porosity* is when there are areas of uneven porosity along the hair's length or on differing areas of the head. This can result in an uneven absorption of chemicals into the hair and may produce an uneven result. A range of pre-chemical treatments are available that will aid in making the hair's porosity even along its length. Hair with other than moderate porosity requires thorough analysis and strand tests before the application of hair cosmetics.

## Elasticity

*Hair elasticity* is the ability of hair to stretch and return to its original form without breaking. Hair can be classified as having high levels of elasticity, normal levels of elasticity and low levels of elasticity. (For more information on permanent waving see Chapter 8.) Hair with normal elasticity is springy and has a lively lustrous appearance. Normal hair, when dry, is capable of being stretched by about 20% of its length; it springs back when released. Wet hair can be stretched 40% to 50% of its length. Porous hair stretches more easily than resistant hair, though it may have a low level of elasticity, as once stretched it often does not return to its original form. Wet hair stretches more easily than dry hair.

## Hair growth patterns

The direction of hair growth will have an effect upon the hairstyle recommended to the client. As a general rule hairstyles will remain in place longer if they follow the direction of hair growth. There are times when additional height can be achieved by styling the hair against this direction.

Strong directions of hair growth, including *nape whorls* and *double crowns* will require special consideration to reduce the adverse effect that they can have on the finished hairstyle. Often additional hair length is required to reduce this effect (for more information see Chaper 13).

## Head and face shapes

The best results are obtained when each of your client's facial features are properly analysed for strengths and shortcomings. Your job is to accentuate a client's best features and play down features that do not add to the person's attractiveness.

You must develop the ability to recommend hairstyles for your clients. Each client deserves a hairstyle that is properly proportioned to their body type, correctly balanced to their head and facial features, and frames their face to its best advantage. The essentials of artistic and suitable hairstyles are based on the following general characteristics:

- shape of the head – front view (face shape), profile, and back view

- characteristics of features – perfect as well as imperfect features, defects or blemishes

- body structure – posture and poise.

# Facial types

Each client's facial shape is determined by the position and the prominence of the facial bones. There are seven facial shapes: oval, round, square, oblong, pear-shaped, heart-shaped and diamond-shaped. To recognise each facial shape and to be able to give correct advice, you should be acquainted with the main characteristics of each.

The face is divided into three areas: forehead to eyebrows, eyebrows to end of nose, and end of nose to bottom of chin (see Figure 3.2). When creating a style for a client, you will be trying to create the illusion that each client has the ideal face shape.

## Oval facial type

The oval-shaped face is generally recognised as the ideal shape. The contour and proportions of this face type form the basis for modifying all other facial shapes.

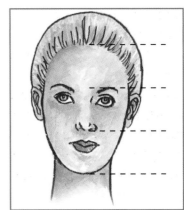

■ Figure 3.2 Ideal face proportions

**Facial contour:** The oval face is about 1.5 times longer than its width across the brow. The forehead is slightly wider than the chin (see Figures 3.3 and 3.4).

A person with an oval-shaped face can wear any hairstyle unless there are other considerations, such as spectacles or the length and shape of the nose or profile. Men's hairstyles have stronger, more angular shapes.

## Round facial type

**Facial contour:** Round hairline and round chin line; wide face.

**Aim:** To create the illusion of length to the face.

■ Figure 3.3 Oval face

■ Figure 3.4 Oval face

Create a hairstyle with height by
arranging the hair on top of the head or by spiking. You can place some over the ears and cheeks, but it is also appropriate to keep the hair up on one side, leaving the ears exposed. Style the fringe to one side (see Figures 3.5 and 3.6).

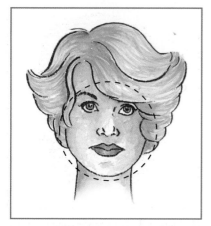

■ Figure 3.5 Round face

■ Figure 3.6 Round face

## Square facial type

**Facial contour:** Straight hairline and square jawline; wide face.

**Aim:** To create the illusion of length and offset the square features.

The problems of the square facial type are similar to the round facial type. The style should lift off the forehead and come forward at the temples and jaw, creating the illusion of narrowness and softness in the face. Asymmetrical hairstyles work well (see Figures 3.7 and 3.8).

■ Figure 3.7 Square face

■ Figure 3.8 Square face

## Pear-shaped facial type

**Facial contour:** Narrow forehead, wide jaw and chin line.

**Aim:** To create the illusion of width in the forehead.

Build a hairstyle that is fairly full and high. Cover the forehead partially with a fringe of soft hair. The hair should be worn with a soft curl or wave effect dressed over the ears. This arrangement adds apparent width to the forehead (see Figure 3.9).

■ Figure 3.9 Pear-shaped face

## Diamond-shaped facial type

**Facial contour:** Narrow forehead, extreme width through the cheekbones, and narrow chin.

**Aim:** To reduce the width across the cheekbone line.

Increasing the fullness across the jawline and forehead while keeping the hair close to the head at the cheekbone line helps create an oval appearance (see Figure 3.10). Avoid hairstyles that lift away from the cheeks or move back from the hairline.

## Heart-shaped facial type

**Facial contour:** Wide forehead and narrow chin line.

**Aim:** To decrease the width of the forehead and increase the width in the lower part of the face.

To reduce the width of the forehead, a centre parting with the fringe flipped up or a style slanted to one side is recommended. Add width and softness at the jawline (see Figure 3.11).

## Profiles

Always look at your client's profile (side view). When creating a hairstyle, the profile can be a good indicator as to the correct shape of hairstyle to choose.

## Straight profile

This is considered the ideal. It is neither concave nor convex, with no unusual facial features. Usually, all hairstyles are suited to the straight or normal profile (see Figure 3.12).

## Concave (prominent chin)

The hair at the nape should be styled softly with a movement upwards (see Figures 3.13 and 3.14). Do not build hair on to the forehead.

Figure 3.10 Diamond-shaped face

Figure 3.11 Heart-shaped face

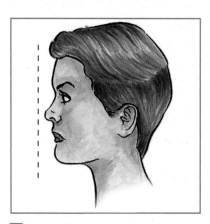

Figure 3.12 Straight profile

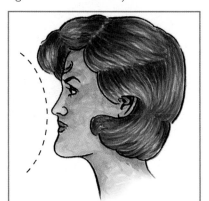

Figure 3.13 Concave profile

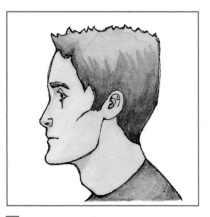

Figure 3.14 Concave profile

## Convex (receding forehead, prominent nose, and receding chin)

Place curls or a fringe over the forehead. Keep the styles close to the head at the nape (see Figures 3.15 and 3.16).

## Low forehead, protruding chin

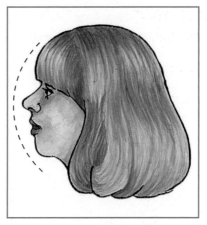
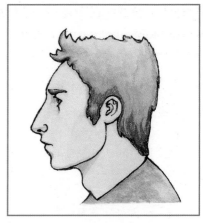

Figure 3.15 Convex profile

Figure 3.16 Convex profile

Create an illusion of fullness to the forehead by building a fluffy fringe with height. An upswept temple movement will add length to the face. Soft curls in the nape area soften the chin. Do not end the style line at the nape – this draws attention to the chin line. Create a line that is either higher or lower than the chin line (see Figure 3.17).

# Nose shapes

Nose shapes are closely related to profile. When studying your client's face, the nose must be considered both in profile and in full face.

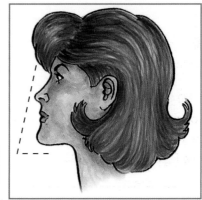

Figure 3.17 Low forehead, protruding chin

## Turned-up nose

This type of nose is usually small and accompanied by a straight profile. The small nose is considered to be a childlike quality, therefore it is best to design a hairstyle that is not associated with children. The hair should be swept off the face, creating a line from the nose to the ear. This will add length to the short nose. The top hair should move off the forehead to give the illusion of length to the nose (see Figures 3.18 and 3.19).

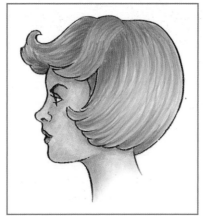
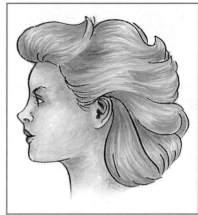

Figure 3.18 Wrong style for turned-up nose

Figure 3.19 Correct style for turned-up nose

## Prominent nose (hooked, large, or pointed)

In order to draw attention away from the nose, bring the hair forward at the forehead with softness around the face (see Figures 3.20 and 3.21).

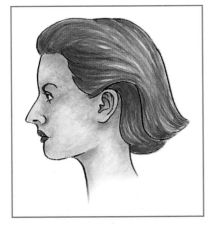

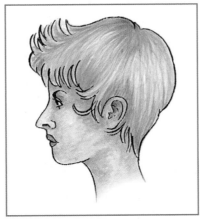

■ Figure 3.20 Wrong style for prominent nose

■ Figure 3.21 Correct style for prominent nose

## Crooked nose

To minimise the conspicuous crooked nose, style the hair in an off-centre manner that will attract the eye away from the nose. Asymmetrical styles are best. Any well-balanced hairstyle will accentuate the fact that the face is not even (see Figures 3.22 and 3.23).

■ Figure 3.22 Wrong style for crooked nose

■ Figure 3.23 Correct style for crooked nose

## Wide, flat nose

A wide, flat nose tends to broaden the face. In order to minimise this effect, the hair should be drawn away from the face. In addition, a centre parting tends to narrow the nose, as well as draw attention away from it (see Figures 3.24 and 3.25).

Figure 3.24 Wrong style for wide, flat nose

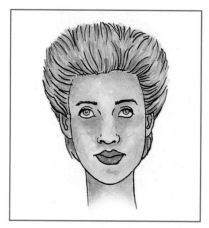

Figure 3.25 Correct style for wide, flat nose

# Eyes

The eyes are the focal point of the face. Be prepared to create hairstyles that bring out the best in a client's eyes.

## Wide-set eyes

Usually found on a round or square face. You can minimise the effect by lifting and/or spiking the top of the hair and fringe area. A side fringe helps to draw attention away from the space between the eyes (see Figures 3.26 and 3.27).

Figure 3.26 Wrong style for wide-set eyes

Figure 3.27 Correct style for wide-set eyes

## Close-set eyes

Usually found on long, narrow faces. Try to open the face with the illusion of more space between the eyes. Style the hair fairly high with a side movement. The hair ends should turn outwards and up (see Figures 3.28 and 3.29).

■ Figure 3.28 Wrong style for
close-set eyes

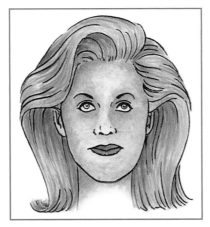

■ Figure 3.29 Correct style for
close-set eyes

# Head shapes

The shape of your client's head is just as individual as other physical features. As with the face, the
oval is considered the ideal shape. Men's hairstyles often follow an angular shape. Your goal when designing hairstyles
should be to give the illusion of an oval. As you evaluate your client's head shape, mentally impose an oval picture
over it. Where there is flatness, plan to build volume (see Figures 3.30–3.35).

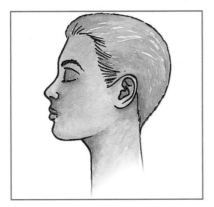

■ Figure 3.30 Perfect oval

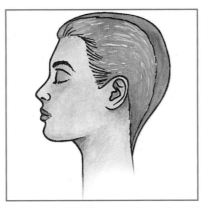

■ Figure 3.31 Narrow head, flat
back

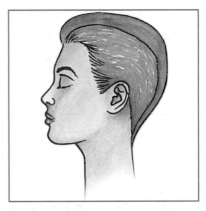

■ Figure 3.32 Flat crown

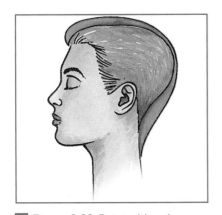

■ Figure 3.33 Pointed head,
hollow nape

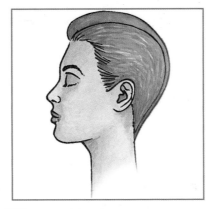

■ Figure 3.34 Flat top

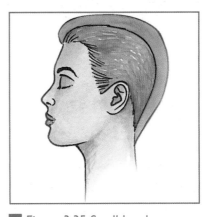

■ Figure 3.35 Small head

# Special considerations

Very few, if any, of your clients will have a perfect set of features. Your goal is to analyse their features and accentuate the best ones. In addition you will need to consider the particular features of various ethnic groups.

## Plump with short neck

**Aim:** To create the illusion of length.

**Corrective hairstyle:** Sweep the hair up to give length to the neck. Build height on top. Avoid hairstyles that give fullness to the back of the neck and hairstyles with horizontal lines (see Figure 3.36).

## Long, thin neck

**Aim:** To minimise the appearance of the long neck.

**Corrective hairstyle:** Cover the neck with soft waves. Avoid short or sculptured necklines. Keep the hair long and full at the nape (see Figure 3.37).

# Educating your client

Your client will require advice on how to maintain their hair and the style that you have created. This will include the correct choice and use of products on their hair. Clients will also need guidance in how frequently they should visit the salon to maintain their hair. Follow-up services for clients with new looks may be offered as a salon policy. All clients should be encouraged to make return appointments before leaving the salon. This will enable you, to plan your work, as well as helping to ensure an ongoing client relationship.

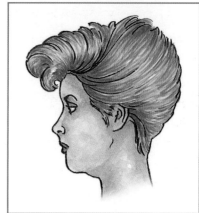

Figure 3.36 Plump with short neck

Figure 3.37 Long, thin neck

*Self review*

1. Suggest two visual aids that can be used to communicate proposed style outcomes.

2. What additional services can often enhance someone's hairstyle?

3. What does hair texture refer to?

4. What does hair porosity refer to?

5. What does hair elasticity refer to?

6.  Which face shape is generally recognised as the ideal?

7.  What is the main feature of a concave profile?

8.  Does hair stretch more easily when wet or when dry?

9.  Name two strong hair growth patterns.

10. How can uneven porosity affect the result of chemical process on the hair?

## Useful contacts

| | |
|---|---|
| HABIA | www.habia.org.uk |
| Institute of Customer Service | www.instituteofcustomerservice.com |

## CHAPTER 4

# Shampooing and conditioning the hair and scalp

## CHAPTER CONTENTS

**Unit H1**    Shampoo and condition hair

**Unit H9**    Shampoo and condition hair and scalp

## WHAT THIS CHAPTER WILL PROVIDE

This chapter will give you the essential knowledge you need to understand and carry out shampooing and conditioning of the hair and scalp. Massage techniques are also described. A variety of products for hair and scalp conditions are suggested.

## The purpose of shampooing

Following consultation, shampooing is usually the first of a great many salon services, and it prepares the hair for hairdressing processes. In salons where the stylist undertakes the shampoo, the client may use this initial experience to evaluate the professional expertise of the stylist. Clients are likely to assume that a stylist who shampoos professionally will perform all additional services with that same level of competency and concern. In salons where a trainee or other member of staff undertakes the shampoo, the client may use the experience to judge the professionalism of the salon as a whole. Therefore, the client who enjoys the shampoo service is more likely to request additional services and to recommend the stylist and the salon to potential clients.

Shampooing is an important preparatory step for a variety of hair services and is performed primarily to cleanse the hair and scalp. However, the psychological effects of a pleasurable and relaxing experience at the shampoo bay will help to ensure that the client visits the salon on a regular basis.

To be effective, a shampoo must remove all dirt, oils, cosmetics and skin debris without adversely affecting either the scalp or hair. It is important to analyse the condition of the client's hair and scalp, and to check for contagious diseases and disorders. A client with an infectious disease of the scalp should not be treated in the salon and should be referred to a medical practitioner.

Unless the scalp and hair are cleansed regularly, the accumulation of oil and perspiration, which mix with the natural scales and dirt, offer a breeding place for disease-producing bacteria. This can lead to scalp disorders (see Chapter 13).

Hair should be shampooed as often as necessary, depending on how quickly the scalp and hair become soiled. As a general rule, oily hair should be shampooed more often than normal or dry hair.

# Water

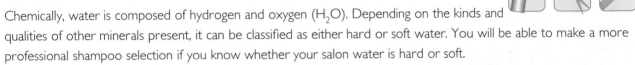

Chemically, water is composed of hydrogen and oxygen ($H_2O$). Depending on the kinds and qualities of other minerals present, it can be classified as either hard or soft water. You will be able to make a more professional shampoo selection if you know whether your salon water is hard or soft.

## Soft water

Soft water is naturally mineral free or water that has been distilled or chemically softened (de-ionised). It contains relatively small amounts of minerals and, therefore, allows shampoos to lather freely. For this reason, it may be preferred for shampooing.

## Hard water

Hard water contains minerals that reduce the ability of shampoo to lather. However, hard water can be softened by a chemical process. Calcium deposits from the hard water can build up limescale, blocking the jets of the shower head (also called the rose).

# Shampooing

## Required materials and implements

Before giving a shampoo, gather all the necessary materials and implements. Don't forget that your client should be properly gowned to protect her or his clothing. The relaxing mood and the professional quality of the shampoo is destroyed if you dash off to get a forgotten item, leaving your client wet and dripping at the basin. The materials and implements required are:

- clean towels
- a clean gown
- the appropriate shampoo and conditioner.

- a hairbrush
- a wide-toothed comb

 REMEMBER!

*Check with your supervisor on the salon procedure for looking after clients' valuables.*

# Chemistry of shampoo

To determine which shampoo will leave your client's hair in the best condition for the intended service, you must understand the chemical ingredients of shampoos. Most shampoos have many common ingredients. It is often small differences in formulation that make one shampoo better than another for a particular hair texture or condition.

The ingredient that most shampoos have in common, and that is usually number one on the list to show that there is more of it than any other ingredient, is water. Generally, it is not just plain water, but purified or de-ionised water. From there, ingredients are listed in descending order according to the percentage present in the shampoo.

# Classification of shampoos

The second ingredient that most shampoos have in common is the base *surfactant* or base *detergent*.

## KEY WORDS

**Surfactant and detergent** – *these two terms mean the same thing: cleansing or 'surface-active' agent*

The term surfactant describes organic compounds brought together by chemical synthesis (combining chemical elements to form a whole) to create wetting, dispersing, emulsifying, solubilising, foaming or washing agents (detergents). Most shampoos are based upon soapless detergents, most frequently lauryl sulphate, for example sodium lauryl ether sulphate and triethanolomine lauryl sulphate. These are manufactured from vegetable oils that are treated with sulphuric acid.

The base surfactant or combination of surfactants determines into which class a shampoo will fall. They fall into four broad classifications: anionic, cationic, non-ionic and ampholytic.

## KEY WORDS

**Anionic** – *lowers the surface tension of water*
**Cationic** – *attracted to the hair, has a positive charge*
**Non-ionic** – *acts as a foam stabiliser*
**Ampholytic** – *acts as a foam stabiliser, makes shampoo less irritating to the eyes*

Most manufacturers use detergents from more than one classification. It is customary to use a secondary surfactant to complement or offset the negative qualities of the base surfactant. For example, an ampholytic that is non-irritating to the eyes can be added to a harsh anionic to create a product that is more comfortable to use.

# Selecting the correct shampoo

Many types of shampoo are available. As a professional hairdresser, you should learn the properties and actions of a shampoo to determine whether or not it will serve your intended purpose. Read the product label and the accompanying literature carefully so that you can make an informed decision.

A pre-shampoo consultation with the client will enable you to decide on the appropriate shampoo to use. Question your client about their hair and scalp: ask when the hair was last shampooed, how often the hair is shampooed and why the hair is shampooed at that frequency (whether it is for cleanliness or for styling). Ask about previous hair treatments. You will probably need to handle the hair to confirm your findings. Shampoo manufacturers give guidance for shampoo selection.

Hair is not considered normal if it has been:

◆ lightened

◆ abused by the use of harsh shampoos

◆ toned or tinted

◆ damaged by improper care

◆ permanently waved

◆ damaged by exposure to sun, cold, heat or wind

◆ chemically relaxed

◆ affected by client ill-health.

Select the shampoo according to the condition of the hair and scalp, bearing in mind any previous treatments. Also consider treatments that are likely to be used after the shampoo. If you intend to undertake a chemical process such as perming, then use either a specialist pre-perm shampoo or a plain soapless shampoo which contains no additives, has a neutral pH 7 and leaves the cuticle flat.

## ✚ HEALTH & SAFETY

Your employer will arrange for you to be instructed in the safe use of chemicals and products. For more information refer to the Control of Substances Hazardous to Health (COSHH) Regulations 2002.

Shampoos available today include those intended for use on the following types of hair.

◆ **Normal hair.** These shampoos are designed to cleanse the average head of hair, leaving it in good condition for subsequent styling. Plain soapless shampoo is often used for this hair type.

◆ **Dry hair.** These shampoos will help nourish the hair, add moisture to the hair and make the hair easier to comb. They often include vegetable oil extracts that help to soften and condition hair, such as palm, almond, coconut, avocado and jojoba.

◆ **Greasy hair.** These shampoos will be effective in the removal of sebum from the hair and scalp, and may contain additives which will help to reduce the activity of the sebaceous glands. They often include egg white and lemon.

◆ **Dandruff-affected.** These shampoos will help to combat the causes of dandruff and to remove dandruff scales from the hair and scalp. Additives such as selenium sulphide and zinc pyrethione are often included within these shampoos.

◆ **Fine hair.** These shampoos are designed to reduce the softening effect of shampooing. Beer is sometimes used in these shampoos.

◆ **Artificially coloured hair.** These shampoos are designed to reduce the colour fade caused by shampooing the hair.

◆ **Pre-perm.** These shampoos are designed to cleanse the hair and to prepare the hair for subsequent permanent curling. They help to even the porosity of the hair without leaving a barrier between the hair and perm lotion.

# REMEMBER!

*Take time to discover what types of shampoo are available for use in your salon. Find out suitability for differing hair and scalp types and conditions.*

*Some two-step shampoos can leave a smoothing residue on the hair and with continued use this will build up on the hair. This build-up can inhibit the penetration of the hair by perm lotion. When its use is suspected, the build-up must be removed before perming.*

# KEY SKILL TASK

*This task could produce evidence that supports C1.1, C1.2, C1.3, & N1.1.*

*Using manufacturers' information leaflets, produce a chart of the range of shampoos used in your salon, and the hair and scalp conditions that they may effectively be used on. Discuss with your supervisor how this chart could be used to train colleagues.*

## Dry shampoos

If your client is unable to get their hair wet, whether due to illness, a lack of water or when there is insufficient time, a dry shampoo may be used. These shampoos are not suitable for preparing the hair for any subsequent chemical service on your client, nor do they enable the 'wetting' of the hair necessary to produce a set or blow-dry.

### Dry spirit shampoo

Dry spirit shampoo is a foaming spirit that, while it wets the hair, evaporates very quickly. The spirit is applied to the hair and massaged through it to produce foam. This foam suspends the dirt from the hair. The foam is wiped from the hair using a cupped hand or a towel, and the hair dries very quickly.

### Dry powder shampoo

Dry powder shampoo is a powder consisting of a mixture of talc and chalk. It is applied to the hair and brushed through (see Figure 4.1). The powder absorbs any grease and attracts the dirt from the hair.

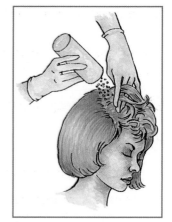

■ Figure 4.1 Applying dry shampoo

Neither of the dry shampoos is as effective a cleanser as wet shampoos.

# Brushing

Hairbrushes made of natural bristles are recommended for hair brushing. Natural bristles have many tiny overlapping layers, or scales, which clean and add lustre to the hair, while nylon bristles are shiny and smooth and recommended for hairstyling.

You should include a thorough brushing as part of every shampoo and scalp treatment, with the following exceptions.

◆ Do not brush before giving a chemical treatment.

◆ Do not brush if the scalp is irritated.

Brushing stimulates the blood circulation to the scalp and helps remove dust, dirt, tangles and hairspray build-up from the hair (see Figure 4.2).

To brush the hair, first part it through the centre from front to nape. Then part a section about 1.25 cm off the centre parting, starting at the nape. Holding this strand of hair in the left hand between the thumb and fingers, lay the brush (held in the right hand) with the bristles well down on the hair close to the scalp; rotate the brush by turning the wrist slightly, and sweep the bristles the full length of the hair. Repeat three times. Then part the hair again 1.25 cm above the first parting and continue until the entire head has been brushed (see Figure 4.3).

■ Figure 4.2 Brushing the hair

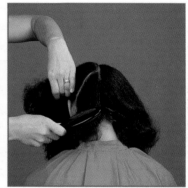
■ Figure 4.3 Hair sectioned and brushing started

Avoid placing the hair under undue tension. If the hair is tangled, commence by removing tangles at the points, then work steadily back towards the root area.

# Shampoo procedure

## Preparation

1 Seat your client comfortably at your workstation.

2 Select and arrange the required materials.

3 Wash/cleanse your hands.

4 Place the shampoo cape around your client's neck (be sure that the client's clothing lies smoothly under the gown and cape) (see Figure 4.4).

5 Remove any hairpins and combs from the hair.

**✚ HEALTH & SAFETY**

Your salon will have preferred ways of working when shampooing. Failure to adhere to these may cause injury to yourself or your client. (See Chapter 1 for more information on health and safety and COSHH.)

6   Ask your client to remove earrings and glasses and put them in a safe place. Your salon may have a policy and procedures for this.

7   Examine the condition of your client's hair and scalp to determine the correct shampoo choice. Check for any contra-indications to shampooing: open cuts or sores on the scalp, contagious disorders, etc.

8   Brush the hair thoroughly.

9   Seat your client comfortably at the shampoo basin, ensuring that s/he is seated in such a position that the neck makes an efficient water seal between it and the basin (assuming that it is a back wash-style basin as illustrated in Figure 4.5).

10   Ensure that towels are correctly located to protect the client. Two towels will be required. Some salons place a towel around the neck at the front of the client and then the second around the neck at the back. Other salons place one towel around the back of the neck, keeping the second in reserve for use when the shampoo is completed.

11   Adjust the volume and temperature of the water spray.

■ Figure 4.4 Completed shampoo gowning

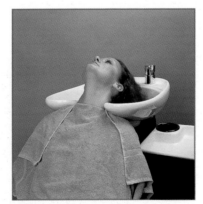

■ Figure 4.5 Client at back wash basin

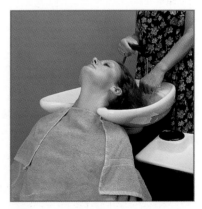

■ Figure 4.6 Testing water temperature

To avoid scalding yourself and the client, turn on the cold water flow first and then gradually introduce the hot water until a temperature which is comfortable to the client is established. Test the temperature of the water by spraying it on the back of your hand or the inside of your wrist, as these areas are more sensitive to temperature than the palm of the hand. The temperature of the water must be constantly monitored by keeping one finger over the edge of the spray nozzle (rose) and in contact with the water (see Figure 4.6).

## Procedure

1   Wet hair thoroughly with warm water spray. Lift the hair and work it with your free hand to saturate the scalp. Shift your hand to protect the client's face, ears and neck from the spray when working around the hairline (see Figure 4.7).

 *REMEMBER!*

*Avoid using water that is too hot or too cold when shampooing, as extremes of temperature can be uncomfortable for your client. Very hot water can cause scalding of the scalp. When shampooing greasy hair use water at body temperature as this will reduce any scalp stimulation.*

2   Apply small quantities of shampoo to the hair. First emulsify the shampoo on the palms of the hands. This will aid distribution and remove any chill. Beginning at the hairline and working back, apply the shampoo with the effleurage massage technique (see page 48). Work into a lather using the pads or cushions of the fingers (the rotary massage technique – see below).

 *REMEMBER!*

*Avoid using excessive amounts of shampoo and conditioner as this is wasteful and can become difficult and time-consuming to remove from the hair.*

3   Manipulate the scalp using rotary massage.

   i   Use the pads of the fingers and thumbs, working them in small rotary movements on the scalp.

   ii  Begin at the front hairline and work in a back-and-forth movement until the top of the head is reached (see Figure 4.8).

   iii Continue in this manner to the back of the head, shifting your fingers back 2.5cm at a time.

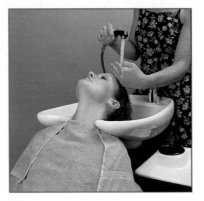

■ Figure 4.7. Shielding client's face during shampooing

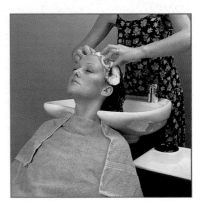

■ Figure 4.8. Rotary massage technique

## HEALTH & SAFETY

To reduce the risk of contracting contact dermatitis always wash and thoroughly dry your hands following shampooing. Always check the manufacturer's guidelines on the use of protective gloves when applying products to the hair.

## REMEMBER!

*When you are shampooing very long hair take care not to tangle the hair by your massage technique. Drawing your fingers from the root area to the hair points will help to untangle the hair.*

iv Lift the client's head, with your left hand controlling the movement of the head. With your right hand, start at the top of the right ear and, using the same movement, work to the back of the head.

v Drop your fingers down 2.5cm and repeat the process until the right side of the head is covered.

vi Beginning at the left ear, repeat the previous two steps.

## REMEMBER!

*Should your client indicate that the shampoo is causing scalp irritation, this may denote a possible allergic reaction. Alternative shampoos should then be used. In severe cases you should recommend that your client seeks medical advice.*

## REMEMBER!

*If personal protective equipment is provided for use when handling certain products you have a responsibility to use these. (For more information refer to the Control of Substances Hazardous to Health Regulations 2002 (COSHH) in Chapter 1.)*

vii Allow the client's head to relax and work around the hairline with your thumbs in a rotary movement.

viii Repeat these movements until the scalp has been massaged thoroughly.

ix Remove excess shampoo and lather by gently squeezing the hair.

4   Rinse the hair thoroughly.

   i   Lift the hair at the crown and back with the fingers of your left hand to allow the spray to rinse the hair thoroughly.

   ii   Cup your hand along the nape line and pat the hair, forcing the spray of water against the base scalp area (see Figure 4.9).

5   Repeat the process.

   i   If necessary, repeat the procedure using steps 2, 3 and 4 as outlined above. You will need less shampoo because shampoo lathers more easily on partially clean hair.

   ii   It may not be necessary to repeat this process when shampooing recently shampooed hair or when the hair is excessively fine.

---

## HEALTH & SAFETY

If shampoo or other products enter your client's eyes use a sterile water wash to rinse this from the eye. Should any eye irritation continue refer your client to her or his doctor. Always report these occurrences to your supervisor.

---

## REMEMBER!

*In massaging the scalp, do not use firm pressure if:*
- *you will be giving your client a chemical service after the shampoo*
- *your client's scalp is tender or sensitive*
- *your client requests less pressure.*

---

6   Apply a surface hair conditioner if required.

   i   Remove excess moisture from the hair by squeezing the hair in the hands.

   ii   Using your hands or a specialised applicator, apply the conditioner to the hair and distribute throughout the hair, using an effleurage massage movement (see page 48).

   iii   Rinse the excess conditioner from the hair, following the manufacturer's instructions. Conditioner left in the hair can make the hair appear greasy and lank, and can cause a flaky effect when dry.

   iv   If you are in doubt about whether a surface-active conditioner is required, consult with the hairstylist.

7   Partially towel dry.

   i   Remove excess moisture from the hair at the shampoo basin.

ii Wipe excess moisture from around the client's face and ears with the towel, taking care not to allow the corners of the towel to touch the client's eyes. Folding the ends of the towel back on themselves will help to prevent this (see Figure 4.10).

iii Lift the towel over the back of the client's head and wrap the head with the towel.

iv Place your hands on top of the towel and massage until the hair is partially dry (see Figure 4.10). Use the effleurage technique described on page 48.

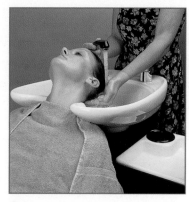

■ Figure 4.9 Rinsing shampoo from the nape area

■ Figure 4.10 Towel drying the hair

## Completion

1 Comb the hair, using a wide-toothed comb, beginning with the ends at the nape of the client's neck. This will help to prevent unnecessary tension on the hair.

# REMEMBER!

*The outermost layer of the hair, the cuticle, overlaps towards the points of the hair. When shampooing long hair always take care not to rub the ends too vigorously as they can easily become entangled and the cuticle interlock.*

2 Change the towel around the client's neck, if necessary.

3 Style the hair as desired.

## Clean-up

1 Dispose of used materials, and place unused supplies in their proper place.

2 Wipe the basin area clear of hair and water.

3 Place used towels in the towel bin.

# REMEMBER!

*Occasionally try to see the salon in the way that your client does. At the shampoo area consider what view of the salon s/he has. From the shampoo chair, does your client see areas that require cleaning? Often from the seated position your client will see under shelves, basins and other fixtures that from a standing position appear perfect.*

**HEALTH & SAFETY**

To reduce the risk of cross-infection always leave the work area clean, dispose of waste materials, put used towels ready for washing, and sterilise combs and brushes. Any equipment used on clients who are found to have head lice should be kept separately from other tools to be used on clients, usually in a sealed polythene bag, until they are washed and sterilised. Check with your supervisor about your salon's procedures for this.

4  Remove hair from combs and brushes and wash them with hot, soapy water, rinse and place in wet disinfectant for the required time.

5  Wash your hands.

**REMEMBER!**

*Throughout the day, top up supplies of shampoo, conditioner and towels. If you note that reserve supplies are running out report this to your supervisor as soon as possible.*

# Conditioning hair and scalp

There are a number of hair and scalp conditions that may be treated by the professional hairdresser. It is essential that, in offering this service, the hairdresser is able to identify those conditions that may be safely treated and those that require referral to a medical practitioner.

**HEALTH & SAFETY**

Take care always to wear protective gloves if recommended by the product manufacturer.

Modern technology has enabled manufacturers to produce a wide range of professional treatments that may be offered by the hairdresser. In some cases these treatments take the form of 'one-off' products that may be applied to either the hair and/or scalp, independently of any other product used with your client. There are also treatment systems available that offer a range of products which may be used in conjunction with each other. These usually take the form of ranges of shampoos (cleansers), treatment lotions or creams, styling aids with a range of 'take home' products which complement those used in the salon. These treatment ranges usually have a regime of use, which leads the hairdresser through the process of analysis of the hair and scalp, selection of the appropriate products and their correct method of application.

## Hair conditioning

### Treatment conditioning

Hair cannot care for itself, and once damaged is unable to repair itself.

Hair that is out of condition is usually rather dry, brittle and rough to the touch. This may be caused by the use of chemical processes on the hair (permanent waving, bleaching and tinting), the use of poor-quality tools (rough combs or brushes with sharp bristles), excessive heat on the hair (too frequent or incorrect use of heated styling tools), effects from exposure to chlorine from swimming pools, your client's ill-health or even the weather (excessive sun).

The result of this may be a roughening of the outside layer of the hair, the cuticle, or, in its worst state, the breakdown of the hair's structure, causing the hair to break.

# REMEMBER!

*Always follow the manufacturer's guidelines when using a product.*

## Surface-active conditioning

# REMEMBER!

*Rotary massage is a surface massage where the pads of the fingers move in rotary movement on the scalp with light pressure. The fingers may regularly be lifted and drawn along the lengths of the hair to remove tangles.*

Following a shampoo, the client's hair is often conditioned to compensate for the drying effect of these processes. A surface-active conditioner would be used. The action of a surface conditioner is to coat the hair. This fills the gaps on the roughened surface of the cuticle, making it easier to comb and less liable to tangle. It also helps to soften the hair. The action of the surface conditioner will usually last until the next shampoo, the effect gradually disappearing as the hair is brushed, combed and subjected to treatment.

To apply a surface conditioner following the shampoo, remove excess moisture from your client's hair by pressing the hair between your hands. Place a small amount of the conditioner on your hands and then distribute this throughout the hair, paying particular attention to those areas worst affected by any dryness. Gently work the conditioner through the hair using your fingers and then rinse thoroughly from the hair. Note that some conditioners are not rinsed from the hair: check the manufacturer's guidelines. A coating of conditioner will be left on the hair until it is next shampooed – during this time it gradually breaks down.

## Penetrating conditioners

These conditioners penetrate the surface of the hair. Their actions are varied but in the main their effect is to build artificial bonds that form in the cortex layer of the hair, replacing those natural bonds which have been lost due to the causes listed earlier. Many of these conditioners also neutralise the effect of chemical treatments on the hair, returning the hair to its normal pH of between 4.5 and 5.5. This helps to prevent any further chemical action by the treatment. (More information about pH will be found in Chapter 8.)

Penetrating conditioners are available in liquid, cream and oil forms. The liquid form is the most suitable where softening the hair is not desirable. The cream format often has the benefit of both the surface-active and the penetrating conditioner in one product. Oil-based products usually consist of vegetable oils. Sulphonated vegetable oils are more easily shampooed from the hair following the treatment as they act both as an oil, conditioning, and a detergent, cleansing. When using a plain vegetable oil, apply to hair before it has been made wet, add shampoo and emulsify this with the oil before adding any water.

# REMEMBER!

*A full awareness of the procedures for using these products is an essential part of offering them as treatments. Always follow the manufacturer's directions.*

## Protective conditioning

Some conditioners may be used to protect the hair during chemical processes. Liquid conditioners, called **pre-treatment conditioners**, may be applied before a permanent wave to even the porosity of the hair. This will produce more even absorption by the hair of the perming solution. Those parts of the hair that are more porous, and therefore require more protection, absorb more of the pre-perm conditioner, therefore being self-selective. Follow the manufacturer's directions at all times when using these products.

Certain cream-based conditioners may be used as protective barriers when perming hair. Those areas of the hair coated with the conditioner will not easily absorb the perming lotion. This technique may be used when root perming or when protecting highly delicate hair during a perming process.

A sunscreen surface-active conditioner may be applied to the hair, either as a cream or as a liquid spray. This lies on the surface of the hair and acts as a screen against harmful rays from the sun, which dry and lighten the hair.

## Scalp treatments

Mild scalp conditions may often be treated by specialist treatment systems. There is a variety of product ranges available, including treatments to combat dandruff (*Pityriasis simplex*), greasy scalp (*Seborrhoea*) and even forms of hair loss (*Alopecia*). As the cause of a scalp condition must normally be established before a successful treatment can be determined, and as this often requires the specialist knowledge of a trichologist, these products may not always be able to offer the remedy required.

## KEY WORDS

**Trichology** – *the study of hair and scalp disorders*
**Pityriasis simplex** – *dandruff*
**Seborrhoea** – *greasy scalp*
**Alopecia** – *hair loss*

Therefore, when offering a treatment to a client, it is advisable to indicate that success is not guaranteed. When using specialist scalp treatments, always follow the manufacturer's guidelines on the method and frequency of application.

Always update the client's record following these treatments.

# Scalp massage

Scalp massage helps to stimulate capillary blood flow, which feeds the hair root and follicle. It will also help to stimulate the production of *sebum* (the hair and skin's natural oil) from the sebaceous glands that open into the hair follicle. (More information is contained in Chapter 13.) Scalp massage will also relax and soothe your client.

Scalp massage may be given by hand or mechanically, and is usually given when the hair and scalp have been treated with a conditioning cream. This lubricates the surface of the hair and scalp, enabling the massage to take place without the client suffering discomfort.

Do not carry out any form of scalp massage if there are open sores or cuts on the scalp, if there is any contagious scalp disorder or if your client complains of pain or discomfort during the massage.

## Petrissage

Petrissage is a massage movement using the pads of the fingers in a co-ordinated gripping, kneading movement (see Figure 4.11). Often when you start the scalp massage, the scalp is tight and therefore this massage should be started gently. As the manipulation loosens the scalp, the massage may become more intense, though never rough. The massage movement should follow an organised pattern over the scalp with both hands using an even pressure. Take care not to exert too much pressure on the sensitive areas of the scalp such as the temporal and mastoid areas.

■ Figure 4.11 Petrissage massage movement

■ Figure 4.12 Effleurage massage movement

## Effleurage

Effleurage is a stroking movement using the fingers and palms of the hands (see Figure 4.12) and has a soothing effect, helping to distribute the increased blood flow.

# The use of heat

During the application of a cream conditioner heat may be used to aid penetration of the hair by the product, as well as speeding up any chemical processes. Moist heat swells the hair shaft, making this action easier. Heat may be provided in several ways, including:

- scalp steamer
- thermal cap
- radiated heat
- scalp heat.

*HEALTH & SAFETY*

Your salon may have procedures for visual checking of electrical appliances and reporting faults. Find out what your salon's procedures are for this.

## Scalp steamer

The scalp steamer is an apparatus with a hood that may be adjusted to fit over the scalp area of your client. It has a reservoir which holds a supply of distilled or de-ionised water. This water feeds into a small boiler that produces steam. This steam is fed to a series of jets that distribute it within the hood (Figure 4.13).

Before use, ensure that the machine is clean. Check the inside of the hood for traces of previously used products and ensure that the reservoir has a sufficient supply of water. Pre-heat the steamer and, once steaming, adjust any temperature settings. Locate the hood carefully over the scalp area, ensuring that the hood and vents are positioned so as to avoid steam escaping on to your client's neck. Be aware of your client's comfort at all times, and ensure that they are able to inform someone should they experience any discomfort.

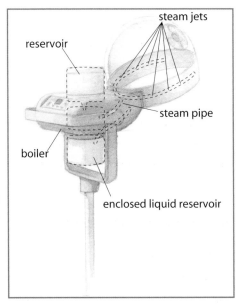

■ Figure 4.13. How a scalp steamer works

*HEALTH & SAFETY*

Never use electrical equipment if you do not know how. Always read the manufacturer's directions or ask your trainer for guidance in correct use.

## Thermal cap

A thermal cap is a close-fitting hood with an electrically heated element, similar to that in an electric blanket, built into the fabric. Once connected to an electrical supply the interior of the cap becomes warm. This heat is conducted to the hair and any products lying on the hair. As the surface is waterproof the moisture is retained. Care must be taken to ensure client comfort at all times.

*HEALTH & SAFETY*

The Electricity at Work Regulations 1989 require that portable electrical tools should be tested regularly for electrical safety (PAT).

## Radiated heat

There are a number of appliances that may be used to radiate heat on to the hair and scalp. Some use specialised light bulbs to generate this heat; others use heating elements (see Figure 4.14). Care must be taken to locate elements correctly around the head, to ensure even heating and to prevent 'hot spots' on the head. As the product's moisture is not trapped within any hood, check to ensure that the hair does not dry out during the process. If this happens, moisten the hair.

## Scalp heat

Scalp heat, if retained, may be used to aid penetration by conditioning products. The scalp area is enclosed within a polythene cap that, in turn, is enclosed within a towel. The polythene cap prevents moisture loss and the towel insulates, reducing heat loss.

■ Figure 4.14 Accelerator in use on client

# KEY SKILL TASK

*This task could produce evidence that supports C1.2, C1.3, & N1.1.*

*Produce step-by-step instructions to guide a trainee in using the electronic heaters (scalp steamer, accelerator, climazone, roller ball) used in your salon to assist scalp conditioning treatments. Include diagrams to illustrate each heater's controls and what functions they fulfil. Remember to include any relevant health and safety features and practices.*

## Useful Tasks

Home-use haircare products may be suggested during the shampoo process, particularly suitable shampoos and conditioners. Watch out for signs of interest shown by your client in the products you are using. Retail lines which complement the products used within your salon should be available.

1. Find out the features and benefits of the shampoos used in your salon, so that you can advise upon and select appropriate products for use on your client, both in the salon and for home use.

2. Many manufacturers produce treatment ranges that have cleansers (shampoos) which are complemented by hair and scalp conditioners and styling products. You should make yourself aware of these and how they are selected for the client.

3. The hairdresser should be aware of what retail haircare products are available from non-salon retail outlets so that comparisons may be discussed with your client.

4. Develop your selling skills; look for signs from your clients of interest in retail products.

5. Produce a fact sheet about the shampoos and conditioning products available in your salon. Include details of specific safety aspects when using these.

## Self review

1. List the range of shampoos used within your salon, and indicate the hair and scalp types for which they are designed.

2. What effect can hard water have on the shower head (rose) at the basin?

3. On what occasions would you use 'dry' shampoos?

4. When shampooing, how is the water temperature tested?

5. Describe 'rotary' massage.

6. List two ingredients often found in 'anti-dandruff' shampoos.

7. What is the pH of normal hair?

8. Describe the action of a surface conditioner.

9.  Give two occasions when protective conditioning may be appropriate.

10. Give two benefits to be gained by the client from scalp massage.

## Useful contacts

| | |
|---|---|
| Clynol | www.clynol.com |
| Goldwell | www.goldwell.com |
| HABIA | www.habia.org.uk |
| Hairdressing Beauty Suppliers Association | www.hbsa.uk.com |
| L'Oréal | www.loreal.co.uk |
| Wella (GB) | www.wella.co.uk |

# CHAPTER 5

# Cutting hair

## CHAPTER CONTENTS

**Unit H6**   Cut hair using basic techniques

**Unit H7**   Cut hair using basic barbering techniques

**Unit H8**   Cut facial hair to shape using basic techniques

## WHAT THIS CHAPTER WILL PROVIDE

This chapter is in three parts. The first looks at haircutting techniques, all of which are relevant for ladies' hairdressing and some of which are relevant to barbering. The second section focuses on the barbering skills of haircutting. The third section focuses on the barbering skills of shaping facial hair.

This chapter provides the essential knowledge of the basic techniques and step-by-step practical skills you will use to cut hair.

# Introduction

This aspect of hairstyling has, arguably, the highest profile with your clients. Clients appear to think haircutting is more important than any other hairdressing skill. Such is the profile of haircutting that there are a number of salon groups specialising in haircutting, often to the exclusion of any of the chemical hairdressing processes.

Haircutting skills are acquired with a thorough understanding of the shapes and effects that may be produced in hair using a range of techniques and a variety of cutting tools. These skills may be developed through practice, initially on wefts of hair (hair attached to a band or thread), then on training heads (lifelike heads with implanted hair, usually human). These tools will enable you, as a trainee hairdresser, to develop the basic techniques and manual dexterity required to create shapes in hair in a controlled manner. Eventually these skills must be applied to a live model. This will provide you with experience of a number of critical influencing factors, including variety of hair textures, hair growth patterns, head and face shapes, and lifestyles.

Learning to cut a number of individual haircuts without an understanding of the principles and processes which support them will produce a skill which may not adapt to suit changing hair fashions and haircutting trends.

# Tools used for haircutting

The quality and selection of tools is important in order for you to accomplish a good haircut. However, good tools will not produce a good haircut unless they are used in the correct manner. To do your best work you should use tools of good quality. However, improper use will quickly destroy the efficiency of any implement, no matter how perfectly it was made in the factory. Therefore when starting to learn to cut hair it may not be advisable to purchase tools of too high a cost until you have developed the skills to use them correctly.

## Haircutting scissors

Scissors come in a variety of sizes, shapes and finishes. The sizes of scissors are measured from the points to the opposite end at the finger grip (see Figures 5.1 and 5.2). The size is described in inches and may range from 3″ through to 10″ by ½″ stages. Your choice will depend mainly upon the following two factors.

1   What feels comfortable to use. The third finger and thumb should fit comfortably, and the thumb should be easily removed from the grip when palming the scissors. Plastic inserts can be obtained for certain scissors, allowing the size of the finger and thumb grips to be varied to suit the user.

2   The technique of cutting to be used. Scissor-over-comb techniques normally require a longer pair of scissors than would be used to produce more textured looks.

The shape of the blade may be straight or curved; the curved shape is often used when club cutting curved shapes

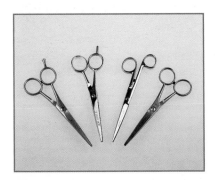

■ Figure 5.1 Range of scissors

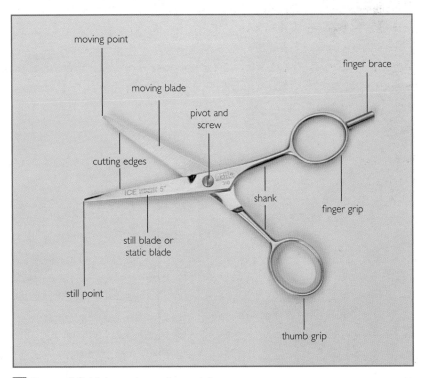

■ Figure 5.2 Haircutting scissors: the parts

in hair. The surface of the cutting edges may be smooth, or one or both of the edges may have micro-serrations. This helps to prevent hair sliding along the length of the blades as they are closed on to the hair (see Figure 5.5).

Scissors may be made of metals of differing hardness. The harder metals retain the keenness of the edge for longer, but are more brittle. Scissors are available in stainless steel, chrome-plated steel and plastic-coated steel. Ceramic blades are also available.

## Care of your scissors

◆     After use, always wipe your scissors dry and place them in their case.

◆     Use light oil on the surfaces at the pivot.

◆     Always keep scissors sharp; the cut of the end of the hair is then much cleaner.

◆     Your scissors have blades which are finely ground; they require specialist sharpening.

## HEALTH & SAFETY

Don't keep haircutting scissors in your pocket, unless they are in a specialised wallet.

## Thinning scissors

There are many types of thinning scissors, the main distinction between types being the serrations on the blade. When the blade is closed, hair slides into the serrations and is not cut. The hair which does not slide into the gap is cut, and this action thins the hair. The more serrations, the less hair will be removed. The wider the serrations and teeth of the scissors, the bolder the cut will be. Closely set, fine teeth will remove much finer strands; a pair of scissors with a single serrated blade will remove a greater bulk of hair than they would if both blades were serrated (see Figures 5.3–5.4).

When used on wet hair, thinning scissors remove more bulk than when used on dry hair. Care must be taken not to over-thin the hair or to cause a definite line of demarcation, which is often the result if the scissors are closed only once on a strand of hair.

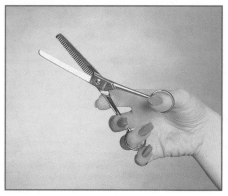

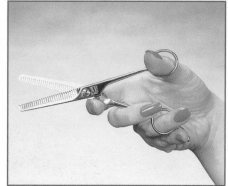

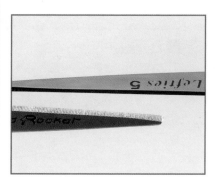

■ Figure 5.3 Thinning scissors with one serrated blade

■ Figure 5.4 Thinning scissors with two serrated blades

■ Figure 5.5 Smooth blade (top) and blade with micro-serrations

# Razors/shapers

There are a number of razors and shapers that you may use on hair. You should only use them when the hair is wet. Traditionally the open razor was used for this, but its use has declined due to the highly specialised sharpening (honing and stropping) process needed and the risks associated with contagious blood-related disorders.

Razors and shapers accept replaceable blades of a variety of types, some of which are highly specialised. Others may be purchased from most retail chemists and personal grooming shops. Some are shaped to replicate the traditional open razor (see Figure 5.6); others are shaped to fit the hand.

# Hair clippers

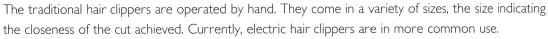

The traditional hair clippers are operated by hand. They come in a variety of sizes, the size indicating the closeness of the cut achieved. Currently, electric hair clippers are in more common use.

## Electric hair clippers

Cordless clippers may safely be used on moist and dry hair, although the battery requires recharging at frequent intervals. They come in a variety of sizes, which varies the closeness and the width of the cut.

Corded clippers may be operated for longer periods. Some types are available with variable degrees of cut and others accept a variety of differently sized cutting heads.

# Combs

A variety of combs are required when cutting hair (see Figure 5.6). Combs with a variety of tooth sizes allow tangles to be removed using the larger teeth, and then the finer teeth can be used to control the hair when cutting. The comb must be small enough to be held easily while also palming the scissors (see Figure 5.8).

Combs that have 'saw cut' teeth are less likely to damage hair than the cheaper, moulded combs, which may have rough surfaces between the teeth.

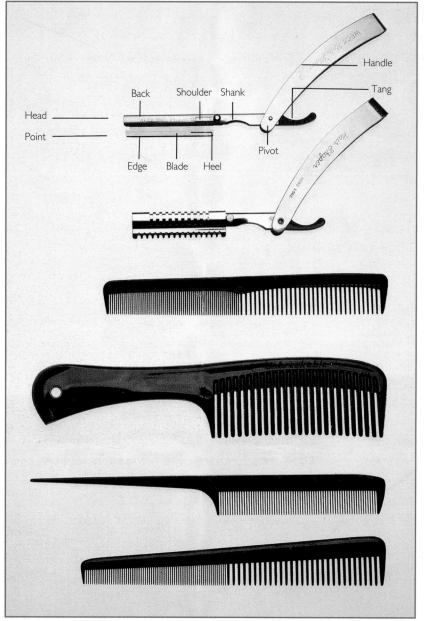

Figure 5.7 Correct scissor hold

Figure 5.6 Top to bottom: replacement blade open razor; open razor with safety guards; all-purpose comb; large-tooth comb; tail comb; hair-shaping comb

# Holding haircutting tools

## Scissors

Haircutting scissors are handled correctly by inserting the third finger into the finger grip of the still blade and placing the little finger on the finger brace (if provided). Insert the thumb into the thumb grip of the moveable blade. The tip of the index finger is braced near the pivot of the scissors in order to give better control (see Figure 5.7).

## Holding comb and scissors

While cutting hair, you will be holding both comb and scissors in the same hand. Practise closing the blades of the scissors, removing the thumb from the grip, and resting the scissors in the palm. Hold the scissors securely with the ring finger. The comb is held between the thumb and fingers, 'palming the scissors' (see Figure 5.8).

## Razor/shapers

### Finger wrap hold

Place the thumb in the groove part of the *shank* and fold the fingers over the handle of the razor. The *guard* faces the hairstylist while working (see Figure 5.9).

### Three-finger hold

Place three fingers over the shank, the thumb in the groove of the shank, and the little finger in the hollow part of the *tang* (see Figure 5.10).

When using the razor, keep the hair moist to avoid pulling the hair and to prevent dulling the razor. When combing the hair *palm* the razor as shown in Figure 5.11.

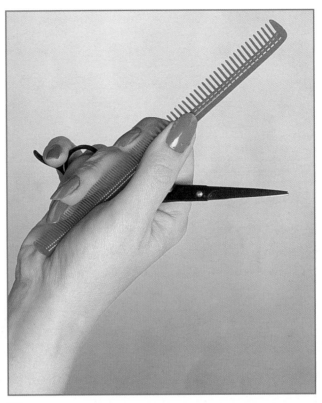

■ Figure 5.8 Holding comb and scissors together (palming)

## KEY WORDS

**Palm** – to securely hold a haircutting implement in the palm of the hand while at the same time holding the comb using the fingers of the same hand; this reduces the need to constantly put the cutting implement (scissors or razor) down while combing the hair

## REMEMBER!

*When combing the hair, hold the comb and scissors in the right hand as shown in Figure 5.8. When cutting the hair, hold the comb in the left hand. To save time, do not put the comb or scissors down during shaping.*

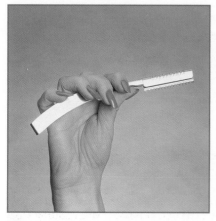

■ Figure 5.9 Finger wrap hold

■ Figure 5.10 Three-finger hold

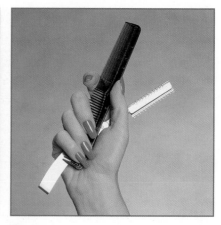

■ Figure 5.11 Razor and comb

# Client consultation and preparation

A good haircut is the foundation of every hairstyle and can change a client's view of themselves and their image.

## Client consultation

In order to be aware of the required hairstyle, you must assess your client's needs and requirements and negotiate how these may best be implemented. Effective communication is essential; there are a variety of tools to help you ensure that this takes place. These include style books, video imaging systems and wigs. Confirmation of the agreed hairstyle should be achieved before commencing the haircut, although this may be reviewed during the cutting as it progresses. Consultation should normally take place before any work is commenced on your client. The following checklist of factors to bear in mind will help you to assess and advise your client:

◆ your client's requirements, personality and lifestyle

◆ your client's face and head shape

◆ your client's body proportions

◆ your client's hair type – texture, thickness and length

◆ any strong directions of hair growth (hair growth patterns)

◆ the suggested hairstyle

◆ your client's ability to manage their hair.

Check the hair and scalp for any contra-indications to the cutting process; these may include contagious scalp disorders and open cuts or sores on the scalp.

 REMEMBER!

*When providing guidance to your client be honest, tactful and sincere. They will respond to factual information that is provided in a clear, understandable and direct manner.*

# Gowning and protecting your client

The purpose of gowning your client prior to undertaking a haircut is to protect her or him and her/his clothing from hair clippings and any products used by you on their hair. Any method of gowning is acceptable provided that it protects your client and their clothing and is hygienic. Differing salons may have their own procedures for gowning the client. If in doubt, consult with your supervisor or trainer.

All items used should be clean, freshly laundered or disposable. Gowns and towels not laundered before reuse may pass infection from one client to the next. All gowning should be secured so that it does not come loose or fall during the cutting process.

A gown that is large enough to cover the client's clothing should be used. Towels may be required when cutting wet hair. However, hairs embed themselves in towels so it may be considered more hygienic to towel dry the hair and use disposable plastic shoulder capes to protect the client. To prevent cut hairs from falling down between the client's neck and their clothing, insert a strip of clean cotton wool or a neck tissue around the neck area. These items are disposable and should be used only once.

## REMEMBER!

*Hair clippings from around your client's neck may be removed by blasting with the hairdryer. Take care, however, that hair clippings do not fly into your client's eyes.*

Throughout the cut, loose hair clippings should be removed from the neck area using a clean neck brush. These brushes should be washed, dried and sterilised regularly. Do not allow quantities of hair clippings to build up around the client's neck during the cut, as this will easily become trapped in clothing. The application of talcum powder to the surface of the skin from a powder blower prior to brushing will help to remove clippings easily from the skin.

# Initial hair analysis

1   Having discussed the style with your client and assessed the hair for quality, quantity and length, gown the client and then shampoo or wet the hair, unless the hair is to be cut dry. The quality or condition of the hair will determine its elasticity and how well it will retain the dried shape. Hair that is dry or porous will lack shine and will not appear smooth and shiny once dried.

2   When wet, the natural fall and movement of the hair may be determined. If this is assessed before wetting, the fall may be confused with the style introduced during the previous styling.

3   Check the hairline (front and back) for unusual hair growth patterns or characteristics that may affect the finished style.

# Haircutting techniques

There are three basic techniques used in cutting hair. These techniques may be achieved with a variety of haircutting tools used in differing ways. Their selection will depend on the required outcome, the preferred technique and salon policy.

# Club cutting hair

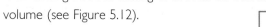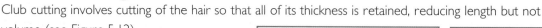

Club cutting involves cutting of the hair so that all of its thickness is retained, reducing length but not volume (see Figure 5.12).

This technique is ideal when producing heavy, smooth hairstyles where curl or movement is not being encouraged. As all of the hair's natural volume is retained, it is ideal for use on thin, fine hair, where maximum volume is required (see Figure 5.13).

# Thinning hair

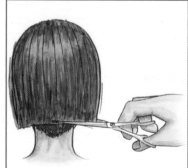

Thinning the hair is cutting it to reduce volume but not length (see Figure 5.14). This may be used to thin hair when it is too thick. It may be carried out over the whole head or just in localised areas (fringes and other hairline areas). Methods of thinning may be used to achieve lift, height or spiky effects in fashion styles. Thinning the point ends of the hair will encourage wavy hair to curl (see Figure 5.15).

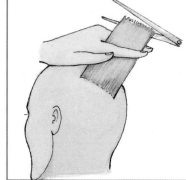

■ Figure 5.12 Club cutting

■ Figure 5.13 Maximising volume by club cutting

# Taper cutting hair

This is cutting the hair to reduce length as well as thickness. This may be carried out in a single operation (see Figure 5.18) or may be carried out as a two-step process, with a club cut followed by thinning. This technique of cutting hair can produce a natural taper to the hair, making it appear more natural for softer shapes. It

■ Figure 5.14 Thinning hair with thinning scissors

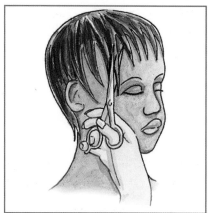

■ Figure 5.15 Point thinning a fringe section

■ Figure 5.16 Thinning with haircutting scissors

will encourage wavy hair to curl, therefore is ideally suited to hairstyles which require movement or curl. Straight hair that is going to be scrunch dried to curl will curl more easily if taper cut or thinned.

Taper cutting will make winding thick hair on to perm rods easier and will also aid the process of back combing.

# Achieving techniques using haircutting tools

Club cutting can be carried out using either scissors (on wet or dry hair) or with clippers (on dry hair). The method of cutting using scissors or clippers over a comb is a method of club cutting the hair, achieving a graduated shape in very short hair (see Figure 5.35).

**Thinning** can be carried out with thinning scissors, haircutting scissors (see Figure 5.17) or a razor/shaper. When using thinning scissors, note that if used on wet hair more hair will be removed than when used on dry hair. The term *texturising* is often applied to the technique of thinning the hair to achieve strong fashion effects, where the thinning gives the hair movement often associated with heavily defined changes in hair length.

**Taper cutting** can be carried out in one step using either a razor/shaper or scissors. Razor/shapers should be used on wet hair only and scissors on dry hair (wet hair does not separate so readily to facilitate the taper with scissors). See Figures 5.18 and 5.19.

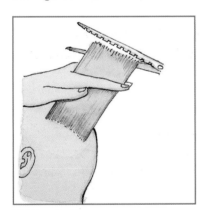

■ Figure 5.17 Thinning with haircutting scissors

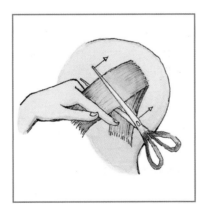

■ Figure 5.18 Taper cutting to aid back combing

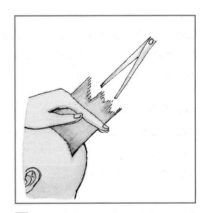

■ Figure 5.19 Taper effect using points of scissors

The critical factors that can affect your haircut are as follows.

◆ Very wavy hair is likely to appear much shorter when dry. Allowance should be made for this apparent reduction in length when planning the haircut.

◆ Strong directions of hair growth, in particular double crowns and cowlicks, may cause hair to spring up when the length is removed. This can be problematic when creating a straight fringe in the presence of the cowlick as, if the hair is cut while held down, it might not lay flat when released.

◆ Strong nape whorls may be easier to control when slightly longer or closely graduated into the neck. Additional length provides weight in the hair to hold the hair down rather than moving sideways as it usually does in the whorl. Close graduation removes the hair length to an extent that any sideways direction is not perceived.

◆ Reducing the bulk, or thinning, very wavy hair can make control of the wave easier. It may be blow dried straight more readily.

◆ Very thick hair may appear too thick when cut to a one-length bob. The hair ends may require thinning.

◆ Baby fine hair may often show cutting marks if club cut.

◆ When club cutting hair that is lightened on the top (often due to sunlight), apparent weight lines or cutting marks may appear at the point where the hair colour changes. Tapering or thinning the hair at these points may reduce this appearance.

◆ During consultation, review the hair's suitability to retain the style required. Consider if the hair has sufficient length, at the relevant points to enable the style to be produced. The texture of the hair will influence the style choice; fine hair may not produce the required volume unless chemical treatments are used, for example a permanent wave style support. You should remember that your client must be able to maintain their hairstyle between salon visits. The potential of very strong hair may be realised by using this strength to produce lift and volume within the style. Dressing the hair against the direction of hair growth may facilitate this volume. Cutting sections of hair within the mesh shorter so as to lift and support the surrounding hair may induce lift.

◆ Creating sudden, definite changes in hair length will normally cause the hair to separate at this change point. You may use this to enhance a style where separation, possibly of a fringe from the remainder of the hairstyle, is required. Wherever there is to be a change in length without causing separation the length changes should be blended by 'over-directing' – that is, drawing the hair at 180° to the direction in which it will fall and connecting to the shorter length that is also drawn in the same direction.

## Producing shapes in hair

Hairstyles are three-dimensional and when cutting hair it is not just the hair's length and outline shape that is changed, but the internal shape as well. There are four basic shapes that may be cut into hair. These may then be used in isolation from each other or may be used in combination, often to achieve fashion effects.

---

**+** *HEALTH & SAFETY*

Sharp-cutting tools can be dangerous if used in confined areas, where there is a real risk that you will be knocked while working. Razors should not be left open on the worktop, but closed and placed in a case or protective cover.

---

## One-length or solid shapes

All of the hair within the style extends to the base line of the hairstyle. This style produces the volume of the style around the design line. If used on its own the hairstyle will tend to be flat on the top and smooth and weighty around the perimeter. If used on wavy or curly hair the result can be a very full effect (see Figure 5.20).

KEY WORDS

**Design line** – *the outline shape of the hairstyle*
**Base line** – *the outline shape at the points of the hair; the furthermost points that the hair extends to throughout the hairstyle*
**Weight line** – *the points in the hair where volume or bulk in the hair is established*

## Uniform layered shapes

All of the hair within this style is cut to the same length (see Figure 5.21). The shape achieved in the style is the same as the head shape. As all the hair is cut to the same length there is no localised build-up of volume in areas of the head, so the hair in the base line will be wispy.

## Layered: internal hair length greater than hair length at hairline (graduation)

The hair at the nape and side design line is the shortest in this hairstyle, gradually getting longer to the top of the hairstyle (see Figure 5.22). Maximum volume is created where the point ends of the top layer reach. This is the weight line within the style. This shape enables the hairdresser to adjust the apparent shape of the head.

Figure 5.20 Achieving a full effect in wavy hair

Figure 5.21 Achieving uniform layered shapes

## Layered: internal hair length less than hair length at hairline (reverse graduation)

The hair on the top of this hairstyle is the shortest in the hairstyle, gradually getting longer towards the style's design line (see Figure 5.23). This enables a long-hair effect to be produced but with volume and movement within the internal structure of the style. The volume is achieved not by creating a weight line within the style but by producing shorter hair which may lift, and hair ends within the style which may curl.

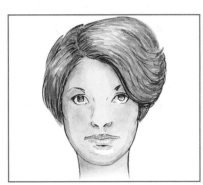

Figure 5.22 Layered hair: graduation where internal hair length greater than at hairline

Figure 5.23 Layered hair: graduation where internal hair length shorter than at hairline

## REMEMBER!

*When cutting wavy and curly hair wet, you must allow for elastic recoil as it dries. The extent of this will depend upon the degree of curl.*

## Cutting the one-length hairstyle

This style requires that the weight be kept at the base line of the hairstyle, so the club cut technique should be used (see Figure 5.24). The hair is best cut when wet as this gives maximum control over the hair. Very long hair will stretch while under tension, so take care not to place too much tension on it when cutting, as when released the hair will retract and the weight line will be lost. The process is as follows.

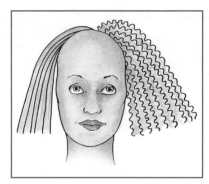

■ Figure 5.24 The one-length hairstyle

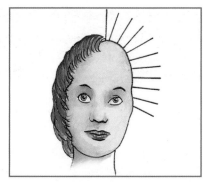

■ Figure 5.25 The uniform layered hairstyle

1   Having sectioned the style, to control the hair the cutting of this style usually commences at the nape. Take small sections of hair, which may easily be controlled.
    Comb smooth, hold down flat to the head or shoulders and cut to the required length, allowing for elastic recoil. When cutting hair that will extend below the level of the nape hairline, it is advisable to keep your client's head upright or inclined forward slightly. The client's head should be central and not allowed to tilt to the side as this may lead to an unbalanced effect.

2   Bring down fine meshes of hair, in controllable sections, hold flat against the head and neck, and cut to the position of the design line. The meshes of hair should be combed downwards to remove tangles and to control the hair. Keep the hair evenly wet while cutting so that you achieve an even level of hair stretch.

3   As you progress up the back of the head, taking fine sections of hair, holding in a downwards direction, the side sections of the head should be incorporated. This will help to ensure that there is no break or step between the back and sides. Hold the hair downwards, first cutting the base line. Allow for the additional hair length required to cover the ears and yet produce an even line at the design line.

4   Check the balance of the sides of the haircut by:

    i   drawing hair from identical areas of each side of the head. If the hair is of even length, the points should meet centrally

    ii  drawing the fingers down strands of the hair from both sides of the head, and check for level using the dressing position mirror.

5   Continue to progress up the head to the parting area. When directing the hair at the top of the head, comb it into the position into which it will fall when dry.

6   Check the cut when it is dry to ensure that all hair extends to the design line. This will allow for any uneven elastic recoil.

7   A fringe may be cut as an integral part of the style, or if it is not to be blended it may be separated off and cut.

8   Hard, solid design lines may be softened (thinned) by *freehand* cutting. This is cutting with scissors, pushing the scissors from within the hairstyle, in the direction of the hairstyle and closing the blades. To remove more hair the scissors may be angled slightly across the line of hair fall. Soft wispy effects on the sides may also be produced in this way.

9   Once completed, or if your client is to be consulted on the progress of the cut, show them the style using the back-view mirror.

# KEY WORDS

**Freehand** – *cutting with scissors from within the hairstyle, in the direction of the hairstyle*

---

## REMEMBER!

*When cutting hair that will extend past your client's shoulders, ensure that your client is upright. It may be more effective for the client to stand, so that their back is in an upright position and your view is not obscured by the chair back.*

---

## Cutting the uniform layered hairstyle

This hairstyle does not produce any weight lines in the style; it follows the shape of the wearer's own head (see Figure 5.25). Additional shape and volume may be added to the style by perming and/or drying in a variety of ways. The hairstyle may be cut on either wet or dry hair, and may be club cut or taper cut, depending on how much volume is required in the style, and on whether the style is to have movement (curl or wave). The process is as follows.

1 This shape may be cut in hair starting at any point of the head. This is normally either at the nape or at the top front of the hairstyle.

2 Take small meshes, which can easily be controlled. Having established the desired length, comb adjacent sections of hair out at 90° to the scalp and, using the adjacent cut section as a guide, cut the hair to the same length. Failure to hold the hair out at 90° can result in the hair's length either becoming longer or shorter than that previously cut.

3 The hair may be tapered or thinned, using scissors or a razor/shaper in a specific area, as required for the hairstyle.

4 Ensure that your client's head is upright when checking for evenness and balance. Use the dressing point mirror to check the balance of both sides, placing the fingers through the hair and drawing the hair outwards.

---

## REMEMBER!

*While cutting hair, watch your client's body language for any indications of discomfort, as this may indicate concern about the progress of the haircut. If this is the case reassure them and address their concerns.*

---

## Cutting the graduated hairstyle

The inner hair length is longer than the outline hair length but the inner hair does not reach to the design line. Graduation creates weight lines in the hairstyle. Figure 5.26 indicates the location of the design line, the weight line, the outline hair length and the inner hair.

The outline hair length or design line may be varied in length and shape depending upon the desired finished hairstyle. The location of the weight line can be varied by the angle of graduation; the weight line will be located at the top of the graduation, where the end of the longest hair reaches in the finished hairstyle.

A graduation may be cut by taking sections that are at 90° to the design line (vertical sections) or by taking sections that are parallel to the design line. Your choice of technique will depend upon:

◆    the technique with which you are most familiar

◆    the technique used in your salon.

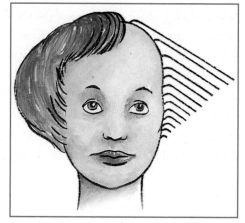

■ Figure 5.26 The graduated hairstyle

Cutting the graduated hairstyle usually commences at the design line, since this is the shortest area of the hairstyle. The actual start point may vary: it may be the nape or the sides or around the ear, depending on the finished hairstyle required, and personal preference. Take small sections that may be controlled easily, comb the hair to remove tangles and then hold it at the required angle. If taking horizontal sections, parallel to the design line, the section of hair should be held at between 1° and 90°, depending upon the required angle of graduation and the position of the weight line. The smaller the angle, the lower the graduation and the lower down the head the weight line will be located. By enlarging the angle, the weight line will be raised. (Figures 5.27–5.30 illustrate this.)

■ Figure 5.27 Producing graduation (1)

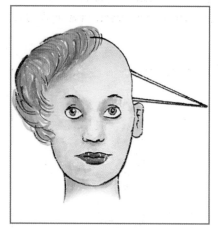

■ Figure 5.28 Producing graduation (2)

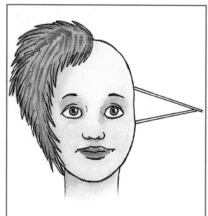

■ Figure 5.29 Producing graduation (3)

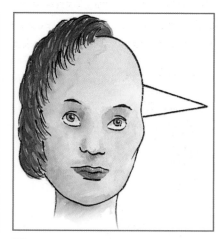

■ Figure 5.30 Producing graduation (4)

# Cutting scissor-over-comb graduation

When a close graduation is required, the hair length being shorter than can be held between the fingers, a graduated result may be achieved by holding the hair in the teeth of the comb and cutting the hair. The comb is pushed upwards from the shortest length, into the longer hair. The cutting point is where the comb's teeth join the back of the comb. The comb's teeth should be angled to reflect the required angle of graduation. The comb should be moved in a steady continuous movement, the teeth angled outwards and the static blade of the scissors in line with the back of the comb (see Figure 5.31). Electric clippers may also be used with this technique.

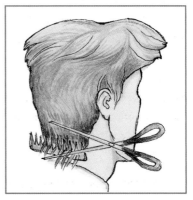

 *REMEMBER!*

*Maintaining weight and volume in hair will often produce straight smooth looks. Reducing volume and layering hair usually encourages hair to curl and lift.*

Figure 5.31 Scissor-over-comb cutting on men's close graduation

# Cutting the reverse graduation

The outer hair length is longer than the inner length. *Reverse graduation* does not create weight lines within the hairstyle; it does, however, allow height and movement within the framework of a longer hairstyle effect (see Figure 5.32).

The outline hair length or design line may be varied in length and shape, depending upon the desired completed hairstyle. The degree of reverse graduation, how much shorter the inner hair length is compared to the outline hair length, may be varied to suit the hairstyle.

The technique of cutting usually starts at the shorter areas of the hairstyle, taking sections that are parallel to the design line. The hair is over-directed at more than 90° to produce the reverse graduation. The greater the angle the greater the degree of reverse graduation (see Figures 5.33 and 5.34).

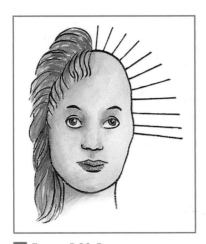
Figure 5.32 Reverse graduation

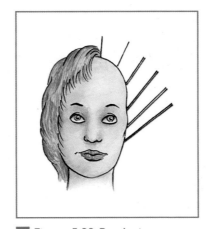
Figure 5.33 Producing reverse graduation (1)

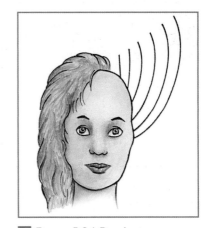
Figure 5.34 Producing reverse graduation (2)

## REMEMBER!

*Hair clippings should be swept away as soon as possible and placed in a covered bin. Do not allow them to remain on your client or on the floor longer than necessary.*

# Combination and fashion techniques

Most hairstyles today require a combination of cutting shapes and cutting techniques to achieve the look. Examples of these are shown in the figures below. Figure 5.35 shows the use of graduation at the sides and back, linked with a uniform layer on the top.

Often a shape can be linked with a specific cutting technique for selected areas of the head. Figure 5.36 shows a technique for producing a one-length cut linked with a fringe which has been texturised to produce a contrasting spiky effect.

You can give separation to those areas that lie on to the skin at the hairline by the use of *freehand* cutting (see Figure 5.37). Whenever the hair is cut while it is in a free unrestrained situation it may be termed *freehand*.

♦ This style of haircutting can be advantageous when cutting very wavy hair that is held taut and likely to retract when released and it is required to lie in a specific point on the head. By cutting *in situ* there is less risk of the elastic recoil moving the cut line.

♦ Carefully stroking the points of the scissors into strands of hair while closing the scissors will reduce volume and encourage curl/wave and a natural effect to hair.

♦ Twisting small sections of short hair and partially closing the scissors on to the mesh will produce a textured effect.

When using any cutting technique it is essential to view the progress of the style and respond to any effects that you did not at first expect. This is particularly true when cutting a client's hair for the first time, when it may not always be possible to predict precisely how the hair will respond to the technique, method and length of the cut. Consult your client, explain what is happening, and gain their confidence and agreement through your responsiveness.

■ Figure 5.35 Graduated haircut

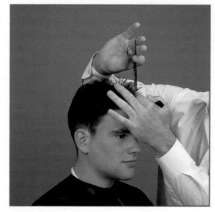

■ Figure 5.36 One-length cut with spiky fringe

■ Figure 5.37 Effect of freehand cutting on hairline

*Useful Task*

Build a portfolio of current and emerging hairstyles and the techniques and methods used to achieve them. This will form a useful reference document for you in your work.

# Barbering

Those traditional skills closely associated with men's hairdressing include developing graduation and sculptured looks, and shaping and removing facial hair. Traditionally the shapes produced in men's hair are squarer and much sharper than those usually associated with other forms of hairstyling (see Figure 5.38). They are produced using techniques that facilitate the easy manipulation of short hair on the scalp or face using the comb and either clippers or scissors.

Barbering invariably involves attention to facial hair, whether it is to level sideburns or, at the other extreme, to shape a full beard and moustache. Facial hair may be used to enhance the wearer's appearance just as with scalp hair. It can alter the apparent shape of the face, drawing attention to or minimising the effects of a range of facial features.

Figure 5.38 A barbering situation

To ignore the total appearance of your client when barbering would be a great error. Having styled the hair on the scalp, neglect of any facial hair, subject to your client's agreement, would equate to failure to complete a hairstyle.

# Preparation

## Seating your client

Barbering skills usually require the use of a hydraulically operated chair for the client (see Figure 5.39). This allows you, the barber, to raise or lower your client and position him to a height and angle which allows you easy and comfortable access to all areas of his scalp and face, no matter how tall he is. To shape facial hair your client should be slightly reclined, as this makes the chin area of the face more accessible. A chair that allows you to do this is a great advantage for the barber and keeps your client comfortable.

**+ HEALTH & SAFETY**

If you are uncertain of the safe working of the chair ask for guidance from your line manager or trainer.

Figure 5.39 Hydraulically operated chair

Always ensure that the hydraulic chair is clean and free from hair clippings. Lower the chair to its lowest position. At this height the chair is at its most stable and least likely to tip or move. In the case of a manual hydraulic chair this may be done by depressing the foot pump and holding it down while the chair falls. Some pressure on the chair may be required to encourage it in its downward journey. Once it is at the desired height, pull the foot lever upwards by placing a foot beneath it and pulling upwards. This locks the chair in position and prevents it from revolving. Electronically operated chairs are available and the manufacturer's directions for use should be followed.

Ensure that the back of the chair is in an upright position and, if you are about to cut the scalp hair, remove the headrest, if attached (its location could prevent you from working with ease in the nape area of your client's hairstyle).

When your client is seated, the chair may be adjusted to a height to suit your work. Pump the foot pedal to do this.

## Client consultation

Discuss with your client the treatment to be given. Listen to your client. (For more guidance about consultation see Chapter 3.)

## Gowning your client

The cutting cloth or cape is usually a square or rectangular shape with a slit in the middle of one side. This slit is to fit your client's neck, being tucked into the client's collar. Ensure that the gown covers your client's clothing.

When cutting, tuck a strand of clean cotton between the gown and the neck. This forms a seal to prevent hair clippings from passing down the neck. A cutting collar may also be used to hold the gown in place while cutting.

When shampooing at a front washbasin it is advisable to protect your client by placing a towel around his chest, followed with a second around the back. At the completion of the shampoo use the towel at the back to towel dry the hair, and move the one from the front to the back. (For more information about shampooing see Chapter 4.)

## Personal hygiene

It is particularly important to be aware of your personal hygiene when shaping facial hair, as you will be very close to your client and often facing into his face. Body odour can offend your client, as can over-liberal use of strong-smelling perfume and cologne. Oral hygiene is also very important. Breath that smells of strong-tasting foods, cigarette smoke or the effects of halitosis or decaying teeth can be very unpleasant to your client.

# REMEMBER!

*Always keep your breath fresh, particularly when working closely with your client or colleagues.*

## Barbering tools

All the tools that you use should be of good quality and hygienically clean. At the workstation there should be a method of sterilising tools easily between clients. Usually you will need a second set of tools, so that you can sterilise one set while continuing to work.

## Scissors

These are described earlier in this chapter. It is advisable to use scissors of 5½ inches or more in length when graduating over a comb. The additional length enables the scissors to be held correctly while close to the head.

## Combs

A range of combs is required. Some should have both fine and coarse-set teeth and vary in size. Fine, flexibly backed combs can flex and fit against the contour of the scalp and neck. This is particularly necessary when close graduating. Rigid-backed combs can cope with strong hair. Combs set with even teeth may be used when producing flat surfaces on the hair (see Figure 5.40). Fashion styling effects may be achieved using specialist styling combs.

Figure 5.40 Barbering combs

## Hair clippers

These act as shears, cutting the hair (see Figure 5.41). Some ranges of electric hair clippers have grader attachments. The grader sets a gap between the scalp and the cutting blade, enabling a consistent length of hair to be cut. The graders vary in size, the smallest (producing the closest cut) being 'number 1' progressing to the much larger 'number 8'. There are graders available which have a graduating effect on the hair if the clipper is inserted sideways into the hair mesh.

## Brushes

A range of brushes is required. Closely set bristle brushes can pick up and hold short graduated hair. Coarser-set bristle may produce textured effects in completed dressings.

You will need a neck brush to dust hair clippings from your client's skin, and you may need other items, such as:

Figure 5.41 Hair clippers

◆ talc puffer, to add talc to the skin, aiding the removal of clippings

◆ pair of thinning scissors (see information earlier in this chapter)

◆ razor (see information earlier in this chapter).

# The barbered haircut

There are two styles of haircut described in this section: one which requires a closely graduated natural hairline effect and one which requires a more sculptured, artistic look – the latter is more closely associated with traditional men's hairdressing competition looks.

While both haircuts may be carried out on dry hair, and in the commercial salon often are, they may also be carried out on hair that is wet. Wet cutting gives more control over the hair and reduces the effect of hair clippings flying over yourself and your client.

Gown your client with a cutting cloth, cotton wool and a cutting shoulder cape (see Figure 5.42).

■ Figure 5.42 Client gowned for cut

Following a consultation, check the hair for strong hair growth patterns, degree of curl, length and texture. The hair should be pre-shampooed if required; this is recommended. You should be aware that within a barbering context there will be a number of clients who do not wish to have their hair shampooed and it may be necessary to lightly spray the hair with water or styling lotion to achieve effective control. Avoid wetting the hair when cutting using electrical clippers.

## HEALTH & SAFETY

Corded clippers should only be used on dry hair, owing to the risk of electric shock.

# The graduated cut 'classic style'

This style is the classic closely graduated hairstyle, having a nape hairline that blends with the neck. The exact point at which the haircut ends and the neckline begins is almost indiscernible.

1   With the hair slightly moist or almost dry, and starting at the centre back of the head, slide the points of the scissors through the hair, close to the scalp at the outermost point of the occipital bone, just down from the crown of the head.

2   Lift the hair section and place it on to the comb.

3   Lift the mesh out from the head at 90° and cut to the required length. Note the position of the back of the comb in the hair (see Figure 5.43).

4   Moving down the head, slide the scissors through the hair at the scalp, 0.5 cm beneath the previous section, and place the hair on to the comb.

5   Lift the mesh of hair, together with the previously cut mesh out from the head, at less than 90° and cut to the same length as the previously cut hair (see Figure 5.44). The lower the hair section is held the shorter the subsequent section of haircut will be. Therefore you control the hairstyle.

6   At all times the section for the meshes should be taken at right angles to the hairline (see Figure 5.45).

7   Continue down the head in the same manner until the hairline is reached. Then, at the hairline, insert a fine-toothed, flexibly backed comb and, pressing it against the scalp with the comb teeth projecting slightly out, move the comb upwards and gradually out from the scalp, cutting continuously with the scissors as you go. A steady and continuous movement of the comb, coupled with a continuous cutting action, will ensure a smooth, even graduation without steps or cutting marks.

8   Move to a point adjacent to the first section cut and repeat the process. Always include a small section of the adjacent cut mesh of hair as a guide to the cut line.

9   Continue around to the side of the head in this manner; remember that the sections and your comb must follow the design or hairline. Ensure that your comb is parallel to the hairline at all times (see Figure 5.46).

10  Once the front hairline is reached, return to the centre back and commence the movement to the other side of the head.

11  Once the lower areas of the hair are cut, the top should be addressed. Starting at the front hairline, take sections of hair 1 cm in depth, hold out at 90° and cut to the same length as the very first cut at the occipital bone (see Figure 5.47).

# KEY WORDS

**Occipital bone** – *the bone just down from the crown of the head*

## REMEMBER!

*For your client's comfort, hair clippings should be dusted from the neck area regularly.*

12  Taking small sections continue from the front in columns, taking meshes of hair at 90° and cutting to the same length as the previous sections until the occipital area is reached (see Figure 5.48). Always include a small mesh of hair that has already been cut within the mesh to act as a guide to the cutting line.

13  Having completed this with one row, start at the front hairline and work back with another row; continue to do this until the top area of the hair is cut and blends with the graduated side areas. The top area will now have a uniform layer and the side and back a graduation.

14  It may be necessary to thin the hair where the uniform layer meets the graduation on the curve of the head, as within this area there will be a considerable volume of hair.

15  For a truly graduated hairline the nape area must be closely blended. This may be achieved by the use of the electric clippers. Using clippers with a variable-cut setting, set for the longest cut, slide the clipper up the neck into the hairline, gradually pivoting the cutting blade away from the hair. Repeat this several times, each time reducing the gauge of the cut and the distance up the hairline that this progresses.

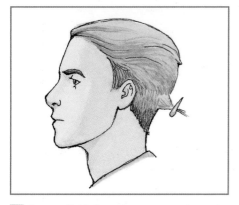

■ Figure 5.43 Step-by-step graduated cut

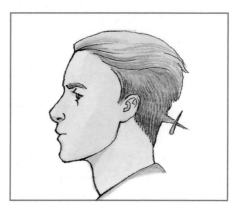

■ Figure 5.44 Step-by-step graduated cut

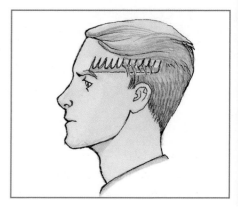

■ Figure 5.45 Step-by-step graduated cut

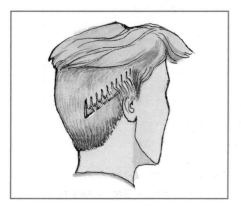

■ Figure 5.46 Step-by-step graduated cut

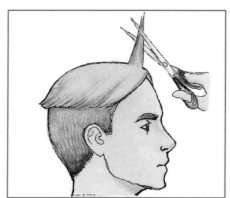

■ Figure 5.47 Step-by-step graduated cut

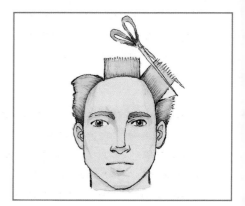

■ Figure 5.48 Step-by-step graduated cut

This task may also be carried out using the very fine teeth of the comb, pushing the comb flat to the neck, gradually tilting the teeth and moving the comb away from the neck and scalp, and cutting the hair that projects through the comb's teeth as you go.

A truly graduated haircut will have a blend with no obvious demarcation lines or *steps* (see Figure 5.49).

The exact end of the hairstyle and the beginning of the neck area should be almost indistinguishable. When a very short-haired result is required, particularly on dark hair, it may be necessary to shave away the hair from just above the ear, behind the ear (on the hairline) and the nape, without producing a definite hairline.

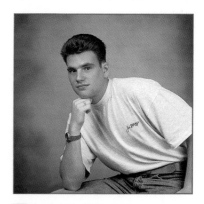

■ Figure 5.49 Finished graduated haircut

# The sculptured haircut

This cut is generally less graduated than the previous one, being more of a uniform layer. The hair is often cut wet, starting with the hair being thinned. This may be achieved by using thinning scissors or a razor.

REMEMBER!

*Consult your client throughout the cutting process to monitor their satisfaction and to check on shape and length.*

## Thinning scissors

Systematically work over the head, cutting each mesh of hair using the thinning scissors. Avoid over-thinning the front hairline, parting area and the crown. To avoid a line of demarcation, use the thinning scissors lightly several times along the entire length of the hair rather that just the once (see Figure 5.50).

## Razor thinning

The razor should be used only on wet or moist hair. Having checked the scalp for any protrusions, section the hair off, starting at the nape, using sections 1 cm deep. Use a co-ordinated comb and razor action (see Figure 5.51).

■ Figure 5.50 Men's thinning technique

Draw the razor over the last three-quarters of the hair's length in the direction in which the hair will lie. Complete this section by section throughout the haircut, taking care in areas where the head curves, as these areas may be over-thinned if a sharp razor is used. The hair on the top of the head is normally combed forward and thinned in this manner, and the hair at the side is combed forward so as to avoid your client's ears (see Figures 5.52–5.54).

Thinning the ends of the meshes in this manner may reduce the curl of over-curly hair, and very straight hair may be styled more easily.

 REMEMBER!

*Before razor thinning the hair, always check the scalp for any lumps or bumps.*

Figure 5.51 Razor thinning

Figure 5.52 Razor thinning techniques (1)

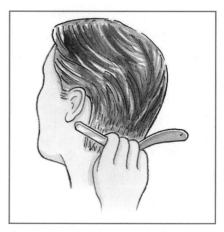

Figure 5.53 Razor thinning techniques (2)

## Layering

The haircut may commence at any part of the head. This is often the nape or front hairline. Take a mesh of hair, comb it at 90° out from the head, and cut to the required length. Continue over the head in this manner, using a previously cut mesh of hair as a guide to the cutting line.

Remember that a square or angular shape is usually required for men; do not round off corners at the side curvature of the head or at the crown.

Once the layering is complete, the hair may require additional thinning to compensate for hair that has been removed by the cut.

You must now outline the hair. Do this by moistening the hair and combing down, using the back of the comb to flatten the hair against the skin. The scissors or inverted clippers may then be used to cut the outline shape. Remember that most men's hairstyles have

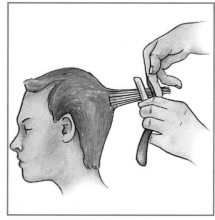

Figure 5.54 Razor thinning techniques (3)

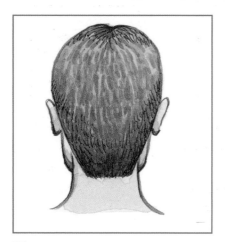

Figure 5.55 Graduated tapered nape hairline

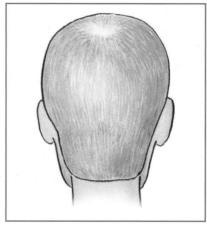

Figure 5.56 Boston neckline

Figure 5.57 Lion's mane neckline

square-shaped necklines. These are either definite square shapes, the line behind the ear being cut in a downward line using the scissors, pointed from the ear down to the nape and then squared across the nape using scissors or inverted clippers, or downward lines either side of the nape with a graduated neckline (see Figures 5.55–5.57).

A *Boston neckline* is a heavy abrupt nape line across the back of the nape, curving slightly to accentuate the width (see Figure 5.56).

# Fashion styling I

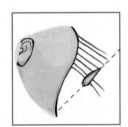

1   Commence the haircut lifting hair from the head in the comb at less than 90° (see Figure 5.59).

2   Using the previously cut section take a section below this and hold the hair at less than 90°, cutting the hair using the previous section as a guide.

3   The result of using a less than 90° angle is that hair will be graduated shorter as you proceed down (see Figure 5.60). Using the previous section as a guide safeguards against steps in hair length (see Figure 5.61).

4   A close result is achieved at sides and nape by sliding the comb up into the hairline and tilting the comb's teeth outwards and cutting the hair as it protrudes between the teeth (see Figure 5.62).

5   Resting the comb back hard against the scalp, with its fine teeth pointing diagonally out, enables hair to be cut closely to the scalp while blending with longer hair higher up within the hairline The result will be an almost invisible nape hairline, with very short hair at the hairline blending with slightly longer hair higher up the head.

6   The hair on the top is cut by taking sections from the crown working forwards, using the previous cut section as a guide (see Figure 5.63). Pulling the mesh slightly back at the front hairline will leave a little more length at this point.

7   Taking small square sections, twisting these and sliding the scissor blade along the outside of this twist develops a textured result in the style (see Figure 5.64).

8   Using the points of the scissors, the front hairline may be *point thinned* (freehand cutting) to provide a softer edge (see Figure 5.65).

■ Figure 5.58 Step-by-step fashion styling, modern short textured look

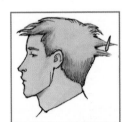

■ Figure 5.59 Step-by-step fashion styling, lifting the hair at less than 90° to decrease hair length down the head

■ Figure 5.60 Step-by-step fashion styling, the graduation in the neck achieved without steps or marks in the hair

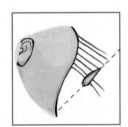

■ Figure 5.61 Step-by-step fashion styling, the hair lengths at the back of the hairstyle

■ Figure 5.62 Step-by-step fashion styling, to achieve a short result use the comb to lift hair

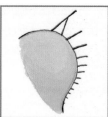
■ Figure 5.63 Step-by-step fashion styling, using the previous cut section to achieve a uniform length on the top

■ Figure 5.64 Step-by-step fashion styling, producing a tapered result for texture

■ Figure 5.65 Step-by-step fashion styling, point thinning to produce a textured fringe area

# Fashion styling 2

1   At the occipital area take a section of hair holding out, in the comb, at less than 90°. Cut the hair as it protrudes through the teeth of the comb (see Figure 5.67).

2   At the hairline the hair should be graduated in. As you progress towards the hairline use the previously cut hair section as a guide to the cutting point. For each section hold the hair at less than 90° (see Figure 5.68).

3   The nape and side hairline may be closely graduated by inserting a comb into the hairline with the back of the comb resting on the scalp, the comb's teeth tilted upwards and outwards, and the hair protruding through the teeth to be cut (see Figure 5.69).

4   From the occipital to the crown area the hair is brought down in sections and cut like the position of the first cut. This may be followed around to the sides (see Figure 5.70).

5   The top hair may be cut by combing sections of the hair up and connecting it into the hair at each side. This will produce a look with lift and movement (see Figure 5.71).

6   Alternatively, the hair may be combed flat to the head and cut to the base line. This will produce a heavy straight look (see Figure 5.72).

The front hairline may be texturised by freehand cutting. This is done by sliding the scissors either down the hair shaft while closing the blade or by point thinning, cutting into the hair from outside the hairstyle (see Figure 5.73).

■ Figure 5.66 Step-by-step fashion styling, modern longer look

■ Figure 5.67 Step-by-step fashion styling, producing a steep graduation at the lower occipital area

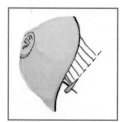
■ Figure 5.68 Step-by-step fashion styling, close graduation at the nape achieved by controlling the hair in the comb

■ Figure 5.69 Step-by-step fashion styling, controlling the side hair using the comb

■ Figure 5.70 Step-by-step fashion styling, producing the weight line

■ Figure 5.71 Step-by-step fashion styling, producing internal layering for lift and movement

■ Figure 5.72 Step-by-step fashion styling, a more solid look will be achieved by cutting the top hair all to one point

■ Figure 5.73 Step-by-step fashion styling, freehand cutting to produce a textured effect at the front

# Style variations

## Partings

When a parting is used in the hairstyle it is usual to cut to this, leaving one side, the heavy side, longer than the other. The heavy side may require more thinning than the other.

## Fringes

Fringes will normally be outlined by cutting on the forehead. Additional length may be required if the fringe is to cover a receding hairline.

## Off-face styles

Hair often dresses more easily back off the face if left a little longer than the rest of the hair.

## Over-ear hairstyles

When cutting hair that will fall over the ear, allowance must be made for the hair to lie out over the ear and yet be level with the rest of the hair. Often hair must be shaped around the ear or left substantially longer in order not to stick out over the ear.

## Added hairpieces

When cutting hair to fit with a hairpiece, additional thinning may be needed so that the hair blends with the lengths of the added hair. Take care not to cut the added hair at the same time as the client's natural hair. Once complete, ensure that the two do blend together.

## Areas of hair loss

Often an additional length of hair must be left to allow an even line to be achieved over an area of hair loss. Discuss the requirements with your client before commencing the cut. Remember tact must be used at all times as hair loss can, for some, cause considerable mental anguish.

# KEY SKILL TASK

*This task could produce evidence that supports C1.1, C1.3, & N1.1.*
*Undertake a consultation with your client regarding their haircut. Record your findings*
*from the consultation, including:*

◆ *client requirements*
◆ *critical influencing factors including*

> *head shape*
> *directions of hair growth*
> *strong hair movements*
> *density of hair*
> *condition of hair*
> *porosity of hair*

◆ *diagram of your planned haircut*
◆ *step-by-step guidelines in undertaking the haircut.*

# Shaping facial hair

To carry out a haircut and neglect the extremities of the hair on the face, for example the base of the sideburns, or to neglect the concept of the total look would be an error. To present the male client, the barber must consider the total appearance of the head and face together. When cutting and shaping facial hair, remember that you are producing a three-dimensional shape on the face, which itself is made of irregular shapes over which you must work.

Discuss the desired shape and effect of the facial hair fully with your client before commencing to shape.

# Tools for use

Facial hair may be shaped using:

◆ haircutting scissors and/or electric clippers, over a comb, to shape

◆ freehand cutting using the scissors, to cut outlines or shape small areas

◆ inverted clippers, to outline the perimeter shape

◆ razor, to remove unwanted facial hair around the perimeter of the shape.

# Beard shaping

## Client preparation

Following consultation, place a lightly coloured towel diagonally across your client's chest. Tuck in one side of the collar, and fold the towel to enclose the other side of the neck. The light towel will reflect light up under the chin area, as well as providing a contrasting surface against which to check the profile of the beard (see Figure 5.74). Ensure that there is no gap between the neck and the towel.

Recline the back of the chair slightly, and then protect your client's eyes from hair clippings by either placing moist cotton wool pads on them or by draping a small hand towel across the eyes. A clean tissue should be placed across the headrest (if in position) to reduce the risk of infection from one client to the next.

Comb the beard to remove tangles. In some cases it may be necessary to lightly moisten the beard to soften dressings. Take care not to over-moisten, particularly if you intend to use electric clippers. While combing the beard, check for any strong or uneven growth patterns that may affect the finished shape. Strong patterns may have an impact upon the beard shape.

■ Figure 5.74 Client with cotton wool pads on eyes

 *REMEMBER!*

*If your client wears a full beard, it may not be necessary to define the outline. Consult with your client.*

## Outline shaping

1    Comb the hair thoroughly to lift it from the face. Check for any areas of thinness that may require special attention. Using the inverted clipper, define the outline shape by pressing the cutting edge into the beard at the required point (see Figure 5.75).

2    Using the clipper, remove the excess hair from this area (see Figure 5.76).

3    Shave this area free of hair (see Figure 5.77).

## Shaping the bulk of the beard

Comb the hair to allow it to lie in its natural position. Insert the teeth of the comb at the position of the required cut and then, using either scissors or clippers, cut the hair to the level of the comb (see Figures 5.78 and 5.79).

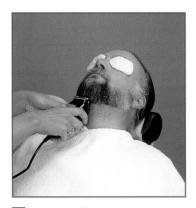

■ Figure 5.75 Outline shaping

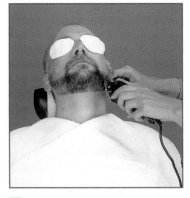

■ Figure 5.76 Shaping the bulk of the beard

■ Figure 5.77 Beard shaping

Your choice of cutting tool will depend upon:

◆ personal preference

◆ the coarseness and thickness of the beard – a coarser beard is easier to cut using electric clippers

◆ the shape to be produced.

■ Figure 5.78 Combing beard

■ Figure 5.79 Trimming goatee beard

 # REMEMBER!

*When cutting very curly facial hair, allow for the hair to spring back into place, producing a closer shape.*

Move the comb slowly over the beard shape describing the shape required, and cut at this point. Take care to observe the profile and balance of the shape being produced, using the mirror and by checking against the light surface of the protective towel. Remember that the beard shape may appear different when the client's head is upright.

Shaping normally commences at the side of the beard, where it joins the hairstyle on the scalp. In most cases the two should flow together. The shape produced on the face may not be that of the face, so care must be

■ Figure 5.80 Moustache trimming – defining the lip outline

■ Figure 5.81 Moustache trimming – reducing volume

taken in holding the comb in the correct position to follow the beard shape. Take care not to shape too short in areas where the beard is thin – the area where the moustache joins the beard is often thinner. Hair in the area beneath the chin will often appear shorter when the head is reclined and once the head is upright will still appear quite full. Take care not to take away corners or points if they are required in the finished shape.

Remove clippings from the client's neck continuously, avoiding a build-up of clippings that may become trapped between your client's skin and clothing.

The line along the top lip of the moustache is defined using either the inverted clipper or by freehand cutting using scissors (see Figures 5.80 and 5.81).

# Completion

Comb the facial hair fully to remove any loose hair clippings. Remove any protective pads from over your client's eyes and wipe any clippings from the face using a tissue. Dust the clippings from your client's neck area and remove the protective towel, taking care not to allow clippings to pass down the collar.

Gently raise the back of your client's chair, and then pass your client a hand mirror with which to view the beard (see Figure 5.82).

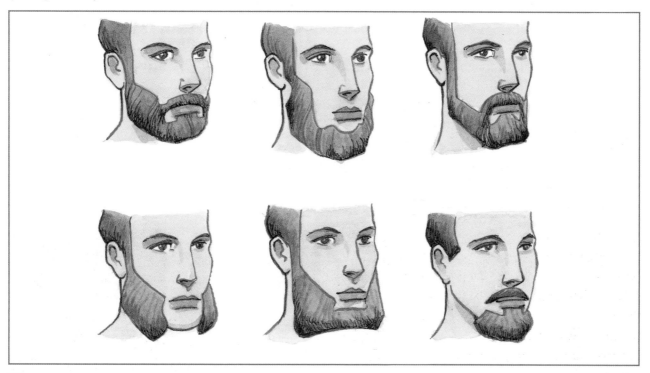

■ Figure 5.82 A range of beard shapes

# Moustache shaping

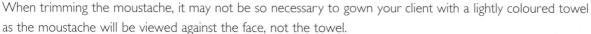

When trimming the moustache, it may not be so necessary to gown your client with a lightly coloured towel as the moustache will be viewed against the face, not the towel.

Having reclined the back of the chair, outline the shape of the moustache area using clippers. The shaping may be carried out above the moustache or between the moustache and the lips. This area may then be shaved free of hair.

Many moustaches have hair that is shaped to extend past the area of actual growth. Take care not to remove this. Comb the hair into place and cut the required length over the lip. If the hair projects on to the lip, scissors should be used, taking care to use the free hand to steady the blades (see Figure 5.83).

Check for balance and evenness of length. Beards may require the application of dressing to produce the required result. Moustache wax may be applied to stiffen the hair to enable *handlebar* effects to be achieved (see Figure 5.84).

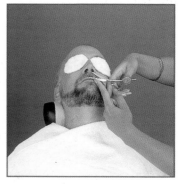

■ Figure 5.83 Trimming the moustache

## Useful Task

There are a number of beard and moustache shapes, most of which have names that are used to identify them. Produce a chart of shapes and their names to use with your consultation.

# Sideburns

For all barbering the finished length of the sideburns must be checked, adjusted and made even. Sideburns that may have appeared quite flat before the haircut will require reduction to be in proportion when the scalp hair has been trimmed. The barber must be able to offer this service.

Figure 5.84 A range of moustache shapes

Following consultation with your client, and cutting using either scissors or clipper over the comb, reduce the bulk of the sideburns. Invert the clipper to cut the lower edge (see Figure 5.85), using the mirror to check balance. Having cut the lower line it may be necessary to soften the line with slight graduation.

Sideburns may be used to add shape to the face. You should consider both their lower line and their profile shape. When removing bulk, use the comb in the section you are cutting to determine the profile shape you want to achieve. Use the mirror to monitor the progress in the shape. The outline shape of the sideburn may require shaving once complete.

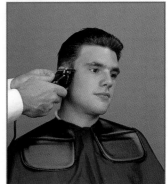

Figure 5.85 Using inverted clipper on sideburns

## Self review

1.  Suggest two factors that may affect your choice of haircut for a client.

2.  What is the purpose of gowning your client for a haircut?

3.  For control, how should haircutting scissors be held?

4.  What is the name given to the haircutting technique that reduces length but retains all of the hair's natural volume?

5.  Which haircutting technique will encourage wavy hair to curl?

6.  What advantage does scissor-over-comb graduation have over other methods of graduating?

7.  Should a haircutting razor/shaper be used on wet or dry hair?

8.  How should the electric clipper be used to outline a beard?

9.  Why is a lightly coloured towel used when beard trimming?

10. What is the essential feature of a graduated neckline?

# Useful contacts

| | |
|---|---|
| HABIA | www.habia.org.uk |
| Pivot Point – follow links, then design forum | www.pivot-point.com |
| Rand Rocket – haircutting tools | www.rand-rocket.co.uk |
| Tondeo – haircutting tools | www.tondeo.de/e/ |
| Toni & Guy | www.toniandguy.co.uk |
| Vidal Sassoon | www.vidalsassoon.co.uk |

## CHAPTER 6

# Styling and dressing hair

## CHAPTER CONTENTS

**Unit H10** Style, dress and finish hair using basic techniques

**Unit H14** Dry hair to shape to create finished looks for men

## WHAT THIS CHAPTER WILL PROVIDE

This chapter provides essential knowledge for understanding a variety of techniques for setting, dressing and finishing hair, including long hair.

## Choice of styling technique

The choice of styling and dressing technique used will depend upon the finished outcome required (this will be agreed with the client by consultation), the hair type being dressed and the preferences of the client. This consultation normally takes place between the hairstylist and client before the hairdressing process begins and may be reviewed throughout the treatment.

 *REMEMBER!*

*Ensure that the client is fully aware of the intended finished result before starting to dry the hair.*

The factors to be taken into account when determining the appropriate styling method include:

♦ haircut and style

♦ hair growth patterns

♦ hair elasticity

♦ head and face shape

◆ hair texture

◆ hair length

◆ hair density.

More information about client consultation is contained in Chapter 3.

# Styling process

The styling process includes the following steps.

◆ **Client consultation.** First you must establish with your client what is the required hairstyle.

◆ **Shampooing.** This cleanses and wets the hair, allowing it to be stretched and formed into a new shape. Hydrogen and sulphur bonds within the cortex of the hair are temporarily broken down by the water, allowing the hair to be stretched (see Figure 6.1). Hair stretches more easily when wet, and shampooing the hair wets it more effectively than merely damping with a trigger spray.

◆ **Drying.** During this stage the hair is stretched into a new shape and dried into that shape. The hydrogen and sulphur bonds in the hair reform and hold the hair in the shape in which it was dried.

◆ **Reforming.** When the hair is wetted again it returns to its natural shape and may be restyled. Hair absorbs moisture from the atmosphere (it is *hygroscopic*) and therefore the hairstyle gradually falls, falling more rapidly in moist damp conditions when there is high humidity. Styling aids often place a coating on the hair to slow down this absorption of moisture, delaying elastic recoil, and therefore extending the life of the style.

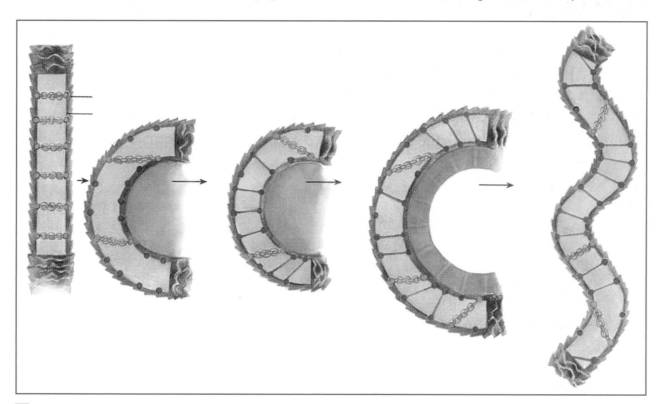

■ Figure 6.1 Chemical bonds within hair

## Gowning your client

The purpose of gowning your client is to protect her or him and their clothing from damage or contamination during the hairdressing process (see Figures 6.2 and 6.3). The exact method of gowning used will depend upon your salon's policy and the nature of the hairdressing processes you are about to carry out, and may be varied during your client's visit to the salon.

■ Figure 6.2 Gowned client    ■ Figure 6.3 Gowned client

When carrying out treatments where the hair is wet, you use a gown to prevent moisture from causing discomfort to the client or damage to clothing. However, when using styling irons, the use of the gown is for different reasons, such as protection from heat on clothing, hair dressings and loose hair.

Gowning will normally be done following your initial consultation with your client, according to your salon's policy. During your consultation, it is useful to be aware of the style of clothing that s/he is wearing, as this can give you a feel for their fashion sense, which in turn can guide you in your style suggestions. However, note that if your client has previously had damage to their clothing while visiting the salon, s/he may not be wearing their usual clothes. Clean gowning materials are used to help prevent the spread of infectious disorders from one client to the next. Different salons' methods of gowning may vary; however, all will endeavour to ensure that the client's clothing is protected.

## Your choice of styling technique (drying hair)

The choice of techniques you will use to achieve the result discussed with your client will depend upon a number of factors. These include the following.

- ◆ **The finished style required.** Some techniques are better suited to particular hairstyles.

- ◆ **The hair texture.** Fine hair may require more support in the drying technique, whereas thick, strong, coarse hair will require less and will produce much of its own volume.

- ◆ **The hair type.** Curly hair may require more tension when drying to control or reduce the natural curl.

- ◆ **Strong hair growth patterns.** For example, a 'double crown' may require more control in the drying process.

**REMEMBER!**

*To enable you to select the most appropriate product for use on the client, you should understand the features of all of the styling aids used within your salon.*

## Styling aids

### Liquid styling aids

Liquid styling aids have the following properties:

◆ making the hair more manageable during the drying process

◆ prolonging the life of the hairstyle (by excluding atmospheric moisture)

◆ giving the hair the necessary stiffness to allow the production of the required hairstyle

◆ helping to condition and moisturise the hair

◆ compensating for the damaging effect that heat can have on the hair; liquid styling aids are usually applied to wet hair that has been towel dried.

Your choice of styling aid will be determined by a range of factors:

◆ the client's hair type

◆ the required hairstyle

◆ the features of the particular product

◆ your personal preference

◆ the salon's policy.

**HEALTH & SAFETY**

The Control of Substances Hazardous to Health Regulations 2002 (COSHH) (see Chapter 1) requires your employer to ensure that you are trained in the safe handling of products and that suitable personal protective equipment is provided if identified as necessary. You should follow these guidelines and use equipment provided in the way indicated.

This information can be obtained by following the manufacturer's guidance notes.

**Blow-dry lotions** are available in liquid form, as a single application phial and multi-application bottles, as well as aerosol and pump-action sprays. Liquids are applied by sprinkling on to the hair, spreading throughout both using your fingers and the comb. Aerosols may be applied by directing the spray on to the hair, ensuring distribution by directing the spray throughout the head of hair and by combing. Take care: avoid applying too much of a product, which will then run on to the client's neck, weigh down the hair and cause waste.

**Mousse** is a blow-dry lotion produced in foam form, making the product easier to apply and distribute by hand throughout all the hair or on specific areas of the hair. Apply by hand a sphere of mousse the size of a golf ball, distributing it throughout the hair using the fingers, followed by a wide-toothed comb (see Figure 6.4). Take care when first applying the mousse as it can be inclined to roll off the hair.

**Gel** is a styling aid that has a heavier consistency than mousse or blow-dry lotions. Applied from the palms of your hands, it is distributed throughout the hair. Gel may also be applied to specific parts of the hair using the pads of your fingers. Gel can be available in both a normal dry look when dry, and a wet look. The crisp finish left on the hair, if the gel is left to dry undisturbed, makes gel very suitable for sculptured or slick looks.

■ Figure 6.4 Applying mousse to the hair

These products are often available for a variety of hair types and degrees of hold, from normal to firm.

 ## REMEMBER!

*If you are unfamiliar with any product you use on a client's hair, always read and follow the manufacturer's instructions.*

*Curl activators* and *moisturisers* are usually available as a pump-action spray. Spray this on to curly hair to give a more controlled, defined curl. Direct the spray throughout the hair and distribute using a wide-toothed comb and the fingers. These products are particularly useful on hair that is dry, difficult to control and fragile.

 ## HEALTH & SAFETY

If you are uncertain about how to use a particular hairdryer follow the manufacturer's advice or ask your line manager or trainer.

## Styling tools

Your choice of blow-dryer will depend upon your personal preference, what is available and the type of style to be produced.

Hairdryers are available with a range of controls including differing air speeds and heat settings. For controlled drying, a *fishtail-style* nozzle can be fitted to concentrate the airflow to a narrow band. *Diffusers* may be fitted to many dryers to reduce the disruption to the hair caused by the airflow (see Figure 6.5).

 ## HEALTH & SAFETY

Do not handle electrical appliances with wet hands.

Select styling tools that will not be adversely affected by the levels of heat used in the drying process. Remember that many plastic- and nylon-based tools will distort if exposed to heat for too long. The fine nylon bristles of brushes may soften or the teeth of plastic combs may bend. Vulcanite (hardened rubber) combs have a slightly higher heat resistance. Metal tools, such as aluminium combs, may be used when controlling short hair or producing waves of raised partings, but they can become very hot, and if then in contact with the client's scalp may burn the skin. Bone combs have a high resistance to heat.

There are a number of brushes designed specifically for use when blow-drying, including *vent-style* brushes which are designed to aid air flow and thus speed up hairdrying,

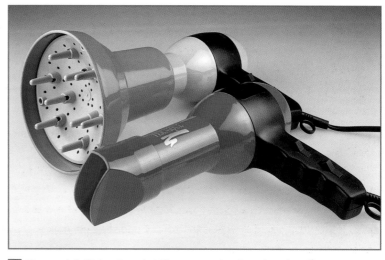

■ Figure 6.5 Fishtail and diffuser nozzles fitted to hairdryers

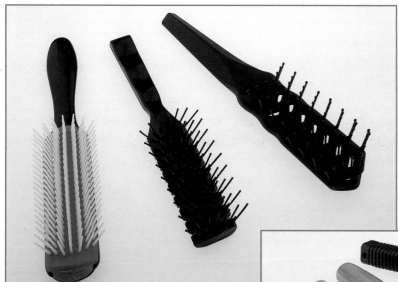

■ Figure 6.6 Vent-style brushes

■ Figure 6.7 Radial brushes

and radial brushes of a variety of diameters which enable you to dry the hair into curved or rounded shapes (see Figures 6.6 and 6.7). Flat bristle brushes are very effective when blow-drying short graduated hairstyles.

## HEALTH & SAFETY

The Electricity at Work Regulations 1989 require that all portable electrical equipment used in the salon is electrical safety-checked regularly. Take care that you do not use electrical equipment that you or a colleague has brought into the salon that has not undergone these safety tests.

## REMEMBER!

*Before use, visually check all electrical equipment for any external damage. If damage is detected, report this to the person responsible for maintenance and ensure that the equipment is labelled and put out of use.*

# Blow-drying

This technique is suitable for a wide range of hairstyles on a variety of hair types and hair lengths. The hairdryer is used together with a variety of tools, including hands, combs and brushes, the choice of which depends on the style required.

Your best results will be achieved on hair that is freshly shampooed. Shampooing prepares the hair by cleansing it and enabling it to be stretched into a new shape. The hair can then be dried into this new shape, delaying elastic recoil, which it will retain until the hair is moistened again.

Following the shampoo, remove the excess moisture from the hair by towel drying. Remove any tangles from the hair using a wide-toothed comb, taking care not to cause discomfort to the client, or damage to the hair, by excessive tension on the hair. Fine porous hair is very easily damaged and broken while wet.

## HEALTH & SAFETY

Never use electrical appliances when the cable is damaged or frayed in any way. Report any damaged equipment to your line manager or the person responsible for maintenance.

Apply appropriate styling aids to the hair, taking care not to allow the product to spill on to the client's face or neck, and comb the hair into the direction of the style. Take care to avoid overheating the hair, as excessive heat can damage the hair and excessive heat on the scalp will cause your client discomfort. Avoid directing the airflow against the hair in one place for too long, as this may cause excessive heating and subsequent damage to the hair.

Having removed excess moisture, start your hairdryer at the lower parts of the hairstyle, those areas that will be on the underneath of the style (see Figure 6.8). If there is an area of the head or a part of the style that is likely to be particularly resistant to styling, this is often best dried first. Ensure that each mesh of hair is dried before moving on to the next, as meshes which are left damp will affect others which lie adjacent.

For smooth results, the airflow should be directed with the direction of the hair. When achieving lift and volume, hold up meshes of hair in turn and direct the dryer into the upheld root area (see Figure 6.9).

Use the dressing mirror to check the shape and balance of the hairstyle being developed.

## Using the radial brush

Using the radial brush will enable you to dry the hair into curls or waves. Your choice of brush will depend upon a number of factors.

■ Figure 6.8 Blow-drying at the nape

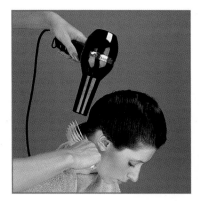

■ Figure 6.9 Blow-drying to achieve root lift

- ◆ The strength of curl achieved will depend on the radius of the brush that you use: the larger the radius, the softer the curl; the smaller the radius, the tighter the curl. Curl strength may also depend on the amount of hair wrapped around the hairbrush when drying.

- ◆ The length of hair may determine the size of brush, as the hair will need to be long enough to be wrapped around the brush.

- ◆ Differing types of bristle material have differing characteristics. Fine, closely set bristle tends to grip the hair; widely spaced bristle may control the hair more easily and remove tangles.

■ Figure 6.10 Blow-drying with a radial brush

- ◆ Your choice will often be personal. If in doubt, check with your supervisor.

Using the fingers, section off a mesh of hair and place it on the brush. Rotate the brush to smooth the ends of the hair in the direction of movement. Wind the hair around the brush and direct the airflow from the hairdryer in the direction in which the hair is lying (see Figure 6.10). Directing the airflow against the direction of the hair will produce a messy result as the shorter hair within the mesh will be dried without control and may produce a fuzzy appearance in the style.

To avoid damage to the hair by excessive heat do not direct the airflow at one place all the time. Keep the airflow moving over the hair. Rotate the brush to ensure that the hair is dried into a smooth finish around it. When working with long or very thick hair, drying can be more effective if you dry the ends of the hair first, gradually winding the hair around the brush and drying it progressively, working towards the root area. Take care when drying very long hair that the brush does not become entangled in it.

When drying fine hair (that drops the curl easily) or hair that is resistant to curl, leaving the brush in place as the hair cools will enhance curl retention.

**HEALTH & SAFETY**

For safety, do not point the airflow directly at the scalp as this may burn the client's skin.

To achieve volume at the roots, lift the mesh away from the head. The higher the mesh is lifted (over-directed) the greater the lift achieved with the particular brush. Larger-diameter brushes will produce more root lift. Flatter results will be produced by using root drag or incorporating the use both of the radial and flat brush on the hair.

## Using the flat brush

Using the flat brush will enable you to produce smooth, straight hairstyles. There are two main styles of flat brush:

1    brushes with closely set, fine bristles, which can be very useful when styling very short hair that may not be long enough to lie easily on the brush

2    brushes with widely spaced, thick bristles, which are ideal when styling smooth, straight styles where the hair length is sufficient to lay on the brush.

Generally, the differences between brushes of these categories lie in their size, the number of rows of bristles and the style of base. Your choice should be the one that is most comfortable for you to use. The styles of base available are rubber-cushioned back, solid back or vented back. The rubber-cushioned back allows the bristles to move slightly and therefore flex with the hair. Both this and the solid back give smoother results on straight hairstyles. The vented back aids speedy drying of the hair.

Using your fingers, take small meshes of hair and lay them on to the bristles of the brush. With the airflow of the hairdryer directed on to the mesh of hair and in the direction of the hair, draw the brush from the roots to the points of the hair (see Figure 6.11). You will produce a smooth, straight result in this manner. When straightening wavy hair, slight tension must be maintained on the hair. If a slight movement is required, for example to turn the ends of a bobbed hairstyle either out or under, then roll the brush in the appropriate direction and direct the air flow

■ Figure 6.11 Blow-drying for smooth bob with vent brush

■ Figure 6.12 Using back mirror

on to the corner of the brush. Use the back mirror to show your clients the completed effect (see Figure 6.12).

Very short hair is best controlled with a flat, closely tufted bristle brush. Using a hairdryer fitted with a fishtail nozzle direct the airflow into the bristles in the direction of the style (see Figure 6.13). Raised partings are produced by placing the brush in the hair 1cm from the roots and drawing it back to raise the roots and place a bend in the hair at the top of the raise. Direct the airflow into the root area, and to keep a clean finish to the hair direct the airflow from one angle (see Figure 6.14).

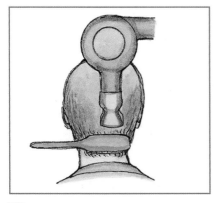

■ Figure 6.13 Directing airflow into the bristles of the brush when drying short hair

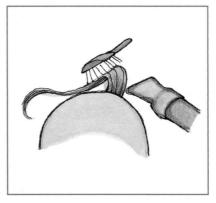

■ Figure 6.14 Directing airflow when producing raised partings

■ Figure 6.15 When blow-drying direct the airflow into the wave trough

You may use either a brush or comb to control wet hair while blow-drying:

◆ brush on long hair

◆ comb on short hair.

Shape the hair and direct the airflow into the trough of the wave (see Figure 6.15). Figures 6.16–6.18 show a range of blow-drying techniques and the use of styling irons.

■ Figure 6.16 Using tension to straighten wavy hair

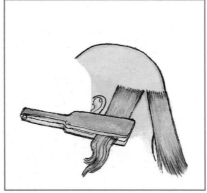

■ Figure 6.17 Using flat irons to produce a fashion style

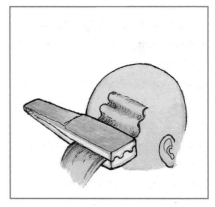

■ Figure 6.18 Using crimping irons

# Finger drying

This technique is best suited to hair that falls into style easily, has some natural volume and movement, and where an informal look is required. Your hands become the tools that guide the hair into position during the drying process. In many cases the body heat from your hands aids the drying of the hair. Drying is often aided by the use of the hairdryer. Your fingers will draw the hair into place either in a claw-like fashion, with the fingers taking on the role of a wide-toothed comb or brush, or the dryer will mould the hair by wrapping it around the fingers to produce movement in the hair (see Figure 6.19). Lift and volume at the roots is achieved by rotary movements of the hair at the root, using either finger pads or the palm of your hand and lifting the hair away from the scalp. Your client's head is normally maintained in an upright position except when producing volume in medium-length and long hair, when the head may be inclined downwards and then brought upright when the root area is dry.

## Scrunch drying

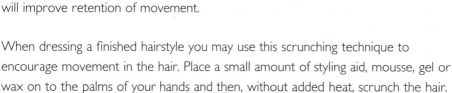

This technique is used when a full curly style is required, usually on medium or long hair lengths. Compress the wet hair into its curled shape in the hand and direct the airflow on to the palm of the hand, opening the hand to allow the access of the warm air and then closing to *scrunch* the hair (see Figure 6.20). Continue to scrunch the hair as the hair cools after the heat has been removed. This will improve retention of movement.

When dressing a finished hairstyle you may use this scrunching technique to encourage movement in the hair. Place a small amount of styling aid, mousse, gel or wax on to the palms of your hands and then, without added heat, scrunch the hair.

## Natural drying

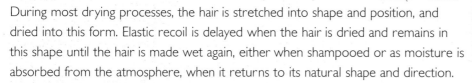

As we have seen, wet hair stretches more easily than dry hair. During most drying processes, the hair is stretched into shape and position, and dried into this form. Elastic recoil is delayed when the hair is dried and remains in this shape until the hair is made wet again, either when shampooed or as moisture is absorbed from the atmosphere, when it returns to its natural shape and direction.

When drying naturally, the hair remains in its unstretched state, having been gently put into shape and dried undisturbed either without heat or by applying radiant heat.

■ Figure 6.19 Finger drying curly hair into style

■ Figure 6.20 Scrunch drying in the hand

---

 REMEMBER!

*When introducing a new hairstyle to your client, provide them with guidance on how to maintain their look between visits to the salon.*

---

## Creating the finished look

Having dried the hair in a controlled manner it will require dressing to give the finished look. Figures 6.21 and 6.23 show two modern dried finished looks.

Depending upon the result that you require, this dressing may consist of brushing the hair into place using a brush of either closely tufted or widely spaced bristles.

For heavy, smooth, one-length looks, the hair is usually brushed with a widely spaced, thick-bristle brush, brushing in the direction of the hair fall. To add texture to the finish, the hair may be brushed at 90° to the direction of fall, usually back from the front hairline, and then allowed to fall into place. To add volume to heavy, smooth one-length styles the brush may be placed into the hair, which already lies in the direction of fall, and slowly lifted up allowing the hair to fall gradually. The surface should be smoothed gently, taking care not to dig the teeth of a widely spaced, large-toothed comb or the bristles of a brush into the volume of the hair.

For shorter looks the hair may be textured by drawing the fingers through the hair, in a claw-like fashion, either in or across the direction of the hairstyle. The *vent* brush may be used in a similar way.

For controlled curly/tousled looks the hair may be scrunched in the hands, your hands may be used to position hair, to separate strands of hair, to add height by rotating the roots or by backcombing the hair, pushing back towards the roots on small meshes of hair.

To produce many fashion effects, combinations of techniques must be used. Be prepared to learn and adapt your techniques to suit emerging fashions. If you are uncertain of the technique to use, ask your stylist/instructor for advice and guidance.

Figure 6.21 A textured look for men

Figure 6.22 Dressing aids

Figure 6.23 A textured look for women

Figure 6.24 Dressing hair

Techniques of backcombing or back brushing may be used when dressing these styles, to achieve more height or control over the hair.

Finishing products can be used to assist you in dressing the hair, to enable you to produce the desired look and to prolong the duration of the finished look. Some products are applied to the hair from the palms of the hands. They may also be applied, using the fingers, to particular areas of the style or to particular strands of hair. Others are applied from an aerosol directed at the hair.

To enable you to select the correct products for the hair texture and for the required result you must learn about the features of the products available in your salon.

◆ Sprays available include hair-fixing sprays that hold the hair in place. Some are available for particular hair types and conditions, and they are often available in differing degrees of hold. In selecting, you will consider the required finished look and whether the style should move or if it should stay fixed in place. Gel spray offers an alternative to hairspray on dry hair, often being firmer. It is designed for use as a sculpting lotion, an aid to dressing the hair into position.

◆ Gel may be used not only when drying wet hair but also as a dressing aid, using small quantities scrunched through the hair to create volume as well as on specific strands of hair to enable them to be moulded into place. Wet-look results may be achieved using these products.

◆ Wax may be used to give separation and definition to the hair and curl. It may be used throughout the hairstyle, having applied a small amount worked through the hair from the palms of the hands. Wax may also be applied to individual strands of hair using the fingers. Flyaway hair may be calmed using a little wax. On fine, soft hair wax can sometimes be too heavy a product for use.

◆ Dressing creams/mousses give control to hair and enable it to be sculpted and moulded into shape. These products are available in a range of strengths and are suitable for differing hair textures and style effects.

◆ Gloss, usually fine oil, is available in liquid and aerosol forms. It gives shine to the hair. Over-generous use of these products can result in a greasy look to the hair.

When applying hair-fixing spray to the finished look, avoid wetting the hair by holding the spray too close or by holding the spray in one place for too long. When using an aerosol on fine, soft hair, the pressure of the spray may move or flatten the hair. Shield the client, their skin and clothing from the products being used.

■ Figure 6.25 Using the brush to control the hair

■ Figure 6.26 Dressing the hair using the fingers

■ Figure 6.27 The finished look

■ Figure 6.28 Rough drying the hair

■ Figure 6.29 Dressing the hair

■ Figure 6.30 The finished look

**REMEMBER!**

*When you use finishing products on the hair that you are unfamiliar with, study the manufacturer's instructions and always follow them. Many finishing products are inflammable and must be used with care.*

# Setting hair

Setting allows a wide range of temporary shapes to be introduced into the hair. These shapes are usually curved or wavy. In some cases they create volume for the hair at the root area and/or in the middle lengths and ends of the hair strand. As it is the shape that the hair is in while it is dried that produces the final style, the possibilities are endless. The hair is wetted, usually with water, stretched into a new shape, and dried into this shape. The hair retains the new shape until it becomes moist again.

There are a number of techniques for introducing shape into hair by setting, including:

◆ roller placement – wrapping hair around a cylinder form to produce a curl or wave

◆ pin curling – shaping the hair into round forms, either flat to the head or with lift at the roots, and securing these in place using clips

◆ finger waving – shaping wet hair into a wave form, against the scalp to produce flat waves.

These techniques may be used on their own or may be combined together to produce the required finished look (see Figure 6.31).

■ Figure 6.31 Hairset in progress

# Setting tools

Tools selected for use when setting depend mainly upon personal preference. Do remember, however, that poorly made tools may have sharp surfaces that damage the hair or scalp, or may be made of materials that are adversely affected by heat from the hairdryer. Select tools that easy to keep clean and that may be sterilised.

## Hair rollers

Hair rollers are cylindrical in shape and vary in diameter. Within a range of diameters there may be several lengths of roller (see Figure 6.32).

### Roller selection
The diameter of the roller will dictate the degree of curl or wave achieved in the hair, and affect the amount of root lift produced. Rollers that have small diameters will produce tight curls and little height in the hair. Large-diameter rollers will produce a soft wave movement in hair but with root lift.

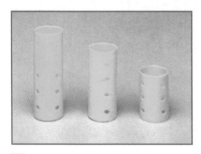

■ Figure 6.32 Rollers of similar diameter and various lengths

Rollers may be made of a variety of materials, with a range of surface finishes:

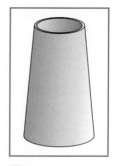

**Figure 6.33**
Tapered roller

◆ smooth plastic – ideal for use on porous hair, which may mark easily; the ideal roller for competition use as it leaves a smooth finish on the hair; it may be difficult to retain in place on the head

◆ spiked plastic – will grip the hair more easily; avoid very long or too numerous spikes as these may mark the hair, cause distortion in the hair or may become entangled in long hair

◆ sponge rollers – will produce a soft set, but due to the porous nature of some they can extend the drying time of hair

◆ metal mesh rollers – will grip the hair but they may mark very porous hair; take care that these rollers do not rest directly on the skin as they may become very hot and burn the client's scalp

◆ flexi/bendy rollers – these are usually made with a plastic-coated, stiff copper wire centre, covered either by foam or cloth; they are easily placed in the hair, do not mark and by bending when positioned do not require any additional fixings to hold them in place

◆ velcro rollers – may be used where a softer set is required; once the hair has been wound, push the roller gently on to the hair mesh at the roots; this action fixes the roller in place; they are often used on dry hair to add slight movement.

Some rollers are tapered, which enables them to fit curved, pivotal setting patterns on the head (see Figure 6.33).

## Roller pins

These are available in metal, plastic or plastic-coated metal. The metallic pins have a coating which prevents them from rusting while on the hair. Take care when using metal pins as they can become very hot under the hairdryer and may burn your client's scalp. Pins are available in a range of lengths, which may be selected to suit the diameter of roller being used. When placing roller pins to hold the roller in place, take care not to distort or break the hair.

## Pin curl clips

These clips are usually made of aluminium with a ferrous metal spring. There are a number available which are made of plastic with a metal spring. Clips are available either with single or double prongs. In selecting, choose the smallest-sized clip necessary to hold the curl in place, as clips can mark the hair. Contoured double-pronged clips are available for use on very thick hair, and have the advantage of being able to close around the hair without flattening the hair or sliding off the curl.

## Combs

The comb used when setting may be determined by personal preference or by salon policy. The comb should enable you to control and mould the hair. When roller setting, a tail comb is often used, as this provides fine-set teeth to comb the hair into place and the pin-tail end to help when sectioning hair and when wrapping the hair smoothly around the roller.

For pin curling, the tail comb or a setting comb may be used. The setting comb has fine-set teeth at one end and coarse-set teeth at the other. This style of comb may also be used when finger waving. Combs should be made of materials that are not affected by the chemicals used in hairdressing. They should not damage the hair or cause static electricity. The most suitable material is vulcanite and the teeth of the combs should be saw cut.

# Preparation

Whatever techniques of setting are used, for ease of dressing and to prolong its life the set should follow the direction of the intended style. The required style should be determined before commencing, through consultation with your client.

Hair sets most effectively when it is thoroughly wet and may be stretched easily into a new shape and then dried into that shape. Shampooing allows the hair to be wetted most effectively, allowing stretching to take place. Stretching and then thoroughly drying the hair allows a new shape to be introduced to the hair. Other techniques are less effective: the less wet the hair is made, the less the hair may be stretched and therefore the softer the set achieved. Hair may be set from dry, applying heat from a hairdryer to induce the set, or heated rollers may be used. Once wrapped around the heated rollers, the natural moisture in the hair is heated, inducing a temporary curl in the hair. Heated rollers may be used in conjunction with fast-drying sprays which moisten the hair, allowing it to be stretched and moulded into shape, and which then dry very quickly.

Hair that is in its unstretched state consists of *alpha keratin*; when stretched, it becomes *beta keratin*, remaining in this state until it absorbs moisture and returns to its natural shape and its alpha keratin form.

## KEY WORDS

**Alpha keratin** – *unstretched hair*
**Beta keratin** – *hair that is in a stretched state*

# Preparing your client

Following consultation, gown your client to protect her or his clothes, and shampoo if appropriate.

# Setting aids

The set will last longer if the hair is protected from the effects of atmospheric moisture, which will cause the hair to spring back to its original shape. Setting aids usually coat the hair with a soluble, water-resistant coating, which will slow down the effects of atmospheric moisture on the hair. They also often contain ingredients that will help the hair to dry, and which help to reduce static electricity and make the hair controllable.

## Setting lotions

These liquids often contain a thermoplastic, polyvinyl pyrollidone, which coats the hair with a film. This gradually breaks down with brushing and is washed away with shampooing. Setting lotions are available with a range of holding powers which offer from a strong hold through to a gentler, mild hold.

When selecting appropriate setting lotions you will often find that when setting fine, delicate hair you need a setting lotion which is not too heavy, but that when controlling strong hair you may need a stronger lotion. Setting lotions are usually applied to towel-dried hair, by sprinkling on to the hair direct from the bottle. When applying, gently massage the hair and scalp; this will help to spread the lotion and prevent it from running down the client's face and neck. Spread the application throughout the head, combing to ensure even distribution.

### Setting mousse

These perform the same task as setting lotions. However, mousse is often more easily controlled when applied to the hair. Use a ball of mouse about the size of a golf ball and apply to towel-dried hair. Work it into the hair strands. Take care when applying mousse to the hair to ensure that the mousse ball does not roll off the hair.

As with setting lotions, mousses are available in varying strengths to suit differing hair types and as temporary hair colourants. See Chapter 7 for more information about hair colour.

### Setting gel

This setting aid can be used when the hair is difficult to control. The gel is usually available either from a tub or tube. To avoid cross-contamination use a spatula to extract gel from the tub.

### Points to remember

◆　Hair sets best when the hair has been shampooed.

◆　The hairset will last longer and be easier to dress if it follows the direction of hair growth.

◆　The set will last longer if protected from atmospheric moisture. Setting lotions can do this.

◆　Keep the hair moist during the setting process.

# Setting techniques

The three setting techniques are:

◆　roller setting (winding)

◆　pin curling

◆　finger waving.

They may be used independently or in conjunction with each other to achieve different effects in the hair.

# Roller setting (winding)

The placement of rollers usually follows the direction in which the root area of the hairstyle moves. The hair should be long enough to be wrapped around the roller at least 2½ times. This will ensure that it holds firmly in place.

 *REMEMBER!*

*As the hair retains the shape in which it is set, any misshapen or distorted ends will also be retained in the finished hairstyle.*

To ensure maximum root movement and control over the hair, the roller section should be the same size as the roller to be used. Remember that the size of roller used will determine the strength of curl and degree of root lift achieved.

Using a comb, take a mesh of hair and comb away from the scalp so that the front of the mesh is at slightly more than 90° to the scalp (see Figures 6.34 and 6.35). Hold the hair firmly and place the roller against the mesh (see Figure 6.36) near the point ends. The mesh of hair should be held centrally but without the points bunched together. Smooth the hair point ends around the roller (see Figure 6.37).

 REMEMBER!

*Buckled hair point ends or distorted hair lengths will not dress smoothly into the finished hairstyle.*

When using rollers with spikes, rotating the roller against the hair can help to ensure a smooth wrap for the hair ends. With the hair point ends wrapped smoothly around the roller, wind the roller down towards the scalp with the hair around it, without bunching. Allow the hair to spread across the width of the roller and ensure that there are no distortions in the hair as it is wrapped (see Figure 6.38).

The angle at which the hair is held when the roller is placed at the ends can vary the degree of lift achieved in the finished style. Over-directing the mesh away from the direction of the style (see Figure 6.39), allows the hair to be controlled further towards the root, and is ideal when working on very curly hair.

Holding the mesh of hair at less that 90° will flatten the root area (see Figures 6.40 and 6.41). This technique may be used when setting overly thick hair to reduce volume without thinning. In cases when no root lift is required at all, the hair may be combed flat to the head, and the roller may be placed on top of the mesh and wound back towards the root area (see Figure 6.42). This technique may be alternated with that in Figure 6.34 to produce deep wave movement at the scalp on long hair.

■ Figure 6.34 Placing rollers

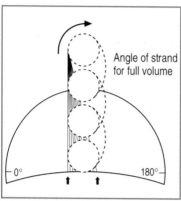

■ Figure 6.35 Roller set for full volume

■ Figure 6.36 Placing roller against mesh

■ Figure 6.37 Smoothing hair point ends against roller

■ Figure 6.38 Winding roller towards scalp with hair on it

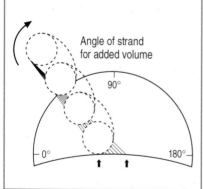

■ Figure 6.39 Over-directing for added volume

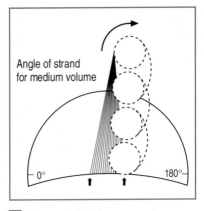

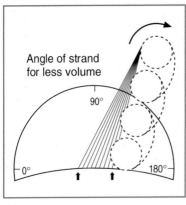

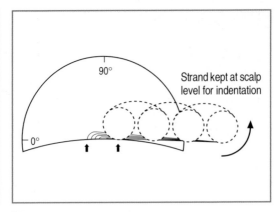

Angle of strand for medium volume

Angle of strand for less volume

90°

90°

Strand kept at scalp level for indentation

0°

180°

0°

180°

0°

■ Figure 6.40 Medium volume

■ Figure 6.41 Less volume-root drag

■ Figure 6.42 Strand curled at scalp level

# REMEMBER!

**Features of good practice**

◆ *Never take sections with too much hair as this will extend the drying time and relax the curl strength towards the roots.*

◆ *For control, roller sections should be no wider than the roller being used.*

◆ *Ensure that all the hair is wrapped with even tension, across the width of the roller.*

◆ *Spread the hair across the width of the roller as it winds.*

◆ *Avoid damaging or distorting the hair when placing the fixing pin (see Figure 6.43).*

## Pin curl setting

Pin curling enables you to place curled hair in the exact position, with the exact degree of curl and the exact direction of root movement, required for the finished dressing. There are three types of pin curl:

◆ **barrel pin curls** – a constant degree of curl throughout the length of hair (see Figure 6.44)

◆ **stand-up barrel curls** – the same effect as that of a hair roller (see Figure 6.45)

◆ **clock-spring pin curls** – a curl which gets tighter towards the hair points (see Figure 6.46).

■ Figure 6.43 Placing fixing pin

Other than the stand-up curl, all others produce little or no root lift. There are three parts to the pin curl: the stem, the body and the base (see Figure 6.47).

The stem direction will determine the direction in which the hair moves, and will normally be determined by the required hairstyle. The size and direction of the body of the curl will determine the degree of movement and how the hair moves from the stem. The size and shape of the base will be determined by the required hairstyle, the thickness of the hair and the direction of the stem.

■ Figure 6.44 Barrel pin curls

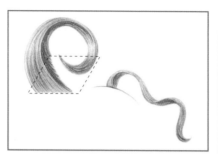

■ Figure 6.45 Stand-up barrel curls

■ Figure 6.46 Clock-spring pin curl

 *REMEMBER!*

*Pressure marks from clips and pins will show as indentations in the finished style. Very porous and bleached hair is particularly susceptible to this.*

## Barrel curls

Take a section of hair and comb to remove any tangles. Mould the stem of the curl in the required direction and, holding the hair mesh at the point where the stem joins the curl body, form a rounded curl shape of the required size (see Figure 6.48).

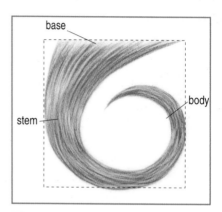

■ Figure 6.47 Parts of a curl

Ensure that all of the hair is smoothly moulded into place and then secure the curl, locating a curl clip over the curl body. Place the clip over only as much of the curl body as is necessary to hold the curl. This will avoid unnecessary pressure marks on the hair (see Figure 6.49). When locating the clip avoid distortion of the stem and root area.

The stems may be directed to support the style, either with a long shaped stem (see Figure 6.50) to produce a flat, directed effect, or over-directed to deepen a movement (see Figure 6.51).

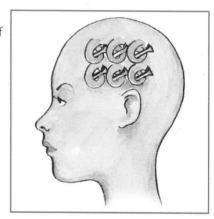

■ Figure 6.48 Forming barrel curls

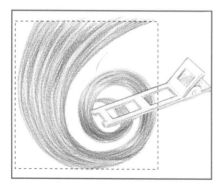

■ Figure 6.49 How to clip curls

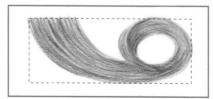

■ Figure 6.50 Curling to produce a flat, directed effect

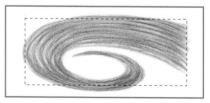

■ Figure 6.51 Over-direction for a deeper movement

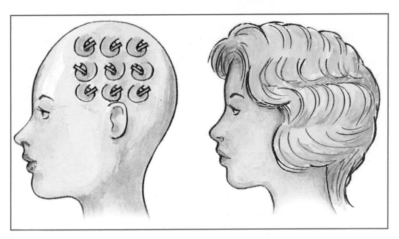

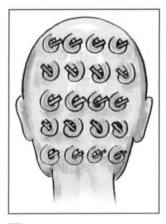

Figure 6.52 Reverse pin curling

Figure 6.53 Reverse pin curling

Barrel curls may be used to produce a flat waved effect in hair, known as *reverse pin curling*. Rows of curls, placed with the body of the curl following the direction of the wave, may be dressed into a corresponding wave movement. The hair may first be moulded into a wave shape, and then the ends of the hair picked up and curled into the wave shape and secured (see Figure 6.52). Alternatively, section the hair into rows at the scalp and then subdivide the rows into pin curl sections. Pin curl the bodies of the curls for each row in alternate directions (see Figure 6.53).

## Stand-up barrel curls

Take sections of hair of a similar depth as that you would take for a hair roller, to produce a similar degree of curl. The width of the section should be no wider than the prongs of the securing clip. Hold the hair up from the scalp and comb to remove tangles and mould the hair together. As for hair rollers, the hair may be over-directed to gain maximum control of hold at less than 90° to produce less root lift (see Figure 6.41).

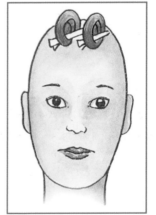

Figure 6.54 Forming stand-up barrel curls

Figure 6.55 Clip-on stand-up barrel curls

Holding the points of the hair, create a rounded shape of the required size and rotate the hair until it rests at the scalp. Locate the securing clip through the curl on to the base of the section. Take care not to mark or indent the curl stem (see Figures 6.54 and 6.55).

Barrel curls may be produced which combine aspects of both the flat and the stand-up effects. This gives subtle degrees of lift where a full effect may not be required (see Figure 6.56).

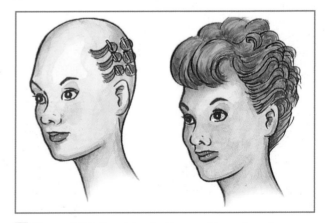

Figure 6.56 Combined effects of barrel curls

### Clock-spring curls

Clock-spring curls are produced in a similar way to barrel curls, but the body of the curl is generally tighter, with the curl getting tighter towards the ends (see Figure 6.57). This type of curl is little used in modern hairstyling.

# Finger waving

Finger waving is the technique of moulding and shaping the hair into wave movements using just fingers, comb, waving lotion and hairpins, clips or tape.

Apply waving lotion to towel-dried hair. Use an applicator bottle to apply the waving lotion and comb through to distribute. This allows the lotion to be distributed smoothly and evenly. Do not use an excessive amount of waving lotion as this may run on to the client's face and neck, causing discomfort.

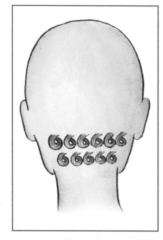

■ Figure 6.57. Clock-spring curls

To determine the natural hair growth, comb the hair off the face, and push the hair forward gently with the palm of your hand; the hair will fall into its natural growth pattern.

### 1 Shaping the top area

Using the first finger of your left hand as a guide, shape the top hair with a comb, using a circular movement. Starting at the front hairline, work towards the crown in 3.7 to 5cm sections at a time until the crown has been reached (see Figure 6.58).

Place the first finger of the left hand directly above the position for the first crest. With the teeth of the comb pointing slightly upwards, insert the comb directly under the first finger. Draw the comb forwards about 2.5cm along the fingertip (see Figure 6.59). With the teeth still inserted in the crest, flatten the comb against the head in order to hold the ridge in place (see Figure 6.60). Remove the left hand from the head, place the middle finger above the crest and the first finger on the teeth of the comb. Raise the crest by closing the two fingers and applying pressure to the head (see Figure 6.61).

■ Figure 6.58 Shaping the top area

■ Figure 6.59 Draw hair towards finger

■ Figure 6.60 Flatten comb against head

■ Figure 6.61 Emphasise ridge

■ Figure 6.62 Comb hair in semi-circular direction

■ Figure 6.63 Complete first ridge at the crown

Without removing the comb, turn the teeth downwards, and comb the hair in a right semi-circular direction to form a dip or trough in the hollow part of the wave (see Figure 6.62). Follow this procedure, section by section, until you reach the crown, where the crest phases out (see Figure 6.63).

The crest and wave of each section should match evenly, without showing separations in the crest and trough parts of the wave.

## 2 Forming the second crest

Start at the crown area (see Figure 6.64). The movements are the reverse of those followed in forming the first crest. The comb is drawn from the tip of the first finger towards its base, thus directing formation of the second ridge. All movements are followed in a reverse pattern until the hairline is reached, therefore completing the second crest (see Figure 6.65).

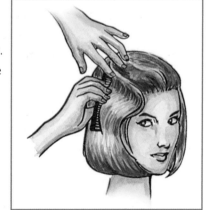

■ Figure 6.64 Start the second ridge

■ Figure 6.65 Complete second ridge

## 3 Forming the third crest

Movements for the third crest closely follow those used in creating the first crest. However, the third ridge is started at the hairline and extended back towards the back of the head, (see Figure 6.66). Continue alternating directions until the side of the head has been completed (see Figure 6.67).

■ Figure 6.66 Start the third ridge

■ Figure 6.67 Complete right side

## 4 Completion

Continue to create these wave movements around the head. The ends of the hair may require pin curling if the hair is too long for you to mould into the nape or on to the side of the face. The waves may be held in place while you are drying them by placing setting tape along the wave troughs or using clips or fine hair pins. Place a net over the hair, taking care not to allow it to press on to the hair, particularly on the front or on the nape, as this will result in marks on the finished hairstyle. Dry the hair thoroughly, using a hood hairdryer. Once dry, remove your client from the dryer, remove the net and any pins or clips, and allow the hair to cool. Using a bristle brush, brush the hair in the direction of the style. Dressing creams or wax may be applied to the hair (to give control) and then, using a dressing comb, reform the waves as they were set. Use the dressing mirror to check the balance of the hairstyle.

# Drying the hair

Always pre-heat the hairdryer. This will speed up the drying process as well as making it more comfortable for your client. If required, place a setting net over the hairset. Secure this, ensuring that the net does not press on to any area of the set, as this may mark the set and affect the finished dressing (see Figure 6.68).

Check that no pins or metal items are pressing on to your client's scalp or hairline. If so, remove them or place a protective pad between the tool and the scalp. Locate the hood of the dryer over the scalp area, ensuring that all of the scalp area is enclosed without it resting on your client's neck or on the face. Inform your client of how to regulate the heat setting and set the timer for the desired time.

Avoid over-drying the hair as this can damage it unnecessarily. However, the hair must be thoroughly dry if it is to be dressed satisfactorily. Allow the hairset to cool slightly before removing the rollers and pins. While the hair is hot, the shape may be relaxed.

■ Figure 6.68 Setting net in place

Having removed the setting tools, brush the hair thoroughly in the direction of the intended style, using a bristle brush.

# Dressing hair

Hair must be thoroughly dry when dressing into style. You may be dressing hair following a wet set, you may be dressing hair which has been set using heated rollers or you may be dressing hair which has little remaining set. It is a distinct advantage to have some set in the hair as this will give you control over the hair.

 *REMEMBER!*

*For some fashion styling techniques, once the setting tools are removed the hair is combed using only the stylist's fingers. This retains the separate effect on the curl.*

Thoroughly brush the hair, using a bristle brush, following the direction of the intended hairstyle. Care is necessary when initially brushing the hair, so as not to cause discomfort when breaking down the crisp effect created by the use of a setting lotion (on freshly set hair) or the effects of hair-fixing spray and tangle (from previously set and dressed hair).

Hair may be moulded into shape using a bristle brush or a wide-toothed comb. Follow these guidelines.

◆ To achieve *control*, brush the hair holding the brush flat to the head.

◆ To achieve *volume*, slowly lift the brush or comb from the head, allowing the hair to fall from the bristles (see Figure 6.69).

◆ To achieve *curve* under, place the brush under the section of hair and draw the hair in, rolling under (see Figure 6.70).

◆ To achieve *wave*, use a comb or brush incorporating a finger wave technique (see Figure 6.71).

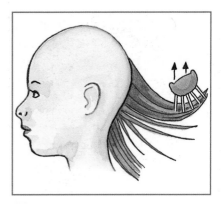

■ Figure 6.69 Using brush or comb to achieve volume

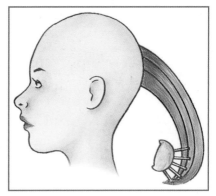

■ Figure 6.70 Using brush or comb to achieve curve under

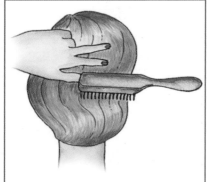

■ Figure 6.71 Using brush or comb to achieve wave

# Backcombing

Control and volume may be achieved in hair by backcombing. Hair that has been tapered or has a natural taper can be backcombed more easily. When building a hairstyle, just as when building a house, build from the bottom up. Use a comb with both widely and closely set teeth; there are specialised combs made with alternate longer and shorter teeth to aid backcombing.

Take a mesh of hair, sufficiently small to be able to hold firmly, and grip towards the points using the first and second finger (see Figure 6.72). The thumb pressing on to the side of the first finger provides added grip. Comb and hold the hair at the angle you wish it to lie; so if you want height, hold the hair in an upright position, and if you want control and flatness hold the hair closer to the head.

Insert the comb, approximately one-third of the length out from the root, into the mesh and push down towards the root (see Figure 6.73). Some of the hair will matt. Continue to do this until the required degree of backcombing is achieved, gradually extending the start position further from the hair root area.

When one section has been backcombed, take an adjacent section and continue. Stagger the section like the bricks in a wall. This will help to prevent gaps and partings in the finished dressing.

 REMEMBER!

*Use a dressing cream, oil or wax to control the hair and add shine.*

Some stylists backcomb all or at least an area of the head before using the wide teeth of the comb or a hairbrush to dress the surface of the hair (see Figure 6.74). Others dress each mesh of hair in turn.

The surface of the hair is smoothed while the backcombing is retained beneath.

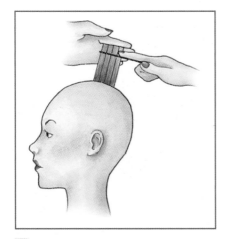

■ Figure 6.72 Taking mesh for backcombing

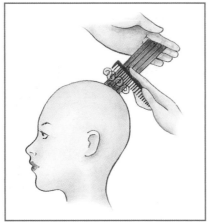

■ Figure 6.73 Inserting comb for backcombing

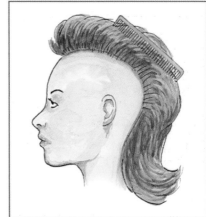

■ Figure 6.74 Dressing the surface of the hair

## Back brushing

A stiff-bristled brush may be used in a similar technique to backcombing. Alternatively a bristle brush may be used on the surface area of the hair to create volume and control.

Starting at the top of the hairstyle, take a controllable mesh of hair, gripping as for backcombing. Hold the hair in the direction and position that you wish to dress it. Lay the bristles of the brush on the top of the section and push towards the root area, rotating the brush slightly, in a flicking action (see Figure 6.75). The higher the section is held from the head the greater the volume potentially created. Before all of the hair within the mesh is used, pick up additional hair from the mesh below. This will produce a continuous back-brushed effect. To control rather than create height, the *flicking* action is reduced. Once completed, the hair may be dressed into place by smoothing the surface and dressing into place using a brush or comb (see Figure 6.76).

 REMEMBER!

*When dressing hair, check the balance of the style using the dressing mirror.*

## Dressing aids

There are a number of control and gloss products available. Some may require care in application to avoid over-use. Oil-based products may make the hair appear greasy if too much is used.

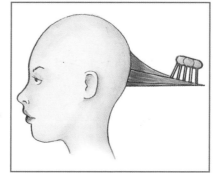

Figure 6.75 Back brushing

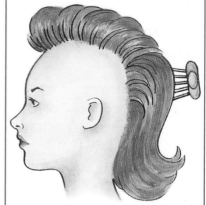

Figure 6.76 Dressing back-brushed hair

A variety of mousse or gel-based products may be used to control and add texture to the hair. These are usually applied either to individual strands of hair (using the fingers) or by spray on the dressed hair. An individually stranded effect may be achieved in the hair by carefully drawing the strands of hair between fingers coated with liquid finishing products, the fingers providing the shaping and the product producing the finish and the hold.

Hair-fixing spray may be used to hold the hairstyle in place. There are a number of types of hair-fixing spray available. Always follow the manufacturer's directions for safe use. Shield the client's face and neck from the effects of the sprays (see Figure 6.77).

Figure 6.77 Spraying dressed hair

*REMEMBER!*

*Take care when using aerosol sprays with clients or colleagues who may suffer breathing problems. Never use them near a naked flame.*

When applying spray to the finished dressed hair, take care not to disturb the hair. On very smooth styles direct the spray with the direction of the hair and follow this by carefully drawing the palms of the hands along the hair in the direction of the hair fall. This can smooth down any stray hairs which may otherwise detract from the effect.

# Dressing long hair

Long hair may be dressed without the need to pre-set, but some preparation will enable you to work more easily and improve the achieved result. If the hair is not to be set beforehand (either wet set or set using heated rollers or tongs) it should be clean, though ideally not freshly washed, as this can make the hair very slippery and more difficult to secure firmly.

The styles that may be achieved will depend not only on your client's wishes but also on the length, texture and density of their hair.

# The scalp plait

You can plait hair so that it either hangs from the head or becomes part of the hairstyle against the head. The scalp plait lays along the scalp. The plait can be created:

◆ from front to back along the centre of the scalp

◆ on either side of the head

◆ diagonally across the scalp.

For this effect the hair does not normally require any pre-setting, but very fine hair can be crimped to add volume. You can achieve different effects by carrying this out on wet instead of dry hair, using gel to produce a crisp-look finish as well as providing control.

# Simple plait

There are a number of techniques that may be used to achieve a simple plait, giving a range of results. The basic principle is the same as for a simple plait: the plait is started at a point of the hairstyle and fresh supplies of hair are added to the plait.

1    Take a small section of hair at the start of the plait and divide this into three even-thickness strands. The hair beneath should be tangle free. Cross these strands over (see Figure 6.78).

2    Cross outer strand 1 over strand 2, which now becomes the central strand; then cross strand 1 with strand 3 (see Figure 6.79).

3    Add additional hair from beneath 2 to strand 2 and then cross over strand 3 to form the central strand (see Figure 6.80).

4    Pick up additional hair to add to strand 3 (see Figure 6.81), and continue in this way.

■ Figure 6.78 Divide into three strands

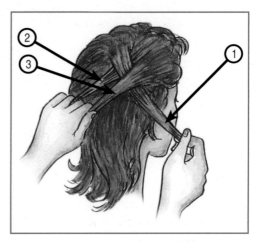

■ Figure 6.79 Starting the braiding

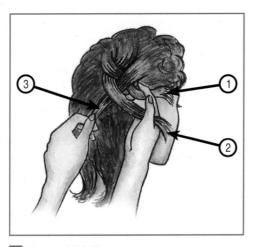

■ Figure 6.80 Drawing over centre strand

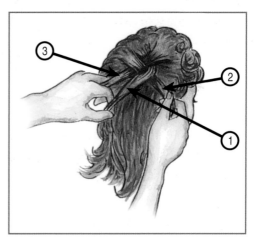

■ Figure 6.81 Pick up strand

For a tight, close effect this is best carried out on moist hair, with the hands holding the hair close to the scalp. The hairstyle may be completed by securing the ends of the plait, rolling and securing them under the plait.

## Vertical roll at the back of the head

For this technique the hair is often backcombed or back brushed prior to dressing (see Figure 6.82).

I    Brush the hair across, horizontally at the back, and locate a row of overlapping hair grips in a line, slightly off-centre, going vertically (see Figure 6.83).

2    Brush the hair back across the back of the head, then in the opposite direction, and twist the hair to form a vertical line up the back of the head. Smooth the hair using a brush or comb, retaining any volume required for the profile shape.

3    Use fine pins to secure the roll, placing the pins in the edge of the top section of hair pointing towards the roll

line, so that the pins penetrate to the lower section. Push the pin into the hair, turning it now away from the roll line (see Figure 6.84). This will place tension on the pin. Take care not to place the pin under too great a tension as this may cause your client discomfort.

## Vertical roll on the top of the head

This is usually produced on the top of the head at the side. For maximum effect it is often located on the *corner* of the head.

1   Brush the hair over the top of the head from one side to the other and secure a line of hair grips, slightly below the roll line.

2   If required, locate and secure a shaped pad over which to build the hair.

3   Dress the hair over the roll's shape, twist the hair ends or tuck them under and secure using fine hair pins (see Figure 6.85).

■ Figure 6.82 Vertical roll at the back of the head

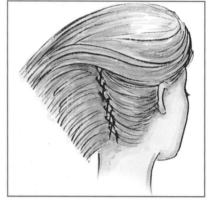

■ Figure 6.83 Full pleat

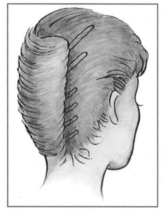

■ Figure 6.84 Full pleat

■ Figure 6.85 Vertical roll on the top of the head

## Helpful hints with long hair

◆   When placing hair pins, ensure that they point downwards, as this will prevent them from loosening.

◆   To prevent hair grips from loosening, overlap or cross them.

◆   Avoid using large quantities of hairspray until the style is complete.

## Self review

1.   How much styling mousse is normally used when blow-drying?

2.   What is the purpose of using a fishtail nozzle with the blow-dryer?

3.   What material are combs best made of if they are to be used when blow-drying hair?

4. When blow-drying for smooth results in what direction should airflow be directed?

5. How can lift be obtained when blow-drying?

6. Which type of hair roller is most likely to mark bleached or very porous hair?

7. When roller setting, what determines the strength of curl achieved?

8. What size is the section taken for a hair roller?

9. What is meant by the term over-directing when setting hair?

10. How should fine pins be located in a finished hairstyle so that they do not fall out?

## Useful contacts

HABIA                                              www.habia.org.uk
Pivot Point – follow links then Design Forum       www.pivot-point.com
Toni & Guy                                         www.toniandguy.co.uk
Vidal Sassoon                                      www.vidalsassoon.co.uk

## CHAPTER 7

# Changing hair colour

## CHAPTER CONTENTS

**Unit H2**   Assist with perming and colouring services

**Unit H3**   Assist with perming, relaxing and colouring services

**Unit H13**   Change hair colour using basic techniques

## WHAT THIS CHAPTER WILL PROVIDE

This chapter provides the essential knowledge necessary for you to understand the hair colouring process. It will guide you in hair colour and product selection as well as in the application techniques available to the professional hair colourist, and their suitability.

## Introduction

Hairdressing is a career that offers you opportunities to develop your creative talents in many different ways. One of the most exciting and challenging areas of creativity in your career as a professional hairstylist will be colouring and lightening hair. There are basically two effects you can achieve by colouring hair:

1   adding colour to and enhancing the existing hair colour

2   permanently changing the hair colour.

Hair colouring includes the processes of any of the following:

◆   adding artificial pigment to the natural hair colour

◆   adding artificial pigment to previously coloured hair

◆   adding artificial pigment to pre-lightened hair

♦ lightening, removing natural pigment and adding artificial pigment in one step.

The terms *tinting* and *colouring* are used interchangeably in this text.

Hair lightening entails the diffusing of the natural pigment or artificial colour from the hair. Hair lightening involves the process of:

♦ lightening the natural pigment to prepare the hair for the final colour (pre-lightening)

♦ lightening the natural or artificial pigment to the desired colour (lightening)

♦ lightening the natural or artificial pigment for corrective colouring

♦ lightening the natural or artificial pigment in selected areas (highlighting).

# Colour theory

## Primary colours

Blue, red and yellow are the primary colours. They cannot be created by mixing other colours together. Blue is a cool-toned colour and red and yellow are warm tones.

## Secondary colours

Green, orange and violet are the secondary colours. They are created by combining two primary colours together in equal proportions.

## Colour strip

The colours opposite each other in the colour strip (see Figure 7.1) when mixed together will neutralise each other. With this information the hairdresser is able to select artificial hair colours that can reduce excessive unwanted tones in the hair. Green ash tones may be used to neutralise excessive red tones, blue ash may be used to neutralise copper tones, and violet ash may be used to neutralise unwanted yellow tones.

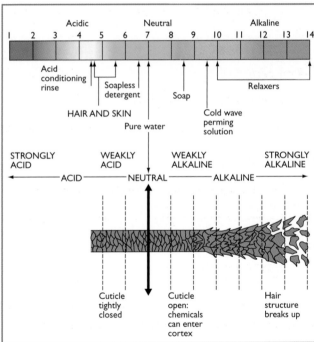

Figure 7.1 Colour strip

## Hair colour consultation

As with all facets of the hairdresser's role, consultation with the client is of crucial importance.

# REMEMBER!

*Hairstylists willing to develop their colouring skills and expertise can serve the needs of a huge and growing market.*

# Reasons clients colour their hair

There are five main reasons why clients wish to colour their hair: to boost self-image, to keep up to date with fashion, for artistic reasons, in reaction to greying and to correct faults in their current colour. These may be subdivided as follows.

## Self-image boost

◆ To alleviate boredom or depression

◆ To promote a more professional appearance

## Fashion

◆ To subtly enhance their existing hair colour

◆ To create a fashion statement or follow a trend which expresses their personality

## Artistic

◆ To accentuate their hairstyle design, making it look more finished

◆ To enhance or minimise their features, using colour to create illusions

## Greying

◆ To conceal premature greying

◆ To keep and enhance their natural white or grey and eliminate yellow

## Corrective

◆ To eliminate the damaged look of sun-lightened hair ends

◆ To remove the unsightly cast caused by chlorine used in swimming pools

◆ To improve upon the results of previous colour experimentation

Almost everyone at one time or another has considered doing something a little different with their hair. Our potential clients may already have done some experimentation at home or in another salon by changing their haircut or style, their hair texture by perming, or their hair's natural colour.

With the emergence and availability of non-professional products that your clients can purchase, why should they come to you, a professional colourist, for advice and service? And who are the typical hair colouring clients today? (See Figure 7.2).

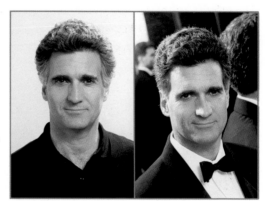

■ Figure 7.2. There are many reasons clients choose to colour their hair; to cover grey is one

## Typical clients

Hair colouring offers a wide variety of choices and therefore attracts the attention and interest of anyone who wants to look good and feel better. Gone are the stereotypes of the obviously tinted client – the damaged hair, the flat or unnatural appearance. Typical clients may want to cover or enhance their grey; they may be teenagers, women, or men who enjoy frequent fashion changes; they are often clients currently unhappy with their natural colour or who want to improve the shine and texture of their hair; they may be current hair colouring clients who come in for their retouch applications and a little relaxation time to themselves. Even the male clientele for hair colour is growing rapidly and is expected to be the fastest-growing category of hair colouring client this decade (see Figure 7.3).

■ Figure 7.3 Hair colouring is a popular service for the male clientele today

As a trained professional hair colourist, you will have access to professional-only products that far surpass those your clients may purchase – in selection, performance and stability. You will know the colour that will look best on your clients, which products and application techniques will best achieve the desired look, how to choose these products and customise them to fit hair conditions at different times of year, and how hair colouring and lightening products will react on clients' hair. The key to your success in hair colouring is communication.

With continuously developing technology and the latest advancements in hair colour education, hair colouring manufacturers are moving to standardise terminology in order to simplify learning and provide greater assistance to colourists.

## The colourist's role in client communication

### Observe

Simple observation gives you a chance to use your training and analyse clients' needs. Your eyes are your primary information-gathering tools. The following is a list of factors about hair that influence colour choice. With time and practice, you will notice certain physical characteristics relevant to hair colour selection when you first see a client. These are items you will need to note when observing clients prior to hair colouring service:

- colour level
- colour tone
- eye colour
- skin tone
- length

- porosity
- density
- texture
- shape
- percentage of grey.

Each of these will be described in detail as we go through a typical hair colour consultation.

The consultation is a time when your greeting and appearance should be at their most impressive. The greeting establishes your credibility and trustworthiness.

You only have one chance to make a first impression on your clients, so make it a good one. You alone are responsible for the image you project. Make sure your clients and potential clients see you as you want them to. Establish and maintain eye contact, make clients comfortable, and listen.

## Listen

Listening allows you to find out how clients view their needs. The finest formulation combined with the most talented application will still result in colour failure if clients are dissatisfied.

Despite all the activity in a busy salon, your clients' thoughts are centred mainly on their own concerns. So, naturally, all clients expect to be treated with courtesy and attention. The hairstylist who recognises this fact and gives clients respect, courtesy and attention will win their confidence. And, when this hairstylist sincerely recommends a hair colour service, clients are likely to listen carefully and seriously consider the recommendation.

 *REMEMBER!*

*Your professional appearance, confident manner and use of professional industry terminology will establish you as an authority in your client's eyes.*

## Make suggestions

To recommend a hair colour service with sincerity means to suggest a colour only when you honestly believe that your client would be happier and more attractive with the colour service. You must be attentive to your clients' needs by listening closely, by being genuinely interested, and by treating every client as you would like to be treated yourself in the same situation. In doing so, you can be confident that your choice will reflect and meet any client's needs, improve your clients' appearance, and enhance your reputation as a colourist (see Figure 7.4).

## Explain the time and monetary investment involved

At the completion of your consultation, you should have an agreement with your client as to what is needed, how long it will take, and how much it will cost. Explain what the service will consist of, each stage, in non-technical language.

## Determine a solution to fulfil the client's needs

Hair colouring is a wonderful service, and can make a tremendous difference to your client. Whether you choose a subtle change or something quite dramatic, the opportunity to create is greatly enhanced by being able to offer a hair colour service.

◼ Figure 7.4 Good communication is essential when discussing a hair colouring service with a client

In the following pages, you will learn how to analyse your client's needs and choose and perform a hair colour service. There are many choices and considerations. Hair colouring is an art, something to be learned over time, not simply by reading books. The people who walk into your salon to become your clients bring not only their hair, but their likes and dislikes, their hopes and dreams – a whole wealth of experiences in which you can share. Take your time, look carefully, listen well, and offer the gift of your art.

## REMEMBER!

*Most hair colouring manufacturers have a telephone helpline to offer professional advice and guidance in the use of their products. Should you experience problems in the use of their products, make use of this facility.*

# Hair colour consultation

The consultation is one of the most important steps in the hair colouring service. But first there are other important elements to consider that will allow you to set the stage for your consultation success.

# Setting the stage: the proper environment

## Adequate lighting

Light, and how it plays with hair colour, is of prime importance to the hair colourist. Bright natural light makes hair colour appear different than does dim light. Electric lights of varying intensities and hues also alter the eye's perception of colour.

Perform the consultation in a well-lit room, preferably with natural lighting. If this is not possible, arrange the lighting so that there is incandescent light in front of the client (around the mirrors) and fluorescent behind the colourist (ceiling fixtures).

Incandescent lighting alone will make the hair and skin tones appear warmer than they truly are; fluorescent lighting alone has a cool cast and will give the skin and hair a pale and unnatural grey appearance. Always remember to consider the lighting in which your clients will see themselves: a beautifully subtle highlight in natural sunlight may disappear under office lighting. Conversely, a strong, attractive colour in your salon lighting could look like neon in the sunlight.

The best mix of lighting for hair colour is to use full-spectrum white fluorescent tubes, or consider adding track-lighting spotlights (incandescent) to existing fluorescent lighting.

## Colour of consultation area

Privacy and good lighting are important. Ideally, a separate room (or area) in the salon should be reserved specifically for consultations. If possible, the walls should be white or neutral, and neutral gowning should be used to conceal your client's street clothes, especially if they are strong colours that may influence your perception of the clients' hair and skin tonality.

# Gathering and using colour consultation tools

In your consultation room or area, you will keep all of your professional hair colouring consultation tools – items that will make communication with your clients go smoothly. Keep a hair colour portfolio of your work, or magazines and picture books with different hair colouring levels, tones, intensities and application techniques, so clients can show you the general hair colour they have in mind. Ink colours on the page will not exactly match coloured pigments in hair, but if you tell your clients this you will both still be able to use these tools as a guide to understanding the desired colour.

Manufacturers' paper colour charts and hair colour swatches, although showing colour on white paper or on white hair, will at least give you an idea of the client's wishes. After all, your idea of red and a client's idea of red may be different – as different as strawberry blonde and burgundy. Manufacturers also make available to colourists their natural colour swatches, to help you judge the natural hair colour depth or level based on their colour product's system (see Figure 7.5). These are usually part of the product shade chart.

A client record card (see Figure 7.6) will be necessary to transfer your hair analysis, testing and consultation information into a permanent file, whether paper based or computerised. You will also want to gather together your materials for strand and predisposition tests, which will be performed prior to each service in this chapter.

Figure 7.5 Hair colourist

| Mr/Mrs/Ms Surname | | Address | | | |
|---|---|---|---|---|---|
| First Name | | Post Code Tel. No. | | | |
| Date of skin test | | Result | Hair type/colour/%grey | | |
| Date | Product | Oxidant | Notes | | Cost |
| | | | | | |
| | | | | | |
| | | | | | |
| | | | | | |

Figure 7.6 Client record card

 REMEMBER!

*Computerised multi-media style selection systems may be used to illustrate to your client the effects of differing hair colour upon their hairstyle.*

# Pre-colour testing

## Test cutting to confirm colour selection

Before applying a tint or bleach, take a preliminary test cutting to confirm your selection. You will learn the following information:

◆ whether the proper colour selection was made

◆ the timing needed to achieve the desired results

◆ whether further pre-conditioning treatments are needed

◆ whether it is necessary to apply a filler (pre-pigmentation).

## Test cutting procedure

1   Mix a small amount of the colour or bleach intended for use with peroxide, according to the manufacturer's directions, using plastic measuring spoons to ensure accuracy of proportions (see Figure 7.7).

2   Apply mixture to a 0.125cm section of hair, usually in the crown area of the head (see Figure 7.8). (Remember to test each area where the hair colour varies. More than one formula may be necessary to achieve even results.)

3   Separate the strand from the rest of the hair using foil or plastic film. Process with or without heat according to the manufacturer's directions, keeping careful records of timing on the client's record card.

 *REMEMBER!*

*It is important that the hair has received all pre-treatments necessary according to your analysis before the test cutting is taken, so that results will be accurate.*

4   Rinse the strand, shampoo, towel dry, and examine the results (see Figure 7.9). Adjust the formula, timing or pre-conditioning as necessary and proceed with tinting on the entire head.

5   If results are unsatisfactory, adjust the formula and repeat the process with a new test.

■ Figure 7.7 Mix colour with peroxide

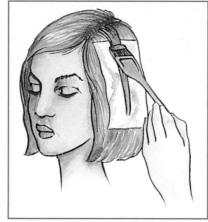

■ Figure 7.8 Apply mixture to strand

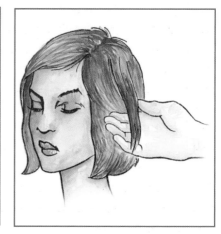

■ Figure 7.9 Examine results

# Predisposition test to check for client sensitivity (skin test)

Allergy to aniline derivative tints is unpredictable. Some clients may be sensitive, and others may develop sensitivity after years of use. To identify an allergic client, a patch, or predisposition, a test should be given 24 to 48 hours prior to each application of an aniline tint or toner. The tint used for the skin test must be the same formula as that used for the hair colouring service. A skin test is not usually required prior to the application of a bleach product that contains no colouring.

## Predisposition test procedure

1 Select the test area – behind one ear extending into the hairline or at the inside bend of the elbow (near a pulse point).

2 Using a mild unperfumed soap, cleanse an area about the size of a one-pence coin (see Figure 7.10).

3 Dry the area.

4 Prepare the test solution according to the manufacturer's directions (see Figure 7.11).

5 Apply to test area with a sterile cotton wool bud or the end of a clean tint brush. Tell your client what to do should a reaction occur. Your client should remove the patch test and, should the symptoms continue, should consult her or his medical practitioner. S/he should also inform you of this occurrence.

6 Leave the area undisturbed for 24 to 48 hours.

7 Examine the test area.

8 Note the results on the client's record card.

A *negative* skin reaction will show no sign of inflammation or skin irritation, and colour may safely be applied. If the skin test is *positive*, you will see any or a number of the following: redness, swelling, burning, itching or blisters. A client with these symptoms is allergic, and should under no circumstance receive the colour service for which the test was performed. Application in this instance could result in a serious allergic reaction for the client, and a professional negligence claim for the hair colourist.

The skin test is also known as an allergy test, a patch test, a predisposition test or a Sabouraud-Rousseau test.

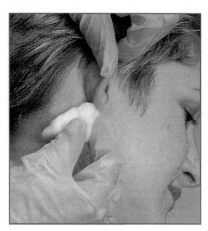
■ Figure 7.10 Clean patch test area

■ Figure 7.11 Mix tint and peroxide

*HEALTH & SAFETY*

A predisposition test must be given before colouring the hair with an aniline derivative product. Operator dermatitis, although rare, involves the same types of reaction as the client can experience. Since the colourist's hands are in water and contact chemical solutions repeatedly throughout an average day, it is important to take proper precautions. You should protect yourself from allergic reactions by wearing protective gloves until the product is completely removed from the client's hair.

## Client record card

Always record the consultation on the client's record card. It is important to keep an accurate record so that successful services can be repeated and any difficulties encountered in one service may be avoided in the next. A complete record should be kept, containing all analysis notes, notes of client's responses to questioning about previous treatments, test cutting and whole-head results, processing, timings, costs, and suggestions for the next service.

# Analysing your client's hair physiology

No two people are exactly alike, and no two heads of hair are exactly the same. Even an individual client's hair will vary from season to season and from year to year. Every person has a natural hair colour that is either a dark, medium or light colour, but no two people have exactly the same hair colour. Inside the hair shaft, where you cannot see, the factors that create or affect hair colour are always different from person to person. That is why the same hair colouring formula and procedure will produce a different result for every client (see Figure 7.12).

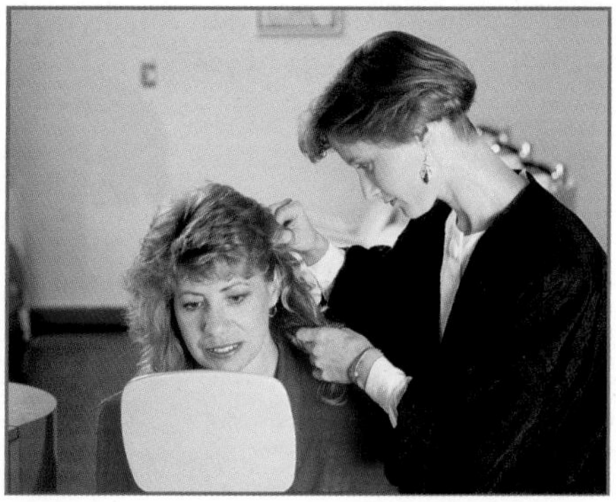

Figure 7.12 Analysing a client's hair physiology

## How hair structure relates to colouring

Hair is a remarkable and resilient fibre. Every hair colour service will affect or be affected by the structure of the hair. Some hair colour products cause a dramatic change in the hair's structure; others affect it very little. When a product significantly changes the hair structure, it usually creates a weaker strand of hair.

Knowing how products affect the structure will allow you to make choices. Your perceptions of what the hair can or cannot tolerate will allow you to be the best judge of what is most appropriate for each client.

Generally every hair on a person's head is composed of three parts: the *cuticle*, the *cortex* and the *medulla*. The medulla is at the innermost layer, centre, of the hair shaft. The cuticle is the outermost layer of the hair. It is made up of overlapping bands of keratinised protein that is very similar to the protein that makes up our fingernails. It is translucent, allowing diffused light to pass through. The cuticle protects the interior cortex layer of the hair. The shiny appearance of the hair depends on this cuticle layer being smooth and intact. A healthy cuticle contributes 20% to the overall strength of the hair.

The cortex is the second layer of the hair. The natural colour we see in the hair is within this layer. The cortex structure is made up of elongated, fibrous cells bundled together. Melanin pigment granules are scattered between the cortex cells. These granules are embedded in the cortex layer like chips in a chocolate chip biscuit. The strength and elasticity of the hair depend on the cortex layer being intact. A healthy cortex contributes 80% to the overall strength of the hair.

## KEY WORDS

**Cuticle** – *Outermost layer of the hair*
**Cortex** – *Fibrous second layer of the hair; contains the natural pigment; the layer affected by permanent colouring and permanent curling*
**Medulla** – *The medulla is at the innermost layer, centre, of the hair shaft; this layer is often missing from very fine hair*

*Hair texture* is described as the diameter of the individual hair strand. The terms coarse, medium and fine are used to differentiate between large, medium and small diameters. Texture has an effect on hair colour because the hair's natural melanin pigment is distributed differently in the different textures. Each diameter also has a different resistance to the changes hair colour chemicals make on the hair shaft (see Figure 7.13).

Fine-textured hair's pigment is grouped more tightly together. Because of this tighter grouping, when you deposit colour you will have a darker result on fine hair. By the same token, fine hair is less resistant to lightening because there is less structure to resist the chemical. When lightening fine hair, a milder lightener can be used successfully.

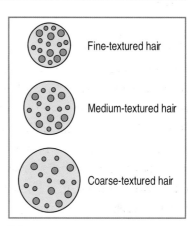

Fine-textured hair

Medium-textured hair

Coarse-textured hair

■ Figure 7.13. Diameters of various hair strands

 *REMEMBER!*

*Due to the compact nature of fine hair, depositing colour molecules in the cortex may cause more damage to the structure than it would in coarser hair textures.*

Medium-textured hair will have average responses to hair colour products. Note any variations in texture throughout the hair. The front hairline is usually finer in texture than hair further back on the head.

Coarse-textured hair has a more open grouping of hair pigment due the larger-diameter hair shaft in which the pigment is located. Because of this open grouping, you will have a slightly lighter result when depositing colour. When lightening the hair, you will encounter greater resistance to the lightener, and a stronger lightening product may be needed.

*Porosity* is necessary for colour to take properly. Each product you put on the hair requires a different degree of porosity.

Porosity, in simple terms, is the ability of the hair to absorb moisture. Porous hair will accept liquid (hair colour, for example) more readily than non-porous hair. Uneven porosity can create problems if even colour results are desired.

As hair grows longer, the ends are subject to frequent shampooing, drying, styling and environmental influences. There will be visual and textural changes. The cuticle will be slightly abraded (worn away), and the rough hair fibre will lose some of its flexibility, body and shine. There will also be some variation in colour from strand to strand and even from the scalp area to the mid-lengths. Hair may be lighter and more faded-out towards the ends.

This longer, older hair is described as over-porous, a condition in which hair reaches an undesirable level of porosity (see Figure 7.14). This hair will respond differently to hair colour products than the newer hair closer to the scalp. Those different responses can only be determined by taking a test cutting. As a general rule, over-porous hair will look duller, flatter and will reflect cooler tones, while the healthier hair will reflect warmer tones.

Occasionally, a client's hair has a cuticle so smooth and compact that you will need to create the proper porosity for the success of your hair colouring service. The hair is considered resistant to the swelling effects of alkalis that allow hair colour to penetrate and, if necessary, cover grey hair. Pre-softening of grey or resistant hair will be covered later.

■ Figure 7.14 It is important to check the porosity of hair before a colouring service is given

 REMEMBER!

*The dense areas of the client's hair will require more product and more careful application. For hair colour to work effectively, each hair shaft must be surrounded by product.*

*Hair density* is the number of hairs per square centimetre on the scalp. Hair can be described as sparsely, moderately and thickly distributed on the head. It is important to notice that hair density varies, even on the same head. For some, the hair around the face line is more sparsely distributed, and the hair over the crown is more densely distributed. For others, the opposite is true (see Figure 7.15).

Hair length will be a factor in your hair colour choice. The hair on heads grows by an average of 1.25cm per month. This translates to 15cm per year. If your client's hair is 30cm long, the hair furthest away from the scalp is two years old.

Longer hair has been exposed to the elements for a longer period of time and is referred to as older hair. Older hair will vary in porosity throughout the length of the hair shaft.

Unequal reactions to liquid and chemicals along the length of the hair shaft are due to variations in porosity. To observe variations in porosity, hold

■ Figure 7.15 Note the variations in hair density prior to a colouring application

several strands of hair away from the scalp by their ends. Note any variations in colour or surface texture. Older, more porous hair will appear lighter in colour and rougher in texture.

Since the hair is longer, more hair colouring product may be needed for the application. Pre-treatment conditioners may be necessary prior to a colour application to help equalise porosity and provide the foundation for even colour results. Many colourists accordingly charge more for colouring long hair (see Figure 7.16).

The shape of the hair as it grows from the follicle is a genetic trait and is described as being straight, wavy or curly. The smoother the hair shape, the more light reflection. The curlier shapes will refract, or bounce back light, and hair colour may not reflect as strongly as on straighter forms. Careful colour choice and application will create satisfactory colour results on any hair texture. To compensate for excessively curly hair, a more intense or stronger tone may be used, as determined by your test cutting. Polymer hair colouring products or those that fill in, or smooth, the cuticle layer may also increase the perception of colour as well as shine (see Figure 7.17).

As a colourist, you should work with the hair's natural attributes, and use texture, shape, density and porosity to your advantage. Follow the hair's natural pattern or style and insert highlights or lowlights to enhance a cut and give a more polished appearance.

Figure 7.16 Hair length will be a factor in your choice of hair colour

Figure 7.17 A curlier hair form may require a stronger tone

# Identifying the natural hair colour

Natural hair colour is the base of the colourist's work. Understanding the science of natural colour will help you develop informed hair colouring choices for each client. It is amazing to realise that nature creates an endless variety of hair colours, with no two alike, using a single substance called *melanin*.

Natural pigments are classified as melanins. Melanin is made of molecules capable of reflecting colour. They are classified into two groups: black-brown, or eumelanin, and yellow-red, or pheomelanin. Special cells called melanocytes receive the amino acid tyrosine from the blood vessels at the bottom of each hair follicle. Within the melanocytes, a chemical reaction occurs. An enzyme known as tyrosinase gives oxygen to the tyrosine, and the result is a change in its molecular structure. This oxidation of tyrosine produces the melanin that creates all the natural hair colour variations.

# KEY WORDS

**Eumelanin** – *Black and brown natural pigment of the hair*
**Melanin** – *Natural pigment of the hair and skin*
**Pheomelanin** – *Yellow and red natural pigment of the hair*

Once the melanin is developed, it is coated with melanoprotein to form a granule. While the hair is forming, these pigment granules, called melanosomes, are pushed up between the cells that are forming as cortex fibres and become a part of the hair structure. These melanin-filled granules are scattered through the cortex of the hair, in no set pattern or amount. This is how nature creates so many hair colour variations from only one natural substance.

The natural hair colour we see (black, brown, blonde or red) will depend upon the type of melanin – eumelanin, pheomelanin or a combination of both. The lightness or darkness (depth) of the hair will depend on the amount and distribution (whether closely packed or scattered) of melanin present in the hair.

The keratin protein of the hair is colourless. It is the melanin alone that gives hair its colour. When hair turns grey, it has the same basic structure as it has always had, except that it does not have pigmented melanin. The melanocytes don't necessarily stop producing pigment all at once. Sometimes they produce less and less until gradually the hair appears lighter. Some hairs have no colour and others do, producing the grey effect sometimes known as *salt and pepper.*

# REMEMBER!

*As our hair colour changes and becomes greyer, our skin colour changes as well. When advising the older client about hair colour suggest the lighter colours rather than the darker.*

Often, clients will wish to colour their hair long before the grey hair is noticeable, because their colour lacks richness. When we lose all the pigment in a few of our hairs, we lose a little pigment in all our hair. This is a great motivation for colouring one's hair.

Understanding melanin is important to the professional colourist because melanin is a contributor to any new hair colour the colourist wants to create.

In hair colouring, hair stylists and hair colour manufacturers use a system to analyse the lightness and darkness of a colour. It is called the *level system.* The materials you receive with your hair colour products will describe your particular manufacturer's system. Generally, in the majority of product labelling systems, a scale of 1 to 10 is used to describe the lightness or darkness. Level 1 colours are the darkest; Level 10 colours are the lightest. Some manufacturers will elect to use a level system starting with zero; others extend their levels beyond 10 to 12. The scale works the same regardless of the starting and ending points – low numbers are darker; high numbers are lighter.

Hair colour manufacturers provide a chart depicting the colours in their product line. This colour chart shows the level and tone of the various colours. Natural hair colours can also be analysed with this tool. By comparing the manufacturer's colour chart with your client's hair you can determine the hair colour level. You can then describe the lightness or darkness (depth) with a number from the level system.

 # REMEMBER!

*The names for the natural hair colour levels may vary from manufacturer to manufacturer. It is important for you to identify the varying degrees of lightness to darkness that distinguish each level. Use the selected manufacturer's colour shade chart as your guide in identifying your client's natural colour level.*

To determine your client's natural colour level, take a few strands of hair and hold them up and away from the head, allowing light to pass through. Holding the hair away from the scalp, take the manufacturer's chart and fan out the hair strands. Place the chart next to the hair closest to the scalp. Sometimes the hair will be a different level due to exposure to the elements or another chemical service. Be certain to identify the natural level at the base of the hair shaft, closer to the scalp. Also identify the level or levels of the middle lengths and ends so you can adjust your formula accordingly.

Do not part the hair or hold it flattened against the scalp: this produces an incorrect reading as, without light passing through it, the hair will appear darker. Hair that is wet or heavily soiled will also appear darker.

The international colour code levels (see Figure 7.18) are:

1 black

2 very dark brown

3 dark brown

4 medium brown

5 light brown

6 dark blonde

7 medium blonde

8 light blonde

9 very light blonde

10 lightest blonde.

| | |
|---|---|
| **10** | Lightest blonde |
| **9** | Very light blonde |
| **8** | Light blonde |
| **7** | Medium blonde |
| **6** | Dark blonde |
| **5** | Light brown |
| **4** | Medium brown |
| **3** | Dark brown |
| **2** | Very dark brown |
| **1** | Black |

Figure 7.18 Natural hair colour levels according to the international colour code

Levels 1, 2 and 3 are considered to be dark hair. Generally, people with dark hair want their hair to stay dark. This is usually the best choice, because their skin and eye colours are also usually strongly pigmented. The dark hair colour in combination with richly toned skin and eye colour creates an intense and exotic combination.

Levels 4, 5 and 6 are medium levels. You will note that the client's pigmentation in skin and eye colour is also in the medium range. There are certainly more options for someone with a medium-level hair colour. Generally, you will select colours with richness or vibrancy for these clients.

Levels 7 and 8 are the light levels. Again you will observe corresponding skin and eye pigmentation in this light range. Clients with light hair generally have most options regarding their choices. Darker or lighter hair works well.

Levels 9 and 10 are very light levels. We do not see many of these people as clients. Their hair colour is generally pleasing until it turns grey. We will discuss grey hair at a later point in this chapter.

The term *tone* is used to describe the warmth or coolness of a colour. The manufacturer's colour chart you used earlier to discover the colour level also describes the hair colours, indicating their tone.

The *warm tones* are red, orange and yellow, although some hair colour labels use different names like auburn, copper, gold or bronze.

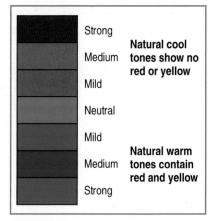

| | Strong |
| | Medium |
| | Mild |
| | Neutral |
| | Mild |
| | Medium |
| | Strong |

**Natural cool tones show no red or yellow**

**Natural warm tones contain red and yellow**

Figure 7.19. The strength or warmth of cool tones is called intensity

The *cool tones* are blue, green and violet, often listed on labels as ash, drab, platinum, pearl or smoky. Those words conjure up visual pictures of the properties or characteristics of the colour tone.

*Intensity* refers to the strength of the tonality in a colour. Intensity is described as being mild, medium or strong. The difference in intensity can be as subtle as an auburn highlight or as strong as a traffic-stopping red. The strength of the warm or cool tone in a hair colour is indicated in Figure 7.19, with neutral (in the centre) representing an even balance of colour tones without showing obvious amounts of either warm or cool colours.

## REMEMBER!

*Most hair colour manufacturers have their own training centres where you may learn how to select and use their own product lines. Some will also visit salons and training centres to give training in the use of their products.*

# Percentage and distribution of grey

Individuals in today's society are constantly being bombarded by advertisements and television commercials that emphasise youth. Because of this, people often seek ways to look younger.

Grey hair can be a curse or it can be a blessing. It is certainly most often the catalyst that convinces clients to colour their hair, which is a blessing to colourists. On the other hand, grey hair can also complicate the hair colour service because it does not respond to hair colouring in the same way as naturally pigmented hair.

Grey hair tends to be coarser, less elastic and occasionally curlier or straighter than other hair on the head. It also becomes more resistant to chemical services, and thus requires special consideration in hair colouring practice.

It is first necessary to determine the amount of grey hair (the actual percentage) on the head, relative to the naturally coloured hair. Then you must determine the distribution of those grey hairs (where they are located on the head). A person who is 50% grey could have their grey hair sprinkled equally throughout the head or located only in the front portion, say, of the head. Each of these requires a different approach to formulating. Therefore, we must identify and note these factors regarding grey hair on the client's record card.

## Determining the percentage of grey

Another consideration when formulating for grey hair is recognising the natural colour that has not yet turned grey. Most people retain some dark hair as they turn grey. The situation in which hair appears grey occurs when there is a mixture of white and dark hair. This salt-and-pepper blending creates different shades of grey depending on the ratio of pigmented to non-pigmented hair. This hair must be analysed for level and tone.

Be careful not to allow the reflection of the white or grey hair next to the pigmented hair to affect your judgement. In many instances this will cause even the most experienced colourist to identify the naturally pigmented hair as darker than it really is, due to the contrast. By misjudging the depth of natural colour, you may not compensate adequately for the undertones present in the hair, which will create a warmer-than-expected end result when you begin to lift the natural hair colour.

## What occurs during the greying process?

The melanin enters the hair shaft void of colour. The melanin pigment granule is still nestled in the cortex of the hair shaft and will still be evident as it is affected by the colouring process. When you lighten hair that is grey or white (non-pigmented hair), the melanin pigment diffuses in the same way as coloured melanin. The strand becomes weakened, the cuticle lifted, and the hair takes on a yellow cast.

Another consideration when formulating for grey hair is what colour the client's hair was prior to turning grey. The hair colourist must recognise that when the hair starts to turn grey, the remaining natural colour changes as well. Grey hair does the masterful job of concealing the undertones that still remain in the hair. The undertones are there and are no less intensified than they were before the hair turned grey.

 *REMEMBER!*

*Each person is born with a particular combination of natural pigment. There is harmony between the hair, eye and skin tones. At the point at which greying clients come to you for colour service, their hair has changed dramatically from the original birth colour. By knowing what colour their hair was when they were younger, you will be able to anticipate the changes that their hair will undergo during treatment with an oxidative hair colour product. The answer to this question will indicate the intensity of pigmentation with which you will be dealing.*

## Selecting colour for desired result

Every hair colouring service must begin with a professional assessment of the client's current hair colour and what changes need to be made. Only then can the best procedure and formula be selected.

## Basic rules for colour selection

◆ Make sure the client's hair is not over-greasy and is dry.

- Look through the hair. To see level as well as tone, raise the hair by pushing it up with the hands against the scalp.

- Analyse the level present in the hair. Does the client want to go lighter or darker?

- Analyse the level of the desired colour. Add or subtract from the natural colour to determine the level of colour necessary.

- What are the natural tones? What highlights does the client want? Select the colour within the level that will supply those tones, or determine which colour concentrate should be used.

- Know the properties of the product you are using. Consult the manufacturer's information on each colour and how it reacts on different hair colour levels (light, medium or dark hair).

- Analyse the condition of the hair, especially its porosity. Does the hair need to be conditioned prior to the service to help the colour be true and prevent excessive fading?

The directions for each colour product will indicate the correct mixing formulas for adequate lift and/or deposit, and what hair colour classification and volume of developer (if any) is required to achieve the desired results, based on your thorough analysis of your client's hair and needs.

 REMEMBER!

*The manufacturer's guidelines require accurate analysis of your client's hair in order to direct you towards the correct colour product choice.*

# Examining the scalp

Examine the scalp carefully to determine the presence of any factors that would make it inadvisable to use a hair colouring product (these factors are called *contra-indications*). An oxidation tint solution should not be used if the following conditions exist:

- positive skin test (predisposition or patch test)

- scalp abrasions, irritations or eruptions

- contagious scalp disorders.

# Examining the hair

Examine the hair to determine what, if any, pre-treatment may be necessary prior to your hair colour service. Elements to consider are:

- evidence of prior chemical treatments (colour, permanent wave or relaxer)

- different degrees of porosity over the length of the hair shaft due to the effects of sun, harsh chemicals or hair length

- variations in texture at the facial hairline, crown or nape.

In some cases it may be advisable to postpone the hair colour service due to excessive damage or the presence of incompatible chemicals in the hair.

The results of such an examination may indicate the need for any of the following:

◆ reconditioning treatments

◆ colour removal

◆ removal of metallic colouring

◆ postponement of service due to breakage or some other problem.

All information about the condition of the client's hair should be recorded on their record card.

# Discuss client's expectations and hair limitations

The difference between your client's current hair colour and what is desired will indicate the hair colour category and formula to use. Does your client want a temporary change or a more permanent one? Does your client want something close to their current colour or a dramatic colour change? Based on your thorough analysis, you can choose the appropriate product and technique to fulfil the client's expectations, but also respect the hair's limitations.

Be realistic in discussing colour selection with your client. It is best to select a general range of colour lightness and tone, rather than to promise an exact shade. Some clients will be able to change their colour in one process, creating the right level and tone at the same time. Others will need two separate products and processes to create the same effect. Be sure to consider carefully all the factors that will influence your client's decisions.

# Consider the client's lifestyle

A colouring procedure that requires a great deal of care may be impractical for a very active person. Pale blonde may be the wrong choice for someone who swims regularly (pool chemicals can turn blonde hair green). An iridescent aubergine colour might be inadvisable for someone who works in a conservative law firm. All of these factors must be considered.

An office job would dictate a more conservative colour choice than a freelance fashion photographer. A full-time mum might need a lower-maintenance colour service. A businessman would wish for an undetectable line of demarcation between the hair colour and his new regrowth.

Sun lovers will have different colour results from people who avoid exposure to the sun. Tennis, boating and convertible cars all mean more sun. People who engage in heavy daily exercise need to shampoo their hair more often; this could cause their colour to fade.

Medicines can affect hair colour results. Sulphur-based drugs can add warmth to light blonde colours. High doses of vitamins and minerals can darken the natural hair colour level. Always ask your clients and note on their record card any medications they are taking.

Home-care products are of great importance for hair colour clients. A shampoo for controlling dandruff or psoriasis may change your colour result. Rapid fading can occur due to highly alkaline, non-professional products. Some mousses, conditioners and hairsprays can build up and coat the hair shaft. This will alter the porosity of hair, causing uneven colour results.

Educating your clients on how to care for their colour-treated hair will improve your results. Healthy, well-cared-for hair will be a positive reflection on your workmanship. Teaching your clients proper maintenance is the most professional approach to beautiful hair colour (see Figure 7.20).

Time spent in the salon for services is a point of discussion. For some, looking good is a form of self-indulgence; for others, it's pure torture. Frequency of maintenance must be presented during your consultation.

Figure 7.20 Discussing hair colour products

The time and money involved in committing to a colour service should be spelled out in advance.

This is a time to make direct eye contact with your client and wait for the answer. If the time or cost is objectionable, alter your suggestion. Continue this conversation until you and your client agree to the maintenance schedule you have presented. At this point, you will have an agreement with your client and can begin your service.

 REMEMBER!

*Your conversation should be something like: 'This colour [show a picture or swatch] can be achieved by [indicate the type of colour service, i.e. weaving, single-process colour, etc.]. The cost of this service will be [state cost]. How do you feel about this?'*

## Choosing level, tone and intensity

If necessary you will adjust the hair colour formula for each individual texture or condition. Remember the findings of your analysis, which are listed on your client's record card. Include the client's current colour in formulating for level, tone and intensity. Generally speaking, a change of 1 to 2 levels will produce the most natural results. Any tone can be enhanced or subdued to the client's wishes by using the 'law of colour' in selecting your formula. Adjust for grey, porosity and length. Natural-looking hair colours are a balance between all three primary colours, including the client's contributing pigment and the artificial colour selected.

## Selecting the appropriate application technique

After a thorough discussion with your client, you must then choose the method that will achieve the desired effect. Sometimes a combination of application techniques is necessary to first cover grey, then add carefully placed highlights, to make the transition from the lightness of grey to the contrasting darkness of a solid colour. Another example would be the use of a double process, blending a pastel colour with a cool tone. Whatever you select, make sure the client understands each step of the procedure and the technique necessary to achieve your objective. This will avoid startled looks from clients when they see unexplained things happening to their hair during a procedure.

 *REMEMBER!*

*Your client may not understand the jargon that you use. Explain the procedure that is about to be used on their hair, in terms that they will understand. This will help to gain their confidence in the process, so they will be more comfortable and therefore more likely to enjoy their visit to your salon.*

# Using colour keys to find the most flattering colour for your client

## Analysing skin and eye colouring

The colour of client's eyes can be a clue as to what their hair colour could be. Eyes are rarely one colour. Usually they are combinations of two or even three colours. Basically there are brown, blue and green eyes. Look more closely. Brown eyes with olive green, reddish brown or gold flecks are quite common. Blue eyes may also have flecks of white, gold or grey. Green eyes can range from grey-green to hazel (with brownish overtones) to yellow-green.

We can categorise eye colour as warm or cool. Warm eye colours contain red, orange, yellow or gold flecks through the iris of brown, blue, or green.

Warm eye colours are:

◆ brown with red, orange, yellow or gold

◆ blue with yellow or gold

◆ green with reddish brown, orange, yellow or gold.

People who have warm eye colours can wear warm hair colours. Cool eye colours contain black, grey-brown, grey-green, blue, violet, grey or white flecks through the iris of brown, blue or green.

Cool eye colours are:

◆ brown with black, grey-brown, grey-green or grey

◆ blue with white, blue, grey or violet

◆ green with blue or grey.

People with cool eye colours look most attractive with cool or neutral hair colours.

The depth of eye colour is another factor in your colour choice. Lighter eyes reflect a lighter pigmentation throughout the client's colouring. A lighter-intensity colour choice would be indicated. Medium eyes reflect stronger pigmentation and more intense colour options are available. Dark eyes reflect the strongest pigmentation. A deeper colour choice is advisable. To choose a colour that will harmonise with the client's natural pigmentation, include the depth of eye colour (light, medium or dark) in your colour equation.

 # REMEMBER!

*Many clients choose coloured contact lenses to enhance their appearance. This can affect your colour choice. If you are not certain of the client's natural eye colour, always ask.*

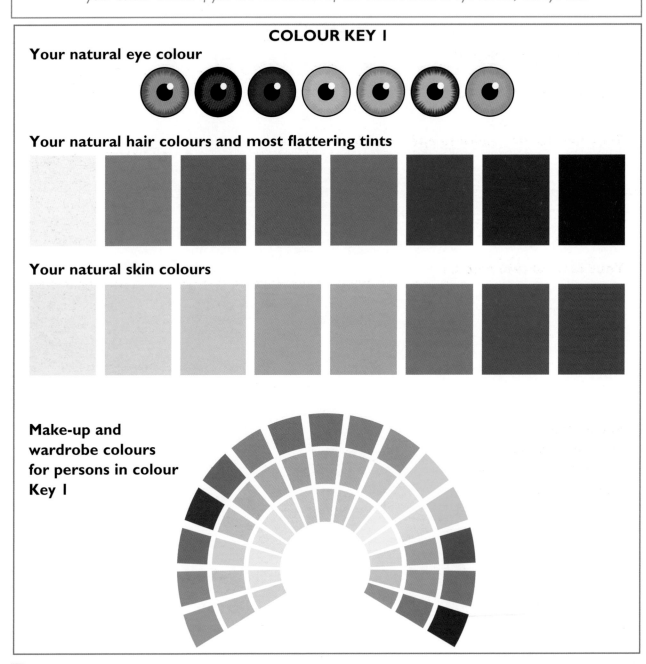

**COLOUR KEY 1**

**Your natural eye colour**

**Your natural hair colours and most flattering tints**

**Your natural skin colours**

**Make-up and wardrobe colours for persons in colour Key 1**

■ Figure 7.21 Colour key 1

Skin tone can be broken down into four simple categories: olive, red, golden and neutral. It is easiest to observe the natural skin tone by looking at the skin on the neck, close to the clavicle. Skin on the face and arm is often affected by sun exposure, which masks the skin tone, making it difficult to determine.

Olive skin tones have an underlying tone of grey, green or yellow. Olive-toned clients look best in cool or neutral colours. If a warm shade is desired, it should be in a darker level.

Red skin tones have an underlying tone of red-brown, red or blue-red. Red-toned clients look best in cool or neutral colours. Warm colours are not recommended for these clients.

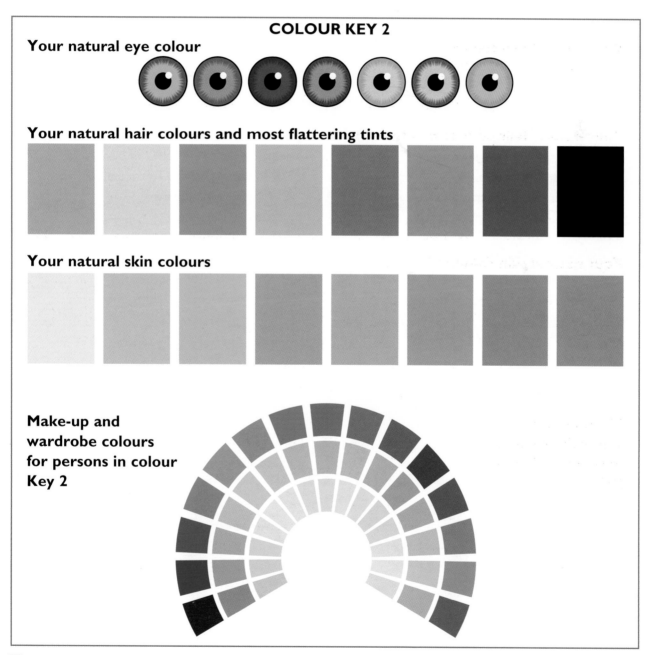

 Figure 7.22 Colour key 2

Golden skin tones have an underlying tone of golden brown, gold or peach. Golden skin tones look best in warm colours. The level chosen would be affected by the client's natural level.

Neutral skin tones are a balance of warm and cool. Neutral skin can have an underlying tone of pink and yellow in combination. You will not observe one predominant underlying skin tone. Generally these skin tones are described as ivory, beige or brown skin. Neutral skin tones look good in either warm or cool colours.

How does this information indicate a colour choice? The charts in Figures 7.1 and 7.2 will help you in your selection. Remember that each person is unique, however, and consult with your trainer or product technician for advice. Gradually, as your skill develops, you will see these features automatically.

# Enhancing your client's natural colouring

When working with hair that has not been coloured, you will notice a natural harmony in the hair tone, skin tone and eye colour tone. Maintaining that natural harmony will give you a pleasing, natural effect. A more avant-garde effect will be achieved by using complementary colour tones. The key to maintaining harmony in colour tone is understanding the 'law of colour'.

Consider how tones change with maturity. Many clients initially want to return to the colour of their youth. They do not realise that the pigment of their skin is ageing in a process similar to that of the hair. To tint the hair back to the natural colour of their youth creates a severe contrast that can be harsh. Generally, a colour of a similar tone but lighter level will be more flattering.

There will always be clients who break these rules. Many do so with great success. Attractiveness is a quality that incorporates the laws of art and balance, along with the client's personality and self-expression.

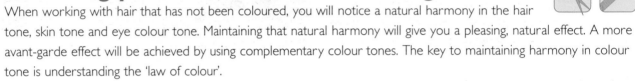

*REMEMBER!*

*The level of your correction must be the same or slightly darker than the problem. For example, if you have a client whose hair is level 6 orange and she wants it to be more neutral looking, you would need to use a level 5 or 6 blue-toned hair colour to correct the warmth. A level 7 in a blue-toned hair colour will not have enough pigment to overcome the level 6 orange.*

# Creating natural-looking hair colour using artificial pigments

Most hair colours represent a balance of colours, which means that they generally contain a balance of each of the primary colours. However, colours will have a predominant base and a level of lightness or darkness that must be identified before formulating a tint for the hair.

Oxidation tints are identified by the predominant base and the level of colour formulated by the manufacturer. Most manufacturers provide literature that identifies the level and base colour for you. You may identify the level and base colour of the client's hair by comparing it to the manufacturer's colour or shade chart (as a guide, not as an absolute).

All colours – warm, cool or neutral – can be formulated in tones that range from the lightest blonde to the darkest black, using the basic theory related to the law of colour (see Figure 7.23).

## Using level, tone and intensity in selecting a colour

When you have decided on which hair colouring products to use, you must next find the correct level, tone and intensity to achieve your desired result. In many manufacturers' product lines, you may find more than one colour choice at each level. However, each of these shades will create a different tonality.

Figure 7.23 A hair colourist using a colour chart

Choose the one closest to what you need to achieve the desired result. To give the new hair colour the exact tonality and intensity desired, the basic shade can be adjusted or modified by adding a small quantity (2.5–5 ml) of a cooler or warmer shade on the same level, or by using a colour concentrate to enrich or drab the final formula. If these are in liquid form they are usually added drop by drop or if in a cream form centimetre by centimetre.

## The four rules for natural-looking hair colour

In order to more easily mimic the characteristics of virgin hair colour, consider the following in determining your choice of colour and application technique.

- The hair should be lighter at the ends than at the base of the hair shaft.

- The hair should be lighter on the surface than underneath.

- Face-line hair should be lighter than the hair behind it (crown and nape).

- The darker hair should always be the dominant colour, i.e. in reverse highlighting, it should always have more dark hair than light on the head.

> ## REMEMBER!
> *Manufacturers identify their hair colours by the use of number. The first number indicates the depth or level, the second number indicates the tone. If there is more than one tonal number, the first number indicates the stronger tone. Therefore a colour 6.43 indicates a colour of level dark blonde with a strong tone of red with a secondary tone of yellow.*

## Classifications of hair colour

Hair colouring falls into three main categories: temporary, semi-permanent and permanent. These classifications refer primarily to staying power (lasting ability) and they also reflect their actions on the hair. These characteristics are determined by chemical composition and molecular weight, or size, of the pigments within the products found in each classification.

# Temporary hair colouring

Temporary colours utilise pigments that have the largest molecules of all classifications of hair colour. The large size of the colour molecule prevents penetration of the cuticle layer of the hair shaft and allows only a coating action on the outside of the strand. The chemical composition of temporary colour is acidic and makes only a physical change rather than a chemical change in the hair shaft (see Figure 7.24).

## Action of temporary colour on the hair

Since the colour remains on the cuticle and does not penetrate into the cortex, it lasts only from one shampoo to the next. However, excessive porosity can allow temporary colour to penetrate, making it last much longer.

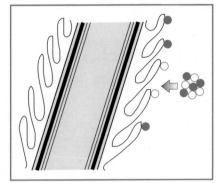

■ Figure 7.24 The action of temporary hair colour

Temporary colours can be used for the following to:

◆ introduce your client to hair colouring

◆ produce short-term fashion colour effects on hair

◆ temporarily restore faded hair to its natural colour

◆ neutralise the yellowish tinge in white or grey hair

◆ tone down over-lightened hair without creating further chemical damage

◆ temporarily add colour to the hair without changing its condition

◆ add red colour when recolouring bleached hair (pre-pigmentation).

Temporary hair colours have several disadvantages:

◆ colour is of short duration; it must be applied after every shampoo

◆ coating is thin and may not cover hair evenly

◆ colour may rub off on pillows or collars and may run with perspiration or other moisture

◆ they can only add colour; they cannot lighten

◆ staining may result if the hair is porous or if a dark colour is used on very light hair

◆ they have a limited ability to darken hair.

Temporary colours come in a wide array of shades from light to dark, warm to cool. They are easy to apply and are valuable as an introduction to hair colouring, or as a short-term solution in corrective colouring situations when the hair may not tolerate a stronger chemical.

An allergy or patch test is not usually necessary for this type of hair colour, except if your client has a history of hypersensitivity.

# Types of temporary hair colouring

A wide variety of products are available within this classification: colour rinses, coloured setting lotions, coloured mousses, colour gels and creams, colour sprays and colour shampoos.

## Colour rinses

*The traditional temporary hair colourings.* There are two forms of colour rinses: basic colour concentrates (water rinses) and prepared ready-to-use colour rinses. This form of hair colouring contains no setting or blow-dry styling lotion.

## Coloured setting lotions

*Temporary hair colouring together with a setting lotion.* The pigment is of mineral origin. These colours are applied direct from the bottle to pre-shampooed and towel-dried hair.

Following consultation with your client, gown them and shampoo their hair. Towel dry the hair and, using a wide-toothed comb, comb the hair back off the face and locate a towel suitable for use when hair colouring. Shake the bottle and then remove the top. Apply to the hair by sprinkling the colour over the hair, gently massaging it on to the hair to distribute the colour throughout the hair as well as to prevent it running down the scalp on to your client's face and neck. Apply the bulk of the colour to the top area of the head and, depending upon the porosity, thickness and length of the hair, apply some to the sides and back. The bulk applied to the top area will comb down. Use a wide-toothed comb to distribute the product through the hair and along its length.

When applying coloured setting lotion to very porous hair, it may be necessary to use a tint brush style application to ensure an even colour coverage and to avoid a patchy result.

Strong red colours may stain the scalp, particularly if used on clients with dry scalps. In these cases a tint brush application, avoiding application to the scalp area, can help to avoid this. To apply the product close to your client's scalp, at the hairline or parting, slide a clean comb into the hair at the scalp and apply the coloration, using a brush, up to and on to the teeth of the comb, then draw the comb down the hair away from the scalp.

Remember to check your client's hairline for any skin staining before placing them under the hairdryer and when removing the setting tools from the hair when dry. Skin staining may often be removed using cotton wool moistened with water. In extreme cases a proprietary skin stain remover may be used.

 *REMEMBER!*

*If you are unfamiliar with the product that you are using consult the manufacturer's directions or your line manager or trainer for guidance.*

While this form of colour is not harmful to the skin, the hairdresser is well advised to wear protective gloves when applying it, in particular when applying strong vibrant shades.

Some coloured setting lotion ranges include a clear liquid version, called a lightener or brightener. It should be noted that while its effect on the hair colour may appear temporary, any lightening of the hair is not temporary and manufacturers will often recommend that no more that three consecutive applications of this be made, so as not to produce a noticeable regrowth.

## HEALTH & SAFETY

Skin and hair are composed of similar types of keratin, with the soft keratin of the skin and scalp even more reactive than the hard keratin of the hair. This allows rinses to stain the scalp and the skin. Therefore, it is advisable to wear gloves to protect your hands even though the solution itself is relatively harmless.

### Coloured styling mousses

These are temporary hair colours within a styling mousse formulation (see Figure 7.25). Most styling mousses are made for use when either blow-drying the hair or when setting. They offer a wide array of colours that are fast and easy to apply. Colour mousses stay on the hair shaft. They do not drip, run or blow off the hair when blow-drying. Some mousses also have detangling and conditioning abilities as well as giving control during drying and style retention.

Prepare your client in the same manner as for coloured setting lotions. Shake the mousse can thoroughly and place a ball, the size of a golf ball, on to your hand. The exact amount to be used will be dependent upon the porosity, thickness and length of your client's hair. Using your hands, in a claw-like action, distribute the coloration throughout the hair. Comb the hair with a wide-toothed comb to ensure distribution.

■ Figure 7.25 A variety of colour mousses and gels are available

This coloration may stain both your client and yourself in the same manner as the coloured setting lotion. Any skin staining should be removed as soon as noticed in the same manner as for coloured setting lotion.

### Coloured gels and creams

These are available in a variety of shades, some natural, others wild and vibrant. These colours are designed to shampoo out completely, but because they tend to be tones of great intensity, they may stain porous, bleached or very dry hair.

### Spray-on hair colouring

This is applied to dry hair from aerosol containers. These are generally used for special or party effects (see Figure 7.26).

■ Figure 7.26 Spray-on hair colouring products are popular for creating special effects

## REMEMBER!

*The metallic salts in some colour sprays can build up after repeated use and cause an adverse reaction with future chemical services. These products are also extremely flammable, so they cannot be used around clients who are smoking.*

### Colour-enhancing shampoos

These combine the action of a colour rinse with that of a shampoo. These shampoos add colour tones to the hair (see Figure 7.27).

# Semi-permanent hair colouring

Semi-permanent colour offers a form of hair colouring suitable for the client who is reluctant to have a permanent colour change. The semi-permanent colour is formulated to be more lasting than temporary colour techniques but milder than permanent ones (see Figure 7.28).

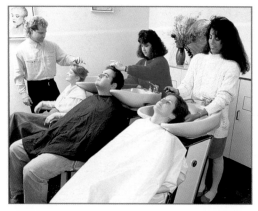

■ Figure 7.27 Colour-enhancing shampoos combine the action of a colour rinse with that of a shampoo

Semi-permanent colour is excellent for clients who feel that their hair is dull, drab or showing grey, but are not yet ready to begin permanent hair colouring. Semi-permanent colour can blend grey and deepen colour tones without altering the natural colour, since there is no lightening action on the hair.

Semi-permanent colour is available in a wide range of shades. It can be purchased as a gel, cream, liquid or mousse. Such products are often chosen by younger clients to produce fashion trend looks. Semi-permanent colour products can deposit a dramatic colour, or can be used for special effects in bright colours. Providing the hair's porosity is normal, the colour will naturally fade without a regrowth, so the client can change the colour at any time or discontinue the effect.

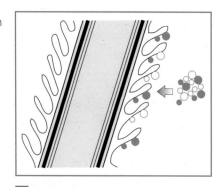

■ Figure 7.28 Action of semi-permanent hair colour formula

Semi-permanent hair colour is formulated to last for between 4 to 12 shampoos. No developer is required. The colour molecules penetrate the cortex and stain the cuticle somewhat, so that the colour gradually fades with each shampoo. Due to this gradual fading of colour tone from the hair, there is no noticeable regrowth (depending upon the colour applied). If the hair is extremely porous, or if heat is used with some types of semi-permanent colour, the results can be more permanent. Results depend on the hair's original colour and porosity, processing time and technique.

Semi-permanent colouring can have the following advantages.

◆ The colour is self-penetrating.

◆ The colour is applied the same way each time.

◆ Retouching is not necessary.

◆ The colour does not rub off on a pillow or clothing.

◆ The hair returns to its natural colour after approximately 4 to 12 shampoos.

◆ This colour does not detract from the hair's condition; in fact these formulations will often condition while colouring the hair.

# Semi-permanent hair colour uses

Semi-permanent hair colour can be used in the following ways.

◆ To enhance hair's natural colour. Semi-permanent colours can be used to add golden or red highlights, and to deepen the colour of the hair. This type of colour is especially effective on African-Caribbean hair and natural hair colour that is too light or too drab to set off the client's complexion.

◆ To tone pre-lightened hair. Semi-permanent colours can serve as a non-peroxide toner for pre-lightened hair. Pre-lightened hair is porous and the toner will penetrate.

◆ To refresh faded tints. Excellent for between permanent colour services and for corrective work, when a non-peroxide alternative is desired.

◆ To add colour to grey/white hair. Most semi-permanent colours are designed to cover hair that is 25% or less grey or create a blending effect on higher percentages. They are also recommended for clients who want to keep and enhance their grey or white hair.

◆ As an alternative to oxidation tinting for hypersensitive clients. Clients who are allergic to oxidation tints may find semi-permanent colour, which is direct colour, a safe alternative. Clients with a history of sensitivity towards hair colour should be skin/patch tested before use.

◆ For pre-pigmentation. Semi-permanent colour may be used, when recolouring bleached hair, to pre-pigment hair.

# Action on hair

Traditional semi-permanent colours are formulated with pigment molecules that are smaller than those of the

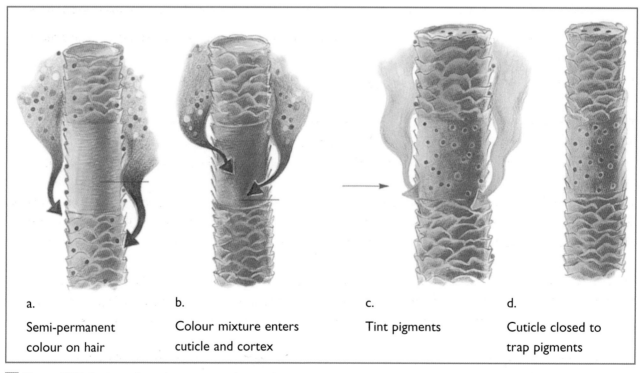

a.

Semi-permanent
colour on hair

b.

Colour mixture enters
cuticle and cortex

c.

Tint pigments

d.

Cuticle closed to
trap pigments

■ Figure 7.29 Action of semi-permanent hair colours

temporary colours but larger than those of the permanent tints. They have a mild penetrating action that results in a gentle addition of colour in the cortex as well as some staining of the cuticle (see Figure 7.29).

The chemical composition of semi-permanent colours falls within the approximate pH range 8.0–9.0, thus causing an alkaline action on the hair. The alkali swells the cuticle, opening imbrications and allowing the molecules to enter the cortex. However, this solution is mildly alkaline, which causes limited swelling and opening. Only a small number of these medium-sized molecules enter and remain in the cortex.

The pigment molecules are trapped within the cortical layer of the shaft as the hair shrinks back towards normal during the rinsing step of the service. A neutral or slightly acid after-rinse helps to close the imbrications and hold the pigment molecules within the cortex. However, even the mild swelling that occurs with shampooing allows some of the colour to fade.

Traditional semi-permanent colours have several distinct differences from temporary and permanent colours. They last longer than temporary colours and do not rub off. They are also easy to use, requiring no retouch application. Because semi-permanent colours make no significant permanent changes in the structure of the hair, they are less damaging. Many brands even give a conditioning effect. They are excellent for toning bleached hair that is too weak or porous to accept another peroxide treatment, and for use on hair that is exceptionally fine or damaged from permanent wave or relaxer services.

## Semi-permanent colour selection

The following steps, used in conjunction with the manufacturer's colour chart, offer a guide to selecting the correct colour with which to take a test cutting.

1    On solid hair (no grey), select a level of semi-permanent colour that is slightly lighter than the desired shade.

2    Due to the absorption of light, the use of an ash or cool shade will create a colour that the eye interprets as darker than if a warm shade is applied.

3    Due to the reflection of light, the warm colours will appear shinier.

The addition of artificial colour molecules to the natural pigment of the hair shaft will create a colour that is darker than the sample on the colour chart. Most colour charts show the approximate colour that will be achieved on white hair. This colour is to be used as a guide to estimate the colour results when it is applied to natural hair.

The natural hair colour must be considered as half the formula. Think of it as half artificial colour and half natural colour. Semi-permanent colours lack the strong oxidisers necessary to lift; therefore they deposit colour and do no substantial lifting. Think back to laws of intensity and remember that colour applied on top of colour makes a darker colour.

Since the take-up of these products is based on the hair's porosity, be careful to avoid creating ends that are darker than the base of the hair. Semi-permanent colours, due to their depositing nature, may also build up on the hair's ends with subsequent applications. A test cutting will determine your formula and timing before each service.

Many semi-permanent colours are used just as they pour from the bottle (i.e. they are direct colours), and the colour medium is the same colour as will be deposited in the hair. However, others require the mixing of an activator prior to their application. These are quasi-permanent hair colours. The activator is an oxidant that helps to swell the cortex and open the cuticle to allow colour penetration. This mild oxidiser also develops the colour pigments within the formula.

Some semi-permanent colours include a colour balancer in the packaging. These crystals need be added only if the semi-permanent colour is to be applied immediately following the removal of a lightening or bleaching product. It stops the residual oxidation that occurs on the hair shaft until the normal pH is completely restored.

Some semi-permanent colours come packaged with an *after-rinse*. This is acid-balanced to close the cuticle and trap the colour molecules within it. This helps prevent fading to a lighter colour as well as fading off-tone. The chemical composition of the after-rinse is designed to leave the hair soft, pliable and easy to comb. Whether or not the product you select is packaged in this way, it is always a good idea to finish your service with a mild conditioning rinse.

## Application of semi-permanent hair colours

| Tools and materials | | |
| --- | --- | --- |
| Colouring towels | Applicator bottle or brush | Finishing rinse |
| Colouring cape | Plastic cap (optional) | Plastic clips |
| Protective gloves | Cotton wool | Barrier cream |
| Wide-toothed comb | Mild shampoo | Record card |
| Timer | Selected colouring product | Colour chart |
| Measure | | |

### Preliminary steps

1   Give a preliminary patch test if required. Proceed only if the test result is negative. (This is not normally required for semi-permanent colours except when using them on clients with known hypersensitivity. A patch test is required prior to each quasi-permanent colour application (see page 150).

2   Thoroughly analyse the hair and scalp and select the appropriate colour product. Record your findings on the client's record card.

3   Assemble all necessary supplies (see table above).

REMEMBER!

*If you are in doubt about your salon's requirements for gowning the client, consult with your line manager or trainer.*

4 Prepare your client. Protect their clothing using caps and towels; most salons have their own gowning procedure. Effective gowning must protect the client and their clothing from risk of damage from the product to be used. Ask your client to remove jewellery and put it away safely.

5 Apply barrier cream around the hairline and over the ears; when pre-shampooing this would be applied following the shampoo.

6 If in doubt about the suitability of the product or its outcome on a particular head, take a test cutting.

 *REMEMBER!*
*When applying strong colours or semi-permanent colours to the hair where the scalp is dry and scaly, avoid allowing the product on to the scalp, as scalp staining often occurs. This may be visible through the finished hairstyle.*

## Procedure

1 Shampoo the hair using a mild shampoo, if required.

2 Towel dry the hair.

3 Put on protective gloves and apply barrier cream to the client.

4 Apply semi-permanent colour to the entire hair shaft (see Figure 7.30).

5 Pile hair loosely on top of the head (see Figure 7.31).

6 Follow the manufacturer's directions about using a plastic cap or heat (see Figure 7.32).

7 Process according to test cutting results or manufacturer's guidelines.

8 According to the timing instructions provided by the manufacturer, when the colour has developed, wet the hair with warm water, and lather.

9 Rinse and (subject to manufacturer's directions) shampoo, then rinse again with warm water until the water runs clear.

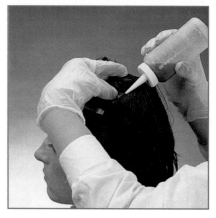

Figure 7.30 Applying semi-permanent colour

Figure 7.31 Applying semi-permanent colour

Figure 7.32 Applying semi-permanent colour

10   Use a finishing rinse to close the cuticle and set the colour.

11   Rinse and towel blot the hair. Style as required.

12   Complete the record card and file it.

**Clean up**

1   Discard all disposable supplies and materials.

2   Close containers, wipe them off, and store safely.

3   Clean implements, tint cape, work area and hands.

# Quasi-permanent (deposit-only) hair colour

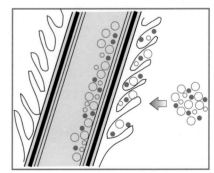

When semi-permanent colours were first introduced some years ago, clients generally shampooed their hair weekly, making the lasting ability of the semi-permanent colour of the time a satisfactory 4–6 weeks. Today, however, with more clients shampooing daily, a colour that lasts 4–6 shampoos may be unsatisfactory. For a colour that will act similarly in nature to the semi-permanent colours but will produce a longer-lasting effect, manufacturers have introduced a new category of hair colours called *deposit-only* or *quasi-permanent colours*.

## Composition and action

The effect of a deposit-only hair colour lies between those of semi-permanent and permanent colour classifications. Deposit-only colours use a form of a catalyst, such as low-volume strength developers, to gently swell and open the cuticle layer and drive the colour into the cortex. Deposit-only hair colours have small- and medium-sized dye molecules. The small molecules penetrate into the cortex slightly, and the medium-sized dye molecules penetrate the cuticle layers, resulting in a colour that has the gentleness of a semi-permanent colour with the longevity of a permanent hair colour. Deposit-only colours last 4–6 weeks, gradually fading from the hair and producing a diffused line of demarcation (see Figure 7.33).

## Selecting and formulating a quasi-permanent colour

Quasi-permanent hair colours are ideal for grey coverage, to refresh permanent tints, for corrective colouring, low lighting and for creating quick fashion effects.

By its very nature, a deposit-only hair colour will darken the natural hair colour when applied. Remember, when formulating, that half of your formula will be the client's natural hair colour and half will be the depositing colour you have selected. Since colour on top of colour always appears darker, select a deposit-only colour lighter than the client's natural level if you intend to keep the same amount of depth but add tone.

Since grey hair has no pigment and appears lighter, it is important to consider the grey hair in your formulation of a deposit-only hair colour. As there is no lift, the resulting depth of colour when covering grey may appear too extreme unless you allow for some brightness in your formulation. It is often inadvisable to make grey hair one even shade when colouring with any product, since natural hair colour has different depths and tonalities that give the hair the added life that grey hair is lacking.

■ Figure 7.33 Action of quasi-permanent hair colour

It is always better when taking a client from lighter to darker to err on the side of lightness, because a darker tone can easily be used to deepen the colour if necessary. A result that is too dark, on the other hand, will involve corrective procedures to lighten or remove the artificial pigment before re-applying to achieve the desired colour.

## REMEMBER!

*When selecting the formulation for the use of these colours on high percentages of white hair, to avoid over-strong or bright results add base tone to any fashion tone selected.*

Hair previously treated with another colour service will have a greater degree of porosity, which must be considered carefully when formulating and applying a deposit-only hair colour.

## Application procedure for quasi-permanent colours

The application procedure for a quasi-permanent hair colour is similar to that of a semi-permanent colour, since neither type of colour alters the hair's natural melanin or produces lift. Follow the manufacturer's application and timing guidelines for the product that you have selected.

For successful hair colouring services, the colourist must follow a definite procedure. A system makes for the greatest efficiency, and the most satisfactory results. Without such a plan, the work will take longer, results will be uneven and mistakes will be made.

## REMEMBER!

*While these colours fall within the semi-permanent hair colour section, most do require a skin test before each application.*

## Permanent hair colouring

Permanent hair colours are prepared from a variety of materials: vegetables, flowers, herbs, salts of heavy metals, organic and synthetic chemicals. All of these permanent colours fall into one of four classifications: vegetable tints, metallic dyes, compound dyestuffs and oxidation tints. Practically all permanent hair colouring is done with the use of oxidising penetrating tints that contain aniline derivatives.

These tints penetrate the cuticle of the hair and enter the cortical layer. Here, they are oxidised by the peroxide added into colour pigments. These pigments are distributed throughout the hair shaft much like natural pigment.

## Vegetable colours

In the past, before technology brought us the hairdressing industry as we now know it, many vegetable materials, such as camomile and henna, were used as hair-colouring ingredients.

### Henna

Henna is the most noteworthy and popular of the vegetable colours and comes from plants grown in moist climates throughout Africa, the Middle East and the East Indies. The henna leaves are removed before the flowering cycle, dried and ground into a fine powder. Hot water is added to create a paste that is applied to the hair.

## REMEMBER!

*Vegetable colours can form an alternative for clients who show an allergy to oxidation colouring.*

Henna is a natural product that appeals to the young client, and consumers who prefer organic products and avoid synthetics. Its natural qualities appeal to many.

Current technology has brought to the market henna in black, chestnut and auburn, plus a lightener. These hennas are made of concentrated herbal extracts that have both a cumulative and a semi-permanent effect. The dye coats the hair and is partially removed by shampooing.

The coating action of henna creates a hair strand that becomes thicker, and thus helps to give body to fine, limp hair. Because it makes no structural changes in the hair, it can be used on weak hair without damaging it. Henna fills in a roughened cuticle and holds together split ends to provide a slick, light-reflective surface. This, coupled with the additional warmth, creates hair that shines.

## REMEMBER!

*The coating effect of henna can make the hair resistant to permanent waving.*

## Metallic hair dyes

Metallic hair colours can be recognised by the descriptive terms used by manufacturers in their packaging even before reading the ingredients list. Metallic dyes are known as *progressive hair colours* and *colour restorers*. They are referred to as progressive because hair progressively turns darker and darker on each subsequent application. The term *colour restorer* is used because the natural hair colour *appears* to be gradually restored. When the desired colour is reached, the consumer needs to reduce the frequency of application to maintain the colour.

Metallic hair dyes comprise a minor portion of the home hair-colouring market and currently are very rarely used professionally. Nevertheless, it is crucial for the professional colourist to be informed of the chemical composition, characteristics and methods of removal, because metals react adversely with oxidation tints.

> ## REMEMBER!
>
> *During your consultation with the client, if you see a progressive darkening of the hair towards the hair ends without a definite line of demarcation, and with a somewhat drab, lacklustre colour, it can often mean that metallic salts are present.*

Clients occasionally request chemical services without knowing the incompatibility of metallic colour with professional oxidation products. Consumers generally do not even realise that they have used a product containing metal. The colourist must be able to analyse and prescribe safe, professional treatments to avoid hair damage and discolouration.

The metallic coating builds up on the surface of the hair shaft. Repeated treatments leave the hair brittle and conflict with future chemical services that include in their formulation hydrogen peroxide, thioglycolate, ammonia and/or most other oxidisers.

Resulting damage might be discolouration, breakage, poor permanent waving results, and even destruction to the point of a melted hair shaft due to the heat created in this adverse chemical reaction.

## Compound dyes

Compound dyes are a combination of metallic salts or mineral dyes with a vegetable tint. The metallic salts are added to give the product more staying power and to create a wider range of colours. Like metallic dyes, compound dyes are not often used professionally.

Many clients use hair colouring products at home. Therefore, you must be able to recognise and understand their effects. Such colouring agents must be removed and the hair reconditioned prior to any other chemical service that involves oxidation. This includes permanent colouring (oxidation tinting), bleaching, and permanent waving and relaxing.

Hair treated with metallic or any other coating dye looks dry and dull. It is generally harsh and brittle to the touch. These colourings usually fade to unnatural tones. Silver dyes have a greenish cast, lead dyes leave a purple colour, and those containing copper turn red.

### Test for metallic salts (incompatibility test)

1     In a glass container, mix 30ml of 20 volume (6%) peroxide and 20 drops of 28% ammonia water.

2     Cut a strand of the client's hair, bind it with tape, and immerse it in the solution for 30 minutes.

3     Remove, towel dry, and observe the strand.

Hair that is coated with metallic salts will lighten or become discoloured. In some instances the solution in which it is immersed becomes discoloured and heated. Bubbling may be observed. The hair may disintegrate.

These reactions demonstrate what would occur if a substance that incorporated an oxidation process were applied to the hair, oxidation tints and perm neutralisers.

Preparations designed to remove metallic salts and non-peroxide dye solvents may assist in the removal of metallic and coating dyes from the hair. Performing an incompatibility test will indicate whether the metallic deposits have been removed.

## REMEMBER!

*The most effective guarantee of future successful chemical services is to cut off the tinted hair.*

## Oxidation hair colour

Permanent oxidation hair colours can lighten and deposit colour in one application, a feat performed by no other classification. This ability to create an infinite array of levels, tones and intensities has made permanent colours irreplaceable in the industry. These tints penetrate the cuticle of the hair and enter the cortical layer (see Figure 7.34). Here, they are oxidised by the peroxide added into colour pigments. These pigments are distributed throughout the hair shaft much like natural pigment (see Figure 7.35).

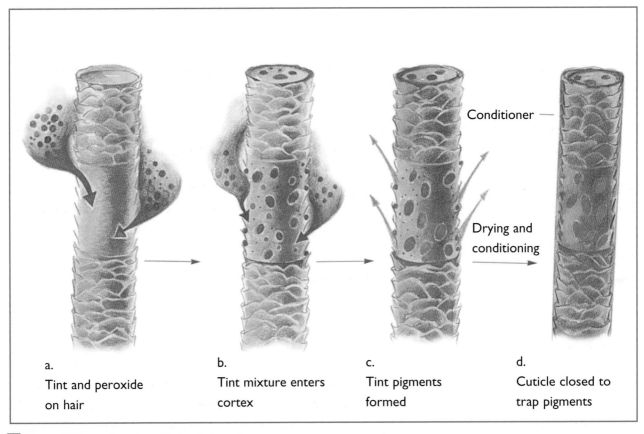

a.
Tint and peroxide
on hair

b.
Tint mixture enters
cortex

c.
Tint pigments
formed

d.
Cuticle closed to
trap pigments

Conditioner

Drying and
conditioning

■ Figure 7.34 Action of oxidation hair colours

## Application classifications

Permanent hair colour applications are classified as either single-process colouring or double-process colouring.

*Single-process colouring* achieves the desired colour with one application. Although the application itself may have several different steps, the desired colour is achieved with a single application. Lightening of the hair's natural pigment and deposit of the artificial pigment in the cortex is done simultaneously as the hair colouring product processes. Some examples of single-process colouring are virgin tint applications and tint retouch applications.

*Double-process colouring* achieves the desired colour on completion of two separate product applications. It is also known as double-application tinting and two-step colouring. Two examples are bleaching followed by a toner application and pre-softening followed by a tint application. Because the lightening action and the colour deposit are independently controlled, a wider range of hair colour possibilities is opened up for each client.

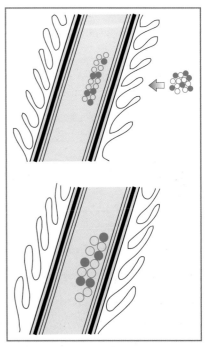

■ Figure 7.35 Action of oxidation hair colour

Bleach is a substance used to lift colour from hair. Once combined with hydrogen peroxide, the mixture causes the hair to swell and raise the cuticle to allow bleach to penetrate into the cortex.

# Hydrogen peroxide

This is available both as a cream and a liquid, and is the most widely used provider of oxygen for the oxidation process that takes place when oxidation tints and bleaches are applied to hair.

In the case of oxidation tints, the oxygen provided by the hydrogen peroxide causes the development of the colour combining with the dye material within the cortex to form a colour molecule too large to exit the hair shaft.

When bleaching, oxygen also changes the natural pigment of the hair, changing the melanin molecule from a coloured to a colourless compound. Those pigments most easily affected are ash tones and brown shades, then reds and finally yellow.

## Peroxide strength

The strength of hydrogen peroxide is described in two ways:

◆ volume

◆ percentage strength.

Volume describes the amount of oxygen released by the product during decomposition. Therefore 1 litre of 20 volume hydrogen peroxide will release 20 litres of oxygen leaving 1 litre of spent product; 1 litre of 60 volume will release 60 litres of oxygen; 5 – 10 – 20 volume hydrogen peroxide is mixed with oxidation tint when adding depth to the natural hair colour (darkening) and 30 – 40 – 60 is used when lightening. Always follow the manufacturer's directions when selecting the strength of peroxide to use.

# REMEMBER!

*A predisposition test must be given before colouring the hair with an oxidation tint. You should protect yourself from allergic reactions and dermatitis by wearing protective gloves until the product is completely removed from the client's hair.*

## Forms of hydrogen peroxide

*Cream peroxide* contains additives such as thickeners, drabbers and an acid for stabilisation. The thickeners help to create a product that is easy to control. This thicker mix is less likely to bleed when producing woven highlights. The creamy formula also tends to stay moist on the hair longer than liquid peroxide.

*Liquid peroxide*, or $H_2O_2$, appears similar to water, a clear liquid to which a stabiliser, usually an acid, is added. The acid reduces oxidation (oxygen loss) until mixed with a product containing an alkali, which neutralises this action and speeds up oxygen release. Once the available oxygen has been released, water is left behind.

## HEALTH & SAFETY

Hydrogen peroxide is an irritant to skin and eyes. If it accidentally comes in contact with anyone's skin or eyes rinse the affected area with sterile water; if the irritation persists seek medical advice immediately.

The strength of hydrogen peroxide can be diluted using distilled or purified water. Dilution rates are as follows:

| 60 volume hydrogen peroxide (mls) | Distilled water (mls) | Resulting volume strength (vol) |
|:---:|:---:|:---:|
| 15 | 30 | 15 |
| 30 | 30 | 30 |
| 30 | 15 | 45 |
| 10 | 20 | 10 |
| 30 | 30 | 15 |
| 20 | 10 | 20 |

| 20 volume hydrogen peroxide (mls) | Distilled water (mls) | Resulting volume strength (vol) |
| --- | --- | --- |
| 10 | 30 | 5 |
| 30 | 30 | 10 |
| 30 | 10 | 15 |

# Bleaching hair

Bleach produces a permanent change in hair colour. It changes a coloured chemical compound into one which is colourless (see Figure 7.36). Oxidation takes place and the natural pigments are gradually changed into colourless molecules in the following order:

BLACK ➡ BROWN ➡ RED ➡ ORANGE ➡ YELLOW

Once lightened, hair does not fade back to its original colour; the lightening effect is permanent. Differing forms of hair pigmentation are more susceptible to the effects of bleach than are others. Blacks and browns are the pigments that are most easily changed. Reds are next and yellows are very resistant to change. Very few heads of hair can be lightened past a pale yellow. The remaining yellow is often neutralised by a mauve ash to produce a white appearance.

Bleaches use the process of oxidation to cause the change in the hair's colour. The greater the oxidation process the greater its lightening ability.

■ Figure 7.36 Special effects hair lightening

## REMEMBER!

*Bleaches are effective in lightening natural hair pigments. Specialist colour reduction products are required to remove artificial hair coloration from the hair.*

Bleach products vary in strength as well as in their ability to maintain the hair's condition. Some products are liquid based, others are based upon powders, others cream, and others based upon oil emulsions. Always follow manufacturer's guidelines in their suitability for differing hair types as well as required results.

# Types of bleach

◆ **Cream bleach** – good for full-head and regrowth applications as well as partial-head applications. Easy to apply and gives between 1–5 shades' lift.

◆ **Oil bleach** – good for full-head and regrowth applications as well as partial-head applications. Easy to apply and gives between 1–3 shades' lift. Take care if using heat to aid action as the bleach will become more liquid when warm and is liable to run on the scalp and hair.

◆ **Emulsion bleach** – good for full-head and regrowth applications as well as partial-head applications. Easy to apply and gives between 1–5 shades' lift. Take care if using heat to aid action as the bleach will become more liquid when warm and is liable to run on the scalp and hair.

◆ **Powder bleach** – good for highlighting and frosting effects and gives between 1–5 shades' lift. Take care not to inhale powder while mixing.

Bleaches do not normally require skin tests to be applied before their use. However, when colouring someone who is know to be hypersensitive it can be advisable to skin test with all colouring products that you plan to use on them.

Application for first-time and regrowth applications are undertaken in a similar manner to oxidation tints.

# KEY SKILL TASK

*This task could produce evidence that supports C1.1, C1.2, C1.3, N1.1 & N1.3.*

*Create a consultation sequence that you can use when undertaking a hair colour consultation with a client. Produce a prompt sheet of questions to ask your client, with the information needed to enable you to make informed decisions about what the client wants, and the products and services that are best suited to produce this result. The prompt sheet should provide the facility to record:*

◆ *your findings from questioning and consultation*

◆ *your findings from inspection of the hair and scalp*

◆ *the results of any tests undertaken*

◆ *the products to be used, including quantities or proportions of products to be used*

◆ *proposed processing times*

◆ *the cost of the service and how this is calculated.*

*Trial the use of this prompt sheet with some of your clients to check its effectiveness. Make any changes you feel will make this more effective and help to support you in your work.*

*Consult with your supervisor before using this with your clients.*

# Oxidation tint application

The Control of Substances Hazardous to Health Regulations 1988 (COSHH) require employers to:

- identify substances in the workplace that are potentially hazardous

- assess the risk to health from exposure to the hazardous substances and record the results

- make an assessment as to which members of staff are at risk

- look for alternative less hazardous substances and substitute if possible

- decide what precautions are required, noting that the use of personal protective equipment should always be the last resort

- introduce effective measures to prevent or control the exposure

- inform, instruct and train all members of staff

- review the assessment on a regular basis.

## Materials preparation

All materials to be used should be in prime condition. Tint product may come in bottles, tubes or cans. Check that no oxidation has already taken place in the product; this may be indicated by a darkening of the product. Ensure that the developer or hydrogen peroxide is in good condition and is of the correct volume (percentage) strength. Materials required are:

- selected tint

- hydrogen peroxide

- cotton wool

- mild shampoo

- after-colour conditioner/colour fixer

- protective cream.

All tools used should be in good repair, clean and dry prior to use. You will need:

- non-metallic bowl

- measuring cylinder/jug

- tinting brush/applicator

- timer

- record card

- tinting cape and towels

◆   protective gloves

◆   plastic clips.

### Client preparation

1   Give a patch test 24–48 hours before the colouring service and record the outcome. Proceed only if the test result is negative.

2   Thoroughly analyse the scalp and hair. Consult and discuss with your client the colour and product to be used.

3   Check the scalp for any cuts, abrasions and contagious disorders. The presence of any of these will contra-indicate the colouring process.

4   Gown your client, following your salon's procedures. This will normally include the use of a client gown, colouring towels and impenetrable tinting cape. Gowning should protect your client and their clothing from contamination from the tinting product about to be used. Jewellery should be removed.

5   Brush the hair, taking care not to scratch the surface of the scalp.

6   Assemble all tools that will be required during the colouring process (see list on page 159).

7   Perform any necessary pre-conditioning treatments.

8   Take a test cutting, if required.

9   Divide the hair into four sections (see Figure 7.37). Apply barrier cream to the hairline and ears when applying dark levels of colour or when the skin is very dry.

10  Prepare the product, mixing the formulation following the manufacturer's directions. Do this at the dispensary, not in front of your client, in case you spill product on them. Ensure that all products that you use are in prime condition and are mixed in clean non-metallic utensils.

■ Figure 7.37 Hair sectioned for tinting

### HEALTH & SAFETY

Take care to avoid inhaling the small amounts of ammonia given off to the atmosphere when mixing tint. Always prepare the product in a well-ventilated area.

Always follow the manufacturer's directions. Accurately measure the quantities of tint product into a non-metallic bowl. If using cream tint, *cream* the tint, as this will aid mixing with the hydrogen peroxide. (Creaming tint means to stir the tint to soften the consistency, to remove tube marks making it easier to mix with liquids.) If preparing colours that are a combination of shades mix the tint product together before adding any peroxide.

## REMEMBER!

*Accurate measurement of product is essential to ensure predictable and consistent results.*

Accurately measure the hydrogen peroxide and then mix with the tint product. When mixing products of differing thickness, add only small quantities of peroxide at a time to the tint, mixing the two together well. In some cases shakers and applicator bottles are used for the mixing process. Once mixed, the oxidation process begins, so mix only quantities that you need to use immediately.

## Procedure for first-time application (virgin hair) adding colour and lightening

# REMEMBER!

*Manufacturers often provide suggested methods of application. If in doubt, read their directions.*

1   Put on protective gloves. This will protect your skin from damage caused by the colouring material.

2   Begin in the section where the colour change will be the greatest or the hair is most resistant, and consult the record card for indication of any particular areas of resistance. If there are no specified areas it is usual to start at the back of the head.

3   Part off a section of hair 0.5cm in depth, using the tail of the application brush.

4   Apply the product to the middle lengths and ends of the hair, to within 1cm of the scalp. Scalp heat will aid and speed up colour development at the root area. Application to the middle lengths and ends first will give this area a greater length of time to develop and therefore produce an even result overall.

5   Ensure that all the hair within each mesh of hair is covered by the tint product. Take care not to apply too much product, as this may result in product dripping on to your client, as well as product wastage.

6   From the nape area progress up one side of the back of the head to the crown area. Take care not to press the tinted mesh of hair on to the untinted root areas of other meshes, as this will bring about an uneven result and over-processing in certain areas.

# REMEMBER!

*Some manufacturers recommend a one-step application when darkening hair in a first-time application. This means applying the product from the roots to the points in one application. Check the manufacturer's directions.*

7   Once the crown area is reached, start at the nape on the other side of the back of the head and progress up this side to the crown area.

8   Apply the product to the two front sections, taking care not to allow the product to drip on to your client's face or ears.

9   Cross-check your application to ensure that all the hair's middle length is covered by the product.

10   Allow the product to develop, usually for 10–15 minutes (check manufacturer's recommendation). Heat may be applied to aid development (subject to manufacturer's directions). This may be applied in the form of a scalp steamer (see page 49 for a description of how to use it). An accelerator/radiant heater may also be used (see page 49). Take care not to allow the product to dry out on the hair.

11  Check the colour development by wiping a strand free of product using moist cotton wool, and checking the colour against the required outcome, using the shade guide.

12  Once sufficient development has been identified, prepare a fresh supply of the product and apply this to the root area, up to the product already on the middle lengths. This is carried out by taking similar-sized sections in the same order as for the first application.

## REMEMBER!

*Avoid sitting your client where draughts of hot or cold air may affect the hair, producing an uneven colour development. A cold room will slow down the development.*

13  Check that all the hair has been coated with the product. Allow to develop, in the same manner as before. A full processing period will be required for this fresh application of product to the hair.

14  Check the development of the colour by wiping a strand of hair free of product using moist cotton wool. Check the resulting colour for evenness and for its match to the desired finished colour.

15  If the development is incomplete, re-apply product to the test strand and leave to develop further. If the development is complete move your client to the basin area.

Your client should view their new hair colour in natural daylight. They should be made fully aware of how their colour will appear once they leave the salon. The hair will be damaged by the chemicals during the colouring process. Most modern colour products reduce hair damage to a minimum, contain buffers to reduce this effect and have conditioners to compensate. Your client may not be accustomed to handling their hair in its new condition and therefore will require guidance in its after-care. Home-care products should be recommended and guidance in their correct use be given to your client, to enable them to maintain their new colour and condition, as well as reduce fade.

Guidance will be required in how frequently your client should make follow-up visits to the salon.

## Procedure for retouch application

The fresh growth of hair will require colouring at intervals of approximately one month. This is the job of the professional hair colourist.

Always consult with your client before undertaking a retouch colour. Check if the colour required is the same as the previous colour service given.

1  Put on protective gloves.

2  Begin in the section where the colour change will be the greatest or the hair is most resistant; consult the

record card for indication of any particular areas of resistance. If there is no specified area it is usual to start at the back of the head (see Figure 7.38).

3   Part off a section of hair 0.5cm in depth, using the tail of the application brush.

# REMEMBER!

*Ensure accurate measurement of product to maintain continuity of hair colour.*

4   Apply the product to the regrowth area. If the regrowth is longer than 1.5cm it should be treated as if it were a first-time application. This is because body heat from the scalp may not affect the hair past this point.

5   Ensure that all the regrowth hair within each mesh of hair is covered by the tint product. Take care not to apply too much product, as this may result in product running down the hair, as well as product wastage.

# REMEMBER!

*Overlapping colour on to previously coloured hair may result in banding of colour, damage to the hair and even hair breakage.*

6   From the nape area progress up one side of the back of the head to the crown area. Take care not to press the ends of the hair on to the tinted root areas of other meshes, as this will result in an uneven result and over-processing in certain areas.

7   Once the crown area is reached, start at the nape on the other side of the back of the head and progress up this side to the crown area (see Figure 7.39).

8   Apply the product to the two front sections, taking care not to allow the product to drip on to your client's face or ears (see Figures 7.40 and 7.41).

9   Cross-check your application to ensure that all the regrowth is covered by the product.

10   Allow the product to develop, usually for 20–35 minutes. Check the manufacturer's recommendation. Heat may be applied to aid development (subject to manufacturer's directions). This may be applied in the form of a scalp steamer (see page 49 for a description of how to use it). An

■ Figure 7.38 Applying tint to root area starting at the back of the head

■ Figure 7.39 Back sections, regrowth application

■ Figure 7.40 Applying tint to regrowth at crown and top section

■ Figure 7.41 Applying tint to front regrowth sections

accelerator/radiant heater may also be used (see page 49). Take care not to allow the product to dry out on the hair (see Figures 7.42 and 7.43).

11 Check the colour development by wiping a strand free of product, using moist cotton wool, and checking the colour against the required outcome, using the shade guide.

12 Once sufficient development has been identified, consider if the colour of the middle lengths and ends requires refreshing. Do not apply colour unnecessarily to the middle lengths and ends as this may result in

■ Figure 7.42 Using the accelerator to assist colour development

■ Figure 7.43 Scalp steamer

damage to the hair and a progressive darkening (colour build-up). Fresh tint, diluted tint or semi-permanent colour may be used to refresh the colour in these areas. The choice may depend upon the degree or amount of colour fade (see Figure 7.44).

13 Check that all the hair has been coated with the product. Allow to develop, in the same manner as before. A full processing period will be required for this fresh application of product to the hair (see Figure 7.45).

14 Check the development of the colour by wiping a strand of hair free of tint using moist cotton wool. Check the resulting colour for evenness and for its match to the desired finished colour (see Figure 7.46).

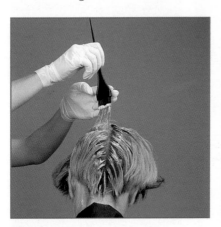

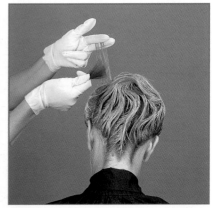

■ Figure 7.44 Applying tint to middle lengths and ends of hair

■ Figure 7.45 Tint applied to all of the hair

■ Figure 7.46 Checking hair colour development

15 If the development is incomplete, re-apply product to the test strand and leave to develop further. If the development is complete move your client to the basin area.

## Removing the product from the hair

1   Massage the product on the hair and scalp, paying particular attention to the hairline, where this process will help to lift any skin staining (moist tint will remove skin staining at this time). This massage will also help to emulsify the product and aid its easier removal from the hair.

2   Follow the manufacturer's directions in product removal. If you are in doubt about the correct process consult with your line manager, stylist or trainer. In most cases this will include adding a small quantity of warm water to the product on the hair. Massage this to emulsify, add more warm water, massage and then rinse away.

 *REMEMBER!*

*At this time the scalp may be a little sensitive, so take care to control the water temperature applied to the scalp, and avoid the warmer temperatures.*

3   Thoroughly rinse the product from the hair.

4   Shampoo the hair thoroughly, using a mild (acid-balanced) shampoo. The acid-balanced shampoo will help to flatten the hair cuticle, prevent any creeping oxidation (continued oxidation action in the hair), and help to return the hair to its normal pH.

5   Apply an anti-oxidation, fixing, finishing rinse to the hair. The exact product to be used may depend on salon procedures and the manufacturer's directions.

6   Style the hair.

7   Complete the record card and file or enter details on to the computerised database.

## Clean-up

1   Dispose of all disposable supplies and materials.

2   Close containers firmly, wipe them clean and put them in their proper place. Never return unused products to their containers as they may be contaminated and will subsequently contaminate all of the product in the container.

3   Wash and dry all equipment, and place soiled linen in the laundry basket.

4   Clean the working area.

5   Wash and dry your hands.

# Highlight and lowlight effects in hair colouring

Highlighting and lowlighting techniques for hair colouring use lighter or darker shades of hair colour to enhance and accentuate your client's hair colour and hairstyle (see Figure 7.47). A combination of lighter and darker shades may be used to give depth and dimension to the hairstyle. A single additional shade may be used to accentuate natural tone in the hair or to define movement in the hairstyle. There are a number of techniques available, some of which produce effects throughout the entire head of hair and others which are designed specifically for small areas of the hairstyle.

# Techniques of highlighting and lowlighting

## Weaving techniques

There are a number of techniques used to weave small strands of hair from the bulk that may then either be coloured or lightened, or a combination of both. There are a variety of specialist tools to produce this effect, but in most cases the point end of a pin-tail comb is used to weave out the strands of hair. These strands are subsequently separated from the bulk of the hair using aluminium foil, fine film wrap, proprietary-brand sachets or tissue.

■ Figure 7.47 Highlights/ lowlights – bold and fashionable

 *REMEMBER!*

*A predisposition test is not normally required prior to the application of a bleach product. However if your client has a history of hypersensitivity a skin test may be advisable.*

### Client preparation

1   Discuss and negotiate the required result with your client. This will include details of the required overall hairstyle, the required colour effect, the density of the woven sections and the cost of the service. Check any colour record cards available for your client.

2   Carry out a predisposition test 24–48 hours beforehand if a permanent oxidation tint is to be used.

3   Gown your client as for a permanent form of hair colouring.

4   Section the hair, according to the required hairstyle, to give control over the hair when weaving.

### Product preparation

1   Prepare the sachets that will be used in the process. When using aluminium foil these may be available in prepared batches, already cut to specified lengths. Others come on a continuous roll which must then be cut to slightly more than twice the length of the hair to be coloured. Fold one end of the foil over at approximately 5 mm deep to produce a more rigid band to hold against the root area at the scalp. When using fine film wrap this is cut as it is required, and is used at its full width. Proprietary brands of sachets consist of a plastic-based sachet with a transparent cover and a mild adhesive strip. If working without assistance, a number of these should be opened ready for use. When working on very long hair it may be necessary to join two of these together. Sachets usually come in a variety of lengths. Tissue may be used to separate strands of coloured hair from the rest. The colour product must be of a thick consistency. For this technique, a spatula is required. The strands to be coloured are placed on the spatula and the colour product applied. The spatula is withdrawn and the coloured hair allowed to fall on to the tissue.

2   Prepare a small quantity of the colouring product. As this process can be quite lengthy, small measured

quantities of product prepared when required are better than preparing a large quantity at the outset which then deteriorates before it is used on the hair.

3    You will require protective rubber gloves.

# REMEMBER!

*Once mixed, the colouring/bleaching product begins to oxidise, and if too long a period elapses before its use, it may have fully oxidised before it touches the hair. It will therefore have little or no effect on the hair.*

## Weaving the highlights

1    It is usual to start at the bottom of the hair section, as the woven meshes will hang down and should not be disturbed. Start at that area of the head where the highest degree of colour change is required, or where the hair is most resistant, if the degree of resistance is known.

2    Using the pin-tail of the comb, draw off a mesh which is 1cm deep and then slice off the top 3mm of this mesh. Allow the larger section to fall and retain the smaller, held firmly outwards from the head, tangle free (see Figure 7.48).

3    Weave out fine strands to be coloured, by pushing the point of the pin-tail (held parallel to the mesh) across the mesh, pressing down at those points when the strand to be coloured is required. When you begin to practise this skill it will be a slow process, however with much practice not only will your speed develop but also your ability to draw off consistent sizes of mesh (see Figure 7.49).

4    Now hold out the woven-off strands from the head while the remainder of the hair is allowed to fall. Place the sachet close to the roots of these strands at the scalp, and then lay the strands on to the foil and apply the colour (see Figure 7.50). Do not apply the colour product all the way to the scalp, as this may result in seepage on to the rest of the hair. Apply to within 5mm of the scalp; the product will be drawn along the hair to the scalp (see Figure 7.51).

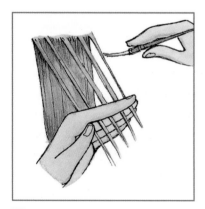

■ Figure 7.48 Weaving the highlights step-by-step; drawing of a slice of hair to be woven

■ Figure 7.49 Weaving the highlights step-by-step; slice now woven off

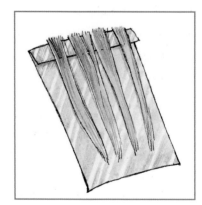

■ Figure 7.50 Weaving the highlights step-by-step; locating sachet close to roots

5   Once the colour/bleach mix has been applied to the strands of hair, fold the sachet to secure it on the hair and to retain the product within it. Avoid pressing on the bulk of the sachet as this may cause the product to ooze from the sachet and contaminate the other hair (see Figure 7.52).

6   Continue to do this throughout the head in a systematic manner (see Figure 7.53). As this can be a lengthy process, check the colour development of those sachets placed earlier as you progress around the head.

7   When making a section at the front hairline, take a parting at a slight angle to the hairline, this will avoid obvious lines of colour appearing. Avoid locating strands of colour on the parting or on the very edge of the hairline, as the regrowth will be very apparent as the hair grows.

8   Allow the hair to process without additional heat as this can cause the product within the sachet to either become more liquid (if it is an oil-based product) or to expand (all oxidation products do this) and therefore ooze on to adjacent hair and cause unsightly patches of colour.

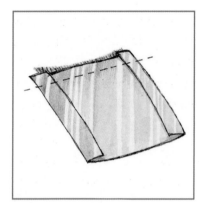

 Figure 7.51 Weaving the highlights step-by-step; pasting bleach on to hair

Figure 7.52 Weaving the highlights step-by-step; folding sachet using tail comb to crease it

Figure 7.53 Weaving the highlights step-by-step; completed head of foil sachets

9   When using permanent hair colours, allow the product to process for the full development period following the application of the final sachet. When using bleach you must check the degree of lift from the earlier sachets, as these may have fully processed before the later ones. If this is the case remove these sachets and, using moist cotton wool, remove the bleach from the hair.

> ## REMEMBER!
> *Too much colour product within the sachet may result in seepage on to the rest of the hair.*

10   Once the colour has fully processed take your client to the basin area. Recline them to the basin and then begin rinsing the hair using lukewarm water. As the water floods the hair the sachets may be removed by sliding them from the hair.

11   Rinse the colour from the hair, shampoo using a post-colour shampoo and follow with a pH balance/anti-oxidation conditioner. This will help to prevent creeping oxidation and to close the cuticle flat.

12   Complete your client's record card, noting the products used, the techniques applied and the results.

## Clean-up

All used materials should be disposed of. Those highlighting sachets made for repeat use should be washed, dried and stored for future use. Used linen should be disposed of in the laundry bin, and all containers returned to their storage area.

## Cap technique

The cap technique involves pulling clean strands of hair through a perforated cap using a hook (see Figure 7.54). This technique is best suited to use on short hair, though there are brands of highlight cap specifically designed for use on long hair. Due to the translucent nature of many brands of highlight cap, it can be difficult to determine the exact position of the highlights in relation to the hairstyle.

### Preparation of the materials

■ Figure 7.54 Drawing strands through holes in a cap

1   Select the type of cap or material to create the cap, the selection of which will often be personal preference. Proprietary brands of highlight cap can usually be used for several applications. For its first use, the holes in the cap will need breaking open using the hook. Take care not to press the hook hard on to the scalp. The areas for the perforations are usually strengthened to avoid tearing and seepage of the colouring product from the outside surface. The interior of the cap should be coated lightly with talc, as this will enable it to slide into position on dry hair. A polythene sheet or fine film wrap may be used in place of the pre-formed cap. The scalp area is enclosed within the wrap and then secured around the hairline using clear adhesive tape. These styles of cap can be susceptible to tearing for those inexperienced with the technique. Other brands of cap may require the application of heat to tighten them to the head shape.

2   Select the hook size relative to the texture of the hair and the thickness of the strands of hair required. The larger the hook size the greater the size of strand drawn through.

3   Select the colouring products, but do not mix the product until all of the strands of hair have been drawn through the cap.

 REMEMBER!

*Check that your client's ears are not trapped or folded under the cap.*

### Client preparation

This is the same as for woven highlights.

### Drawing through the highlights

1   Brush the client's hair in the direction of the hairstyle and then ease the highlight cap into place. You will need to locate a *latex* cap by placing your hands on the inside, palms open, and easing the cap into place. Ensure that the cap is tight to the scalp, particularly at the crown area.

2   *Plastic* caps are rather like bonnets which are located firmly over the hair and then held in place by a tie under

the client's chin. Polythene sheeting and fine film wrap is located on to the scalp area as firmly as possible and while it is held in place clear adhesive tape is bound around the hairline. Excess sheet or wrap is then trimmed off, taking care not to cut the hair beneath.

3   Lengths of hair which hang from beneath the cap should be gathered together at the nape and protected from colouring product.

4   Draw the strands of hair through the cap starting at the top of the hairstyle. Gently but firmly push the hook through the cap. As you collect hair in the hook, to ensure that the full length of the hair is coloured, gather hair at the root area. Ease this hair through the cap. The closeness and thickness of the strands depends on the thickness of your client's hair and the required outcome. When a subtle effect is required more fine strands may be drawn through. For a more obvious result, fewer thicker strands are drawn through.

 # REMEMBER!

*Avoid using colour mixes which are too thin as these may seep through the holes in the cap and cause a blotchy result.*

5   When all the strands are drawn through, check to ensure that the cap is still firmly against the scalp. Gently grasp the strands between the fingers and pull to ensure that they are fully through the cap, and using the fine teeth of a comb, gently comb the hair to ensure that there are no tangles or partly pulled-through strands.

6   Mix the colouring/bleach product and apply this to the hair strands which have been drawn through the cap (see Figure 7.55). Start the application of the product to the top of the head and, section by section, paste the product on to the hair in an upward direction. In this manner the product-coated hair will lay on the cap instead of hanging down on your client's face and neck.

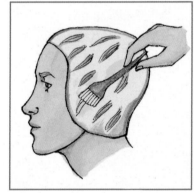

■ Figure 7.55 Applying bleach to plastic cap highlights

7   Process as for other forms of permanent hair colouring. Take care: the heat applied may cause oil-based colouring products to become more fluid and these may drip on to the client or seep through the holes in the cap.

8   Check the colour development as for other forms of permanent hair colouring. Once the processing is complete, rinse the product from the hair and cap. The use of high water pressure may result in wetting your client.

9   Apply a conditioning cream to the strands of hair if no subsequent colouring is required, and ease the cap off the head. The cream acts as a lubricant, preventing drag on the hair that might otherwise cause discomfort and hair damage due to over-stretching.

10   Continue as for the removal of other forms of permanent hair colour.

## Clean-up

Dispose of all disposable items in a covered bin. Reusable highlight caps should be rinsed clean, dried and then a fine film of talc applied. Place used linen in the laundry basket and return part-used containers to the storage area.

| Outcome | Cause | Action |
|---|---|---|
| Scalp irritation | ◆ high strength of peroxide<br>◆ allergy to product | ◆ remove product immediately and rinse with cold water<br>◆ seek medical advice |
| Hair breakage | ◆ over-processing<br>◆ overlapping on to previously coloured hair<br>◆ too early comb-through of product<br>◆ incompatible chemicals | ◆ remove immediately<br>◆ use restructurant<br>◆ use penetrating conditioner |
| Uneven result | ◆ poor application<br>◆ uneven application<br>◆ uneven mixing of product<br>◆ too large hair sections<br>◆ seepage of product during highlight process<br>◆ too much product<br>◆ incorrect product<br>◆ uneven application of heat to product<br>◆ one-step application used when two-step was appropriate | ◆ spot colour to produce even result |
| Poor coverage | ◆ hair resistant<br>◆ tint under-processed<br>◆ poor-quality product<br>◆ lack of red (white/blonde hair) | ◆ pre-soften hair<br>◆ recolour<br>◆ spot colour<br>◆ pre-pigment |
| Incorrect tone | ◆ under-processed<br>◆ base too dark (yellow cast)<br>◆ base too light (green cast)<br>◆ incorrect $H_2O_2$ | ◆ recolour/bleach if hair tests confirm tensile strength<br>◆ pre-pigment and recolour |

## Useful Task

### Keeping up to date

Colouring manufacturers are always willing to promote and inform the professional about their products. Use this facility to develop your skill and to maintain the currency of your product knowledge and your application technique skills. Manufacturers are generally very keen to inform and update the hairdresser. As a professional hair colourist you should ensure that you constantly update your skills and make yourself aware of what is available so that you can advise both the business and your clientele of the most recent developments and technology.

## Self review

1. State five factors about your client that may affect their choice of hair colour.

2. What is the name of the test used on hair to determine the result of using a particular colour formulation on the hair?

3. When should a predisposition test be carried out?

4. What is the term that describes hair's ability to absorb moisture?

5. What is meant by *level* when hair colouring? What does the term level 7 mean?

6. Provide another term to describe a green tone in hair.

7. List the categories of artificial hair colour.

8. How do oxidation tints act on the hair?

9. Why is a two-step application required when applying lightening oxidation colour to virgin hair?

10. During hair colouring, how may tint staining be removed from the skin?

## Useful contacts

Clynol          www.clynol.com
Goldwell        www.goldwell.com
HABIA           www.habia.org.uk
L'Oréal         www.loreal.co.uk
Wella (GB)      www.wella.co.uk

## CHAPTER 8

# Changing hair curl

## CHAPTER CONTENTS

**Unit H2**   Assist with perming and colouring services

**Unit H3**   Assist with perming, relaxing and colouring services

**Unit H12**  Perm and neutralise hair using basic techniques

**Unit H15**  Perm, relax and neutralise hair

## WHAT THIS CHAPTER WILL PROVIDE

This chapter provides the essential knowledge needed to understand the permanent waving and hair relaxing processes. It describes the procedures for carrying out a range of basic perms and straightening techniques, and guides you in selecting appropriate techniques and products.

# Chemical treatments that affect hair curl

Chemical processes, including permanent waving and relaxing, enable you to offer a wide range of hairstyles and effects to your clients. This in turn enables you to satisfy your clients' needs, which from a business point of view are very important.

The wide variety of products and techniques available enable you to produce many differing effects, from those that are subtle but support the style to those which have a dramatic, obvious effect. The properly completed perm or relaxer provides many valuable benefits, including:

◆   the ability to achieve a wide range of fashion effects

- long-lasting style retention

- easy manageability for your client when styling at home

- additional volume and fullness for styling soft, fine hair textures

- greater control in styling hair that may be naturally curly, coarse, wiry and hard to manage.

These processes must be carried out with due care, as the chemicals used when permanently curling and relaxing hair, if used incorrectly, may cause damage to the hair and even injury to your client and yourself. Always follow the manufacturer's directions for safe use.

 **REMEMBER!**

*The word perm is now popularly used to indicate permanent waving with either alkaline- or acid-balanced solutions.*

# History of the permanent wave

There have been attempts to wave and curl straight hair dating back to early civilisation. Egyptian and Roman women were known to apply a mixture of soil and water to their hair, wrap it on crudely made wooden rollers and then bake it in the sun. The results, of course, were not always permanent.

## The machine age of permanent waving

In 1905 Charles Nessler invented a heavily wired machine that supplied electrical current to metal rods around which hair strands were wrapped. These heavy units were heated during the perming process. They were kept from touching the scalp by a complex system of counterbalancing weights suspended from an overhead chandelier mounted on a stand (see Figure 8.1).

Two methods were used to wind hair strands around the metal units. Long hair was wound from the scalp to the ends, a technique called *spiral winding* (see Figure 8.2). After World War I, when many women cut their hair into the short bobbed style, the *croquignole winding* technique was introduced (see Figure 8.3). Using this method, shorter hair was wound from the ends towards the scalp. The hair was then styled into deep waves with loose end curls.

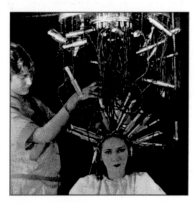

■ Figure 8.1 Machine permanent wave

■ Figure 8.2 Spiral flat wind

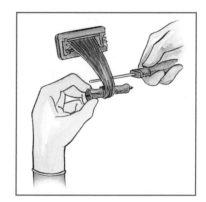

■ Figure 8.3 Croquignole wind

The client's fear of being tied to an electrical contraption with the possibility of receiving a shock or a burn led to the development of alternative methods of waving hair. In 1931, the *pre-heat method* of perming was introduced. Hair was wrapped using the croquignole method, and then clamps, pre-heated by a separate electrical unit, were placed over the wound curls. This was known as the *falling heat* or *wireless system*.

## The first machineless perm

An alternative to the machine perm was introduced in 1932 when chemists Ralph L. Evans and Everett G. McDonough pioneered a method that used external heat generated by chemical reaction. Small, flexible pads, called *exothermic pads*, containing a chemical mixture including calcium oxide, were wound around hair strands. When the pads were moistened with water, a chemical heat was released. This process created long-lasting curls. Thus the first machineless permanent wave was born. Salon clients were no longer subjected to the dangers and discomforts of the Nessler machine.

## Cold waves

In 1941 scientists discovered another method of permanent waving. They developed the *waving lotion*, a liquid that softens and expands the hair strand. After the waving lotion has done its work, another lotion called a *neutraliser* is applied. The neutraliser hardens and shrinks the hair strand, allowing it to conform to the shape of the rod around which the hair is wrapped. It also stops the action of the waving lotion.

This perm is called a *cold wave* because it does not use heat. Cold waves replaced virtually all predecessors and competitors, and cold waving and permanent waving became almost synonymous terms. Modern versions of cold waves, usually referred to as alkaline perms, are still very popular today.

## Acid-balanced perms

For many years, manufacturers sought to develop a permanent wave solution that would minimise hair damage and permit hair that had been damaged by lightening or tinting services to receive a perm. To achieve these goals, they developed a waving lotion that was not as highly alkaline as earlier lotions.

Acid-balanced permanent waves with pH levels ranging from 4.5–7.9 were introduced in 1970. They did not contain strong alkalis and therefore were less damaging to the hair. Acid-balanced lotions were, however, slow to penetrate hair, and processing time was longer. To overcome this problem, the client is placed under a pre-heated hood dryer to shorten the processing time. Often the curl pattern achieved from acid-balanced perms is softer than that achieved from an alkali wave; therefore a size smaller perm rod is often advised.

## Modern perm chemistry

Perm chemistry is constantly being refined and improved. Perms are available today in many differing formulas for a wide variety of hair types. Waving lotions and neutralisers for both acid-balanced and alkaline perms are being formulated with new conditioners, proteins and natural ingredients that help to protect (or *buffer*) and condition the hair during and after perming.

Stop-action processing is incorporated in many waving lotions to ensure optimum curl development. Curling takes place in a fixed time without the risk of over-processing or damaging the hair. Special pre-wrapping lotions have been developed to compensate for hair that is not equally porous all over, and therefore protect the hair.

Virtually all permanent waves are achieved with a two-step chemical process:

1  **waving lotion** – softens or breaks the internal structure of the hair

2  **neutraliser** – rehardens or rebonds the internal structure of the hair.

Some perming systems have wrapping lotions that help to pre-soften the hair making it easier to wind and ready to receive the perming agent.

### The pH scale

This 14-point scale is used to indicate the acidity or alkalinity of a substance. The symbol pH (potential Hydrogen) refers to the quantity of hydrogen ions present. The centre of the scale (7) is neutral and is a point which is neither acid nor alkali. The further from the central point the higher the level of either acidity (pH of less than 7) or alkalinity (pH of over 7). Figure 8.4 shows the relative pH of a number of hairdressing-related substances.

### Alkaline perms

The main active ingredient (or *reducing agent*) in alkaline perms, ammonium thioglycolate, is a chemical compound

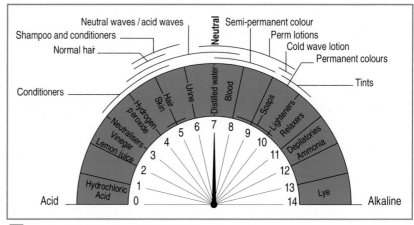

Figure 8.4 Relative pH of hairdressing substances

made up of ammonium hydroxide and thioglycolic acid. The pH of alkaline waving lotions generally falls within the range 8.2–9.6, depending on the amounts of ammonium hydroxide present. Because the lotion is more alkaline, the cuticle layers swell slightly and open, allowing the solution to penetrate more quickly than acid-balanced lotions. Some alkaline perms are wound with perm lotion (*pre-damping*), others are wound with water, with the perm lotion applied after all the hair has been wound (*post-damping*). Some require a plastic cap (to retain scalp heat) for processing, others do not. Therefore, it is extremely important to read the manufacturer's instructions for use before beginning.

The benefits of alkaline perms are:

◆  strong curl patterns

◆  fast processing time (varies from 5–20 minutes)

◆  room-temperature processing.

Generally, alkaline perms should be used when:

◆  perming resistant hair

◆  a strong/tight curl is desired

◆  the client has a history of early curl relaxation.

## Acid-balanced perms

The main active ingredient in acid-balanced waving lotions is glycerol monothioglycolate, which effectively reduces the pH. Lower pH is gentler on the hair and typically gives a softer curl than alkaline cold waves. Acid-balanced perms have a pH range of approximately 4.5–7.9 and usually penetrate the hair more slowly. They require a longer processing time and heat to develop curl. Heat is produced in one of two ways.

1   The perm is activated by heat created chemically within the product. This method is called *exothermic*.

2   The perm is activated by an outside heat source, usually a conventional hood-type hairdryer. This method is called *endothermic*.

Recent advances in acid-balanced perm chemistry, however, have made it possible to process some acid-balanced perms at room temperature without heat. These newer acid-balanced perms usually have a slightly higher pH but still contain glycerol monothioglycolate as the active ingredient.

Most acid-balanced perms are water-wrapped, require a plastic cap (to retain scalp heat), and may or may not require a pre-heated hood dryer for processing. Read the manufacturer's perm directions carefully before starting.

Benefits of acid-balanced perms are:

◆   softer curl patterns

◆   slower, but more controllable processing time (usually 15–25 minutes)

◆   gentler treatment for delicate hair types.

Generally, acid-balanced perms are used when:

◆   perming delicate/fragile or colour-treated hair

◆   a soft, natural curl or wave pattern is desired

◆   style support, rather than strong curl, is required.

## The chemistry of neutralisers

Neutralisers for both acid-balanced and alkaline perms have the same important function: to permanently establish the new curl shape. Neutralising is a very important step in the perming process. If the hair is not properly neutralised, the curl will relax or straighten after one or two shampoos. Generally, today's neutralisers are composed of a relatively small percentage of hydrogen peroxide, an oxidising agent, at an acidic pH. An alternative oxidising agent is sodium bromate. As with waving lotions, there are slightly different procedures recommended for individual products. To achieve the best possible results, read and follow the manufacturer's directions.

# Hair structure and perming

Whether using an acid-balanced or alkaline formula, all perms subject the hair to two different actions:

1   **physical action** – wrapping sections of hair around a perm rod

2   **chemical action** – created first by reducing agent (waving lotion) and second by an oxidising agent (neutraliser).

Since both of these actions work together to create a change in the internal structure of the hair, it is important to understand the composition of hair and how it is affected during perming.

## The physical structure of hair

Each strand of hair is structurally subdivided into three major components (see Figure 8.5).

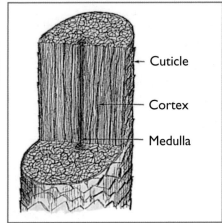

Figure 8.5 Structure of a hair

◆   The cuticle, or outer covering, normally consists of seven or more overlapping layers. Although it comprises a small percentage of the total weight of the hair, the cuticle possesses unique structural properties that protect the hair. During perming, the waving lotion raises the cuticle layers and allows the active ingredients to enter the cortex.

◆   The cortex, the major component of the hair structure, accounts for up to 90% of its total weight. The cortex gives hair its flexibility, elasticity, strength and resilience, and contains the colour. It is in the cortex that the physical and chemical actions take place during the perming process to restructure the hair into a new curl configuration.

◆   The medulla is the innermost section of the hair structure. The function of the medulla, if any, is unknown. In fact, it is not at all unusual for an otherwise normal, healthy hair to be without a medulla.

## The chemical composition of hair

Hair consists almost entirely of a protein material called keratin, which is made up of approximately 19 amino acids. When many acids are bonded together, they form a polypeptide chain. These chains twine around each other in a spiral fashion to assume a helical shape very similar to a spring. Hair contains a high concentration of the amino acid cystine that is joined together crosswise with disulphide linkages or bonds. Disulphide bonds add strength to the keratin protein, and it is these bonds that must be broken down to allow the perming process to occur.

## Processing

The chemical action of a waving lotion breaks the disulphide bonds and softens the hair. When the chemical action softens the inner structure of the hair enough, it can mould to the shape of the rod around which it is wound (see Figures 8.6–8.9).

■ Figure 8.6 Each hair strand is composed of many polypeptide chains; this series of illustrations shows the behaviour of one such chain

■ Figure 8.7 Hair before processing; chemical bonds (links) give hair its strength and firmness

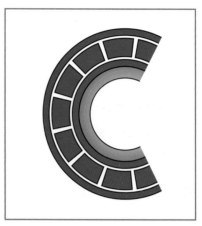

■ Figure 8.8 Hair wound on rod; the hair bends to the curvature and size of the rod

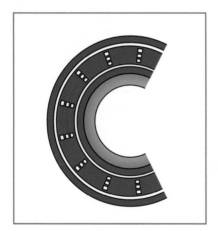

■ Figure 8.9 During processing, waving lotion breaks the chemical cross-bonds (links) permitting the hair to adjust to the curvature of the rod while in this softened condition

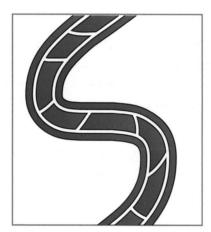

■ Figure 8.10 The neutraliser reforms the chemical bonds (links) to conform with the wound position of the hair, and rehardens the hair, thus creating the permanent wave

# Neutralising

When the hair has assumed the desired shape, the broken disulphide bonds must be chemically rebonded. Neutralising rehardens the hair and fixes it into its new curl form. When the neutralising action is completed, the hair is unwrapped from the rods, and you have a new curl formation (see Figure 8.10).

# Choosing the right perming technique

The stages of perming are:

1    client consultation

2    selection of equipment and products

3    preparation of the hair

4    perm wind/wrap

5    application of perm lotion

6    processing

7    neutralising.

In order to decide which perming technique is right for your client you must be able to evaluate and analyse your client's hair. You will consult with your client to establish what they expect to accomplish with a perm – a tight, curly look or a loose, wavy look. This information helps you to select the correct perm product and technique.

## Basic manual perming skills

Successful perming requires manual dexterity. With practice, your skills in handling and manipulating hair will improve. Before actually applying a perm lotion, you will probably spend considerable time practising pre-perming skills like pre-perm sectioning, curler sectioning and winding/wrapping. Your ability to give successful perms depends on mastering these important skills.

## Client consultation

Every perm client has a different idea of how s/he wants the perm to look. The only way to meet your client's expectations is to determine what those expectations are. Talk to your client in a friendly but professional way (see Figure 8.11). Take a few minutes to discuss the following points.

◆    **Hairstyle.** How much curl does your client want? Photos or magazine pictures help to make this clearly understood by both of you.

◆    **Client's lifestyle.** Does s/he have a lot of leisure time, or a demanding schedule that requires a low-maintenance style?

◆    **Personal image.** How does your client's hairstyle relate to their overall personal image? Is your client concerned about current fashion trends?

◆    **Previous experience with perming.** What did s/he like or dislike about past perm services?

Once you learn what questions to ask and how to ask them, the consultation with your perm client takes only a few minutes. It is time well spent, however, because the consultation helps establish your credibility as a professional.

■ Figure 8.11 Pre-perm consultation

**PERMANENT WAVE RECORD**

Name ...............................................................................Tel. ...........................................................

Address ..............................................................................................................................

.........................................................................................................................................

**DESCRIPTION OF HAIR**

| **Length** | **Texture** | **Type** | | **Porosity** |
|---|---|---|---|---|
| ☐ short | ☐ coarse | ☐ normal | ☐ very porous | ☐ slightly porous |
| ☐ medium | ☐ medium | ☐ resistant | | |
| ☐ long | ☐ fine | ☐ tinted | ☐ moderately porous | ☐ resistant |
| | | ☐ highlighted | | |
| | | ☐ bleached | ☐ normal | |

**Condition**

| ☐ very good | ☐ good | ☐ fair | ☐ poor | ☐ dry | ☐ oily |
|---|---|---|---|---|---|

Tinted with ...........................................................................................................

Previously permed with ........................................................................................

**TYPE OF PERM**

| ☐ alkaline | ☐ acid | ☐ body wave | ☐ other |
|---|---|---|---|

No. of rods .............................. Lotion ........................................ Strength ......................

**Results**

| ☐ good | ☐ poor | ☐ too tight | ☐ too loose |
|---|---|---|---|

| Date | Perm used | Stylist | Date | Perm used | Stylist |
|---|---|---|---|---|---|
| ................ | ................ | ................ | ................ | ................ | ................ |

Other side of Record, continue with:

| Date | Perm used | Stylist | Date | Perm used | Stylist |
|---|---|---|---|---|---|

Figure 8.12 A client record card

It inspires your client's confidence in your technical and creative abilities, and makes the perming experience more satisfactory for both
of you.

Keep the vital information you learn during the client consultation as a permanent record, either written or computerised, along with other important data, including the client's address, and both their home and business telephone numbers. Figure 8.12 shows an example of an organised format for maintaining client records.

# REMEMBER!

*If the presence of previous, unknown chemical treatments is apparent, carry out an incompatibility test to test for the presence of metallic salts on the hair. See page 153 for details of this test.*

# Perm preparation

## Pre-perm analysis

After the client consultation, you must analyse the overall condition of your client's hair and scalp. This analysis is essential for you to determine:

◆ if it is safe and advisable to proceed with the perm service; the hair must be in good condition and have the necessary strength to accept a chemical alteration to achieve a successful perm

◆ which perm product should be chosen for the best results on the particular hair type

◆ which perm technique should be used – curler/rod and parting sizes, and winding/wrapping pattern.

First, examine the scalp for abrasions, irritations, open sores or contagious disorders. If any of these exist, do not go ahead with the perm. Minor abrasions may be protected by using petroleum jelly BP as a barrier between the skin and the lotion.

Next, judge the physical characteristics of the hair with regard to these important criteria: porosity, density, texture and length.

Finally, determine the overall condition of the hair. Observe if the hair has been treated previously with chemicals: perm, tint, bleach, highlighting (frosting, dimensionally coloured). This will guide you in choosing the appropriate perm.

Question your client about previous use of products on the hair that may be incompatible with the perming process. Products that contain metallic salts (compound henna, hair colour restorers, progressive hair dyes and metallic-coloured hairsprays) leave traces of salts on the hair which react with the process. If the presence of these salts is detected it is not safe to proceed with the perming process until all traces are removed. If you are in doubt about the presence of salts, carry out an incompatibility test on a sample of the hair.

Check any existing salon records regarding previous treatments and their outcomes.

 *REMEMBER!*

*As your salon retains information relating to clients it will be registered with the Data Protection Commissioner. Your salon will have rules regarding who has access to client information, this information's security and for what purpose the information may be used. Familiarise yourself with these as you have a responsibility to comply with them.*

# Determining porosity

Porosity refers to the hair's capacity to absorb moisture. There is a direct relationship between the hair's porosity, the type of perm (acid-balanced or alkaline) you will use, and the strength of waving lotion you will choose.

The processing time for any perm depends more on hair porosity than any other factor. The more porous the hair, the less processing time it takes, and the milder the waving solution required. Hair porosity is affected by such factors as excessive exposure to sun and wind, previous use of harsh shampoos, tints and lighteners, perms and use of thermal styling appliances.

## Porous hair

Porous hair may be dry – even very dry. If hair is tinted, bleached, or has been exposed to the sun or was over-processed by a previous perm, it will absorb liquids readily. Soft, fine, thin hair usually has a thin cuticle so it will absorb liquids quickly and easily. Rough, dull-looking hair and hair that tangles easily is also likely to be porous.

While the hair is dry, check porosity in three different areas: front hairline, in front of the ear and in the crown area. Select a single strand of hair, hold the end securely between the thumb and first finger of one hand, and slide the thumb and first finger of the other hand from the hair end to the scalp.

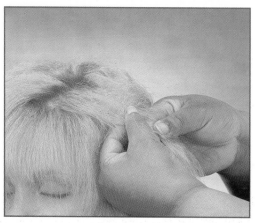

If the hair feels smooth and the cuticle is dense and hard, it is considered resistant and will not absorb liquids or perm lotion easily. If you can feel a slight roughness, this tells you that the cuticle is open and that the hair is porous and will absorb liquids more readily (see Figure 8.13).

■ Figure 8.13 Testing for hair porosity

## Poor porosity (resistant hair)

This refers to hair with the cuticle layer lying close to the hair shaft. This type of hair absorbs waving lotion slowly and usually requires a longer processing time and/or a strong waving lotion.

## Good porosity (normal hair)

Hair with the cuticle layer slightly raised from the hair shaft can absorb moisture or chemicals in an average amount of time.

## Porous (tinted, lightened or previously chemically treated) hair

Hair that has been made porous by various treatments or styling absorbs lotion very quickly and requires the shortest processing time. Use either an acid-balanced perm or a very mild alkaline wave.

## Over-porous hair (a result of over-processing)

This type of hair is very damaged, dry, fragile and brittle. Until the hair has been reconditioned, or the damaged part has been removed by cutting, it should not be permed.

If hair is unevenly porous (usually porous or over-porous at the ends with good to poor porosity near the scalp), a pre-wrap lotion, specifically designed to even out the porosity, is recommended to achieve even curl results and help prevent over-processing porous ends (see Figures 8.14– 8.17).

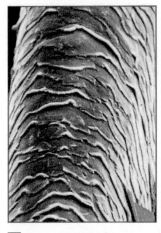

■ Figure 8.14 Normal (moderate porosity)

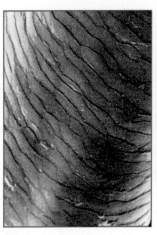

■ Figure 8.15 Resistant (poor porosity)

■ Figure 8.16 Tinted (extreme porosity)

■ Figure 8.17 Damaged (over-porous hair)

## Determining texture

Texture refers to how thick or thin (in diameter) each individual hair is. Fine hair has a small diameter; coarse hair has a large diameter (see Figure 8.18). You can feel whether hair is fine, coarse or medium when a single dry strand is held between the fingers.

The texture and porosity together are used to determine the processing time of the waving lotion. Although porosity is the more important of the two, texture does play an important role in estimating processing time. Fine hair with a small diameter becomes saturated with waving lotion more quickly than coarse hair with a large diameter, even if both are of equal porosity. However, when coarse hair is porous, it processes faster than fine hair that is not porous.

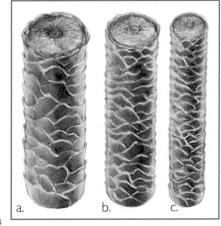

A perm adds body to hair that appears limp and lifeless, and does not hold a style very long. For coarse, wiry hair, a perm provides greater manageability in styling.

■ Figure 8.18 a. Coarse; b. Medium; c. Fine

 REMEMBER!

*If pre-perm analysis is not correct, poor curl development or hair damage can result.*

## Testing elasticity

Elasticity is the ability of hair to stretch and then return to its original length. To test for elasticity, stretch a single dry hair. If the hair breaks under very slight strain, it has little or no elasticity. Other signs of poor elasticity include a spongy feel when the hair is wet and/or hair that tangles easily. When hair is completely lacking in elasticity (for example, extremely damaged hair), it will not take a satisfactory permanent wave. The greater the degree of elasticity, the longer the wave will remain in the hair, because less relaxation of the hair occurs. Hair with good elastic qualities can be stretched by 20% of its length without breaking (see Figure 8.19).

## REMEMBER!

*Your employer will have arranged a review of the risks associated with the use of chemicals in your salon. This is part of the Control of Substances Hazardous to Health Regulations 2002 (COSHH). If personal protective equipment is provided you are advised to use this.*

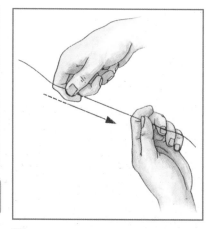

■ Figure 8.19 Testing for elasticity

## Assessing density

Density, or thickness, refers to the number of hairs per square centimetre on your client's head. Density is one characteristic that determines the size of the partings you will use. Thick hair (many hairs per square centimetre) will require small partings on each rod. Too much hair on the rod can result in a weak curl, especially near the scalp.

If hair is thin (few hairs per square centimetre), slightly larger partings can be used, but avoid stretching or pulling the hair towards the rod because this can cause hair breakage or straight, misdirected hair at the scalp.

## Hair length and perming

Hair that is 5 cm to 15 cm long is considered ideal for perming. Hair should be long enough to make at least 2.5 turns around the rod. To perm hair longer than 15 cm, smaller partings must be used to allow the waving lotion and neutraliser to penetrate more easily and thoroughly.

## Perm lotion selection

The type of perm lotion you choose depends on the total evaluation of your client's hair and wishes during the consultation and pre-perm analysis. The following is a general guide to help you decide whether to use an alkaline or an acid-balanced perm.

Today's perm products offer a wide selection of special features and formulas for all hair types. There are alkaline formulas for resistant hair and acid-balanced formulas for bleached hair. Each formula gives excellent results if you choose the perm carefully and follow the manufacturer's directions.

## REMEMBER!

*Your employer will have arranged for training, if required, in the correct use of chemicals. You should follow the guidance provided in their correct use.*

| Hair type | Type of perm lotion |
|---|---|
| Coarse – resistant | Alkaline lotion wind or alkaline post-damp |
| Fine – resistant | Alkaline lotion wind or alkaline post-damp |
| Normal | Alkaline post-damp or acid lotion |
| Normal – porous | Alkaline post-damp or acid lotion |
| Normal – delicate | Acid lotion |
| Tinted – non-porous | Alkaline post-damp or acid lotion |
| Tinted – porous | Acid lotion |
| Highlighted, frosted, dimensionally coloured | Acid lotion |
| High-lift tinted | Acid lotion |
| Bleached | Acid lotion |

# Pre-perm shampooing

Today, there are shampoos specifically formulated for pre-perm cleansing that thoroughly yet gently cleanse the hair. Use of these shampoos is recommended for optimal results. If a specialist shampoo is not available use a plain soapless shampoo that contains no additives as this will clean the hair without leaving any traces that may inhibit or block the penetration of the perm lotion.

## REMEMBER!

*While shampooing or undertaking any pre-perm preparation of a client's hair, you should avoid vigorous brushing, combing, pulling or rubbing that can cause the scalp to become sensitive to perm solutions.*

When analysing a client's hair before perming, you may notice that the hair looks and feels coated. This coating might be the build-up of shampoo or conditioners, improper rinsing, resins from styling products or hairspray, or mineral deposits from hard water. This coating can prevent penetration of the waving lotion and interfere with perm results. It is very important for the hair to be free of all coatings before beginning any perm.

Begin the process by wetting the hair, applying the shampoo and gently working it into a lather. If the hair is extremely coated let the shampoo remain in the hair for several minutes before rinsing. Rinse thoroughly to remove all shampoo and dissolved build-up. Towel blot excess water from the hair. For more information about the shampooing procedure see Chapter 4.

# Pre-perm cutting or shaping

If your client has chosen a hairstyle that is the same or very similar to the design s/he currently has, reshape the style using either scissors or a razor. If the finished style requires texturising or thinning of the ends, wait until after giving the perm to texturise. Over-tapered or thinned ends are more difficult to wrap smoothly and accurately. Irregular effects cut into hair can be difficult to wind without distortion of the hair. Lightly tapering thick hair before winding can aid the winding process.

If your client wants a completely new style, rough cut the hair into an approximation of the final shape. After the perm is completed, you can finish shaping the style more exactly.

# Perm curlers and rods

Correct selection of perm curler or rod size is essential for successful perm results. The size of curler determines the size of curl created by the waving process. Perm curlers are typically made of plastic and come in varying sizes. They range in diameter (distance through the centre of the curler from side to side) from 0.3–1.9cm. They are usually colour-coded to identify their size easily (see Figure 8.20).

Perm curlers are also available in three lengths: short, medium and long (4.4–8.8cm). Curlers of all diameters are available in long lengths. Medium and short lengths are not always available in all diameters. These shorter curlers are used for wrapping small or awkward sections.

As well as the traditional shape of perm curlers, there is a range of alternatives, some designed especially to achieve specific shapes in the hair. These include spiral curlers, rickrack sticks, triangular curlers, flexible curlers and crimping shapers.

# Types of curler

There are two types of curler: concave and straight. Concave curlers (as in Figure 8.20) have a small diameter in the centre area and gradually increase to their largest diameter at the ends, resulting in a tighter curl at the hair ends, with a looser, wider curl at the scalp. The diameter of the straight curlers is the same throughout their length, creating an even-sized curl from end to scalp.

All curlers have some means of securing the hair on the curler to prevent the curl from unwinding. Usually an elastic band, with a fastening button or loop attached to the end, stretches across the wound hair and secures it when the button or loop is inserted into the opposite end of the curler. Rounded curler rubbers are less likely to mark and break hair than are the flat ones.

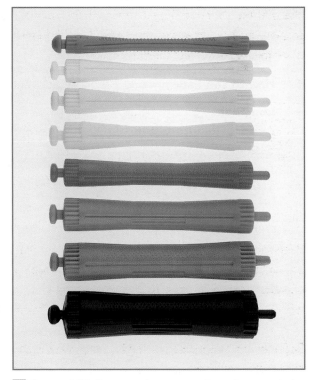

■ Figure 8.20 Perm curlers, or rods, colour coded according to size

## Selecting curler size

When selecting curler size, two things must be considered.

1   The amount of curl desired. The amount of wave, curl or body needed is determined between you and your client during the consultation. Your success in creating a style depends primarily on the curler sizes you choose, the number of curlers used and where the curlers are placed on the head.

2   Physical characteristics of the hair. Of the hair characteristics described earlier, three are important to curler size selection:

    i   hair length

    ii  hair elasticity

    iii hair texture.

## Suggested hair sectioning and curler size

Although the hair length, elasticity and texture must be considered in the choice of curlers, the texture should be the determining factor.

♦   **Coarse texture, good elasticity.** This type of hair requires smaller (narrower) sections and larger curlers to permit better placement of curlers for a definite wave pattern.

♦   **Medium texture, average elasticity.** Medium or average textured hair requires sections that are the same size as the size of the curler.

♦   **Fine texture, poor elasticity.** This type of hair requires smaller sections and curlers wound without any tension on the hair.

♦   **Hair in the nape area.** Use short sections and short curlers.

♦   **Long hair.** To permanently wave hair longer than 15cm, use small sections. This permits the waving lotion and neutraliser to penetrate more easily and thoroughly. Spiral winding, piggy-back or double-winding techniques may be used to achieve an even curl pattern from points to roots.

## Sectioning and parting

Pre-sectioning is the division of hair into uniform working areas at the top, front, crown, sides, back and nape. Pre-sectioning makes the winding easier as it ensures that the curlers will fit on to the client's head in the direction that you intend. It also secures the hair out of the way and keeps it off your client's face while winding.

 *REMEMBER!*

*When selecting perm rods for use with acid perms, choosing a size smaller than the required curl size can help to reduce the effect of curl drop, sometimes experienced with this type of perm.*

# Winding

## Winding patterns

Just as the curler size and sectioning size determine the size of the curl, the winding pattern determines the direction or flow of the curl.

Three basic winding patterns are:

1   orthodox wind (nine-section)

2   brick wind

3   directional wind.

All winding patterns may be adapted to suit particular head shapes and to allow the blocking to follow the direction of the required hairstyle or the natural fall of the hair.

### Orthodox (conventional) wind

This traditional sectioning pattern is perhaps the most widely used when perming. The hair is divided into nine sections to allow the curlers to fit easily on the head. This allows the curlers to be wound in a downward direction, following the natural fall of the hair, and back off the face. The top/front section may also be wound in a forward direction if required to follow the direction of the hairstyle or to follow the natural fall of the hair on the top. (See Figures 8.21 and 8.22.)

■ Figure 8.21 Orthodox wind 1

■ Figure 8.22 Orthodox wind 2

### Brick wind

This technique does not use pre-sectioning. The curlers are located on the head in a staggered 'brickwork' pattern. This technique prevents the occurrence of continuous partings in the end curl pattern and this makes the technique very suitable for use when perming hair which will be dried naturally, especially short hair.

The wind commences at the focal point of the hairstyle, usually at the front. The skill of the hairdresser is to position the curlers in a brickwork pattern that will follow the direction of the required hairstyle without placing the hair under tension. (See Figures 8.23 and 8.24.)

■ Figure 8.23 Brick wind 1

■ Figure 8.24 Brick wind 2

## Directional wind

Sectioning patterns may be devised to enable the curlers to fit on to the head in directions that will support the direction of the hairstyle. Pre-sectioning will ensure that all curlers fit on to the head without placing the hair under tension. (See Figures 8.25 and 8.26.)

# Winding the hair

To create a uniform wave or curl pattern, the hair must be wrapped smoothly and cleanly on

 Figure 8.25 Directional wind I

Figure 8.26 Directional wind 2

each perm rod without stretching. As noted earlier, the action of the waving lotion expands the hair. Hair that is wound tightly interferes with this action: the hair may be damaged, and the tight wind may prevent penetration of the waving lotion and neutraliser.

When winding with acid wave a slight tension may be used.

## REMEMBER!

*To prevent breakage, the band should not press into the hair near the scalp or be twisted (flat rubbers) against the wound hair.*

## Hair strand parting in relation to the head

The term *base* refers to the area of the head or scalp where the curler is placed in relation to the head. The curlers can be wrapped on-base, off-base or one-half off-base. Each of these curler positions creates a slightly different scalp wave direction, which will influence the overall curl pattern results.

## Curl on-base

When the strand is held in an upward position (at 90° to the head) and wound on the rod, the curl will rest on-base (see Figure 8.27). Hair wound in this manner will produce curls that start close to the scalp for hairstyles that require fullness, height and upward movement. When perming very curly hair, over-directing the hair (holding the hair at more than 90° to the head) will enable the perm to control the curl even closer to the scalp.

## Curl off-base

When the strand is held in a downward position and wound on a curler, the curl will rest off-base (see Figure 8.28). Hair wound in this manner will produce a curl that starts further away from the scalp than hair wound on-base. Off-base winding produces close-to-the-head hairstyles that do not require fullness of height.

Figure 8.27 Curl on-base

## Curl one-half off-base

When the strand is held straight out from the head and wound on a curler, the curl will rest one-half off-base (see Figure 8.29). Hair wound in this manner will produce a combination of the previous two.

## End papers

End papers or end tissues are porous papers used to cover the ends of the hair to ensure smooth, even winding. End papers minimise the danger of buckled or distorted ends and help to form smooth, even curls and waves. They are especially important in helping to wind uneven hair lengths smoothly.

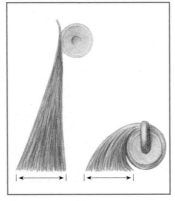

■ Figure 8.28 Curl off-base

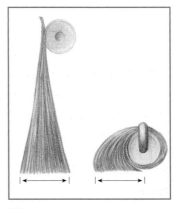

■ Figure 8.29 Curl one-half off-base

There are three methods of end-paper application in general use today. Each method is equally effective, if used properly.

1    Double-end paper wrap

2    Single-end paper wrap

3    Book-end wrap

Hair should be shampooed and left moist (not saturated) for wrapping. Section hair, then begin by making your first parting (blocking). Remember, each parting should be no longer than the length of the curler. If the parting is too long, the hair will not wave evenly and hair may be placed under undue tension. If the hair should become dry while you are winding, moisten the hair lightly using water from a trigger spray.

## Double-end paper wrap

1    Part off and comb the parted hair up and out until all the hair is smooth and evenly distributed (see Figure 8.30). Do not pinch the ends together.

2    Place one end paper under the hair strand so that it extends below the ends of the hair. Place the other end paper on the top (see Figure 8.31).

3    With your right hand, place the curler under the double end papers, parallel with the parting at the scalp (see Figure 8.32).

4    Wind the strand smoothly on the curler to the scalp without tension (see Figure 8.33).

5    Fasten the band on the top of the curler.

The preparation and winding of curls for a single-end paper wrap and book-end wrap are the same as the double-end paper wrap, with the following exceptions.

## Single-end paper wrap

Place only one end paper on top of the hair strand and hold it flat between the first and second fingers to prevent bunching (see Figure 8.34). The hair is wound in the same manner as the double-end wrap.

## Book-end wrap

Hold the strand between the first and second fingers; fold and place an end paper over the strand, forming an envelope. Take care not to indent into the hair with the folded side of the paper. Wind the curl as in the double-end wrap (see Figure 8.35).

## Preliminary (pre-perm) test curls

Preliminary test curls help determine how your client's hair will react to a perm. It is advisable to carry out a test on hair that is tinted, bleached, over-porous or shows any signs of damage.

Preliminary testing gives you the following additional information:

◆ actual processing time needed to achieve optimum curl results

◆ curl results based on the curler size and perm product you have selected.

### Procedure

1 Shampoo the hair and towel dry.

2 Following the perm direction, wrap two or three curlers in the most delicate areas of the hair.

3 Wind a coil of lightly moist cotton wool around the curlers.

■ Figure 8.30 Combed hair ready for end tissue

■ Figure 8.31 Two end tissues, one above hair, one beneath

■ Figure 8.32 Locating and winding perm rod at the hair ends

■ Figure 8.33 Winding rod, middle length, smooth even tension

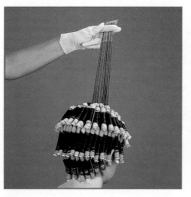
■ Figure 8.34 Single-end tissue in place

■ Figure 8.35 Book-end wrap

4   Apply waving lotion to the wrapped curls, being careful not to allow the waving lotion to come into contact with the unwrapped hair.

5   Set a time and process the hair according to the perm directions.

6   Check the hair frequently.

To check a test curl, unfasten a rod and carefully (remember, the hair is in a softened state) unwind the curl about 1½ turns of the curler. Do not permit the hair to become loose or unwound from the curler completely. Hold the hair firmly by placing a thumb at each end of the curler. Move the curler gently towards the scalp so that the hair falls loosely into the wave pattern. Continue checking the curlers until a firm and definite 'S' is formed. The 'S' reflects the size of the rod used (see Figure 8.36). Be guided by the manufacturer's directions.

When judging test curls, different hair textures with varying degrees of elasticity will have slightly different 'S' formations. Fine, thin hair is generally softer and has less bulk. The wave ridge might be less defined and more difficult to read. Coarse, thick hair has better elasticity and seems to reinforce itself, falling into the wave pattern more readily. The wave ridge will be stronger and better defined. Long hair may produce a wider scalp wave than short hair, because larger curlers are used and the diameter of the wave widens towards the scalp.

When the optimum curl has been formed, rinse the curls with warm water, blot the curls thoroughly, apply, process and rinse the neutraliser according to the perm directions, and dry these test curls gently. Evaluate the curl results. If the hair is over-processed (see below), do not perm the rest of the hair until it is in better condition. If the test curl results are good, proceed with the perm, but do not re-perm these preliminary test curls.

■ Figure 8.36 Unwinding hair carefully, without pushing or pulling

## Over-processing

Any lotion that can properly process the hair can also over-process it, causing dryness, frizziness or hair damage. Over-processed hair is easily detected. It cannot be combed into a suitable wave pattern, because the elasticity of the hair has been excessively damaged, and the hair feels harsh after being dried. Reconditioning treatments should begin immediately.

Causes of over-processing are:

◆   lotion left on the hair too long

◆   improperly judged pre-perm hair analysis and/or waving lotion that was too strong

◆   test curls were not made frequently enough or were judged improperly.

## Under-processing

Under-processing is caused by insufficient processing time of the waving lotion. After perming, under-processed hair has a limp or weak wave formation. The ridges are not well defined and the hair retains little or no wave formation. Typically, after a few shampoos, the hair will have no curl pattern at all (see Figure 8.37).

Under-processed hair, even if there is no curl, has been chemically treated. If, in your professional judgement, you decide the hair can be re-permed, condition it first, choose a milder lotion and test the curls frequently.

## Important safety precautions

Remember that the lotions used for perming contain chemically active ingredients and therefore must be used carefully to avoid injury to you and your client. The following precautions should always be taken.

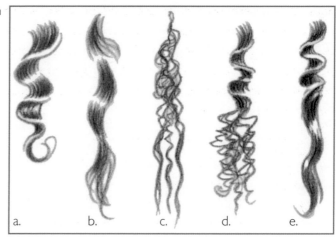

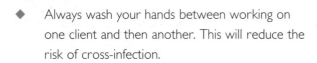
■ Figure 8.37 Good results (a), under-processed curl (b), over-processed curl (c), porous ends (d), improper winding (e)

♦ Always wash your hands between working on one client and then another. This will reduce the risk of cross-infection.

♦ Protect your client's clothing with a plastic shampoo cape.

♦ Ask your client to remove glasses, earrings and necklaces to prevent damage.

♦ Do not give a perm to a client who has experienced an allergic reaction to a previous perm.

♦ Do not save any opened, unused waving lotion or neutraliser. These lotions can change in strength and effectiveness if not used within a few hours of opening the container.

♦ Do not dilute or add anything to the waving lotion or neutraliser unless the product directions tell you to do so.

♦ Keep waving lotion out of eyes and away from the skin. If waving lotion contacts these areas, rinse thoroughly with cool, clean water.

♦ Do not perm and apply hair colour to a client on the same day. Perm the hair first, wait one week, then apply hair colour. There are products available today which combine perming and colouring within the one process.

## Perming

Before you begin perming, make sure you have all the necessary materials at hand. Good organisation and planning will help to develop precision and speed in completing a perm. At the perming station the following equipment should be laid out in an organised, easily accessible fashion:

♦ perm product

♦ client's record card

♦ towels

♦ curlers (organised by size)

♦ plastic hair clips and pins

♦ end papers

♦ pin-tail comb

♦ cotton wool

♦ protective gloves

♦ perm lotion applicator.

Some alkaline perm product directions call for water winding, some are lotion wound, and others require pre-wind lotions. Some wave lotions come in two parts that must be mixed just prior to use. Some need dryer heat. (Note: the dryer should be pre-heated.) Some perms require that a plastic cap be placed over the curlers during the processing, others do not. Considering all the variables, it is not a good idea to trust your memory. Make it a practice to check the printed directions that accompany every perm each time you give a perm.

 REMEMBER!

*Always read and follow the manufacturer's directions carefully.*

# Partial perming

Perming only a section of a whole head of hair is called *partial perming*. Partial perming can be used on:

◆ clients (male and female) who have long hair on the top and crown and very short, tapered sides and nape

◆ clients who need volume and lift only in certain areas

◆ designs that require curl support in the nape area but a smooth, sleek surface.

Partial perming uses the same techniques and wrapping patterns that have already been described. There are a few additional considerations, as described below.

1 When you are winding the hair and reach the area that will be left unpermed, go to the next-largest curler size so that the curl pattern of the permed hair will blend into the unpermed hair.

2 After wrapping the area to be permed, place a coil of moist cotton wool around the wrapped curlers as well as around the entire hairline.

3 Before applying the waving lotion, apply a heavy, creamy conditioner to the sections that *will not* be permed to protect this hair from the effects of the waving lotion (waving lotion softens and straightens unwrapped hair).

# Applying perming lotion

The technique used in applying perming lotion will vary, depending on a number of considerations.

## Pre-saturation

Used when perming strong straight hair. By applying the lotion to all of the hair before commencing winding, the hair begins to soften uniformly and offers less resistance to winding.

## Pre-damping

Wetting the hair with perm lotion as you wind. This enables more resistant areas, if wound first, to begin to soften before the less resistant areas, therefore producing an even curl development throughout the hair. This method may also be used when perming hair using winding patterns to which it may be difficult to apply the perm lotion after winding. In some cases a mild-strength lotion may be used as a winding lotion followed by a stronger lotion, post-damping. This is often used when perming hair with differing rates of porosity along the hair's length.

## HEALTH & SAFETY

Whenever winding with perm lotion, either pre-saturation or pre-damping, wear protective gloves to protect your skin.

## Post-damping

The hair is water wound, and then the lotion is applied after the wind is completed. This gives time for the winding process to take place. Care must be taken to ensure that lotion is applied to all wound curlers.

After shampooing, shaping and wrapping the hair, place a coil or band of moist cotton wool around the entire hairline. To prevent skin irritation and for added protection, apply a barrier cream to skin around the hairline before applying the cotton wool band. This safety precaution prevents waving lotion from coming into contact with the skin and possibly causing irritation. If lotion is applied accurately there should be a minimum of dripping, but the cotton wool assures your client's comfort and safety. After the waving lotion has been applied, remove the cotton wool, gently pat the skin with water-soaked cotton wool, and replace with fresh.

## HEALTH & SAFETY

Should perm lotion enter your client's eyes, rinse with sterile water from an eye bath. Should eye irritation continue inform your line manager and, if required, seek medical advice.

Unless otherwise specified in the product instructions, apply waving lotion with care to the wound hair. Systematically apply lotion to each curler in turn, using an applicator bottle. Run the nozzle along the top of the curler, releasing lotion on to the hair. To ensure lotion penetration on thick hair, rock the curlers gently and apply lotion carefully to the underside of the wound curlers. Avoid allowing lotion to flood on to the scalp. Coverage will be assured by making three applications to the entire head, a little at a time. Remember, dry hair will not absorb moisture easily. By gradually adding lotion to the hair, it will be more readily absorbed, ensuring thorough distribution and coverage (see Figure 8.38).

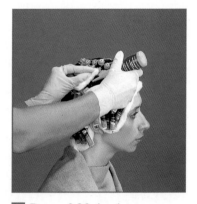

Figure 8.38 Applying perm lotion to wound hair

## HEALTH & SAFETY

Care should be taken when handling any substance the pH of which falls near the extremes of the scale, as it may cause injury to the skin.

## Processing time

Processing time is the length of time required for the hair strands to absorb the waving lotion (softening). It depends on the hair type (porosity, elasticity, length, density, texture and overall condition) and the specific perm lotion you are using. Again, follow the manufacturer's directions closely. It is usually safe to anticipate that the processing time will be less than suggested by the manufacturer or a client's previous record card. Some perms have stop-action processing so that all you have to do is set a timer (see Figure 8.39). Some perms give you a general timetable to follow and require that you do a test curl during processing. It is very important to time the perm process accurately to help prevent over- or under-processing.

The ability of the hair to absorb moisture may vary from time to time in the same individual, even when the same lotions and procedures are used. A record of the previous processing time is desirable, but should be used only as a guide.

It is sometimes necessary to saturate all the curlers a second time during processing. This might be due to:

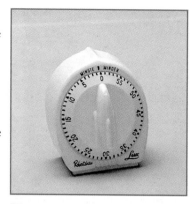

■ Figure 8.39 Processing timer

◆   evaporation of the lotion or dryness of the hair

◆   hair poorly saturated by the hairstylist

◆   no wave development after the maximum time indicated by the manufacturer

◆   improper selection of solution strength for the client's hair

◆   failure to follow the manufacturer's directions for a specific formula.

A reapplication of the lotion will hasten processing. Watch the wave development closely. Negligence can result in hair damage.

Most manufacturers provide instructions with their product. Here are some you will encounter.

◆   'Process at room temperature'. Make sure that your client is not sitting in a draught or too close to a heater. A room that is cool slows down the processing.

◆   'Place a plastic cap over the wrapped curlers'. Be sure that the plastic cap covers all the curlers and that the cap is airtight. Secure the cap with a non-metallic clip. The cap holds in scalp heat. If it is too loose or if all the rods are not covered, processing might take longer. A dry towel placed over the plastic cap will increase the effect and will reduce the influence of blasts of warm or cold air on parts of the head (producing uneven development).

◆   'Use a pre-heated dryer'. Turn the hood dryer to a high setting and medium airflow. Allow the dryer to warm up for approximately 5 minutes before placing your client under it. Cover the wound curlers with a plastic cap secured in place, locate the hood to enclose all of the curlers and reduce the heat to a medium setting. (Note: dryer filters should be cleaned frequently so that optimum heat and airflow will remain constant.) Take care not to over-process the hair, in particular porous hair.

◆   'Use an accelerator'. This may be used to aid the process of the perm. The curlers are not usually covered with a plastic cap. The accelerator must be located correctly and evenly around the head. Use the correct heat setting process, taking care not to allow the hair to become dry. In some cases these machines are programmable to particular lotions and hair types. Having located a sensor on the hair, it will regulate the processing.

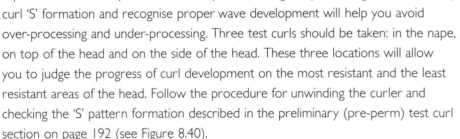

## Useful Task

Find out your salon's procedures for dealing with accidental spillage of lotions on to your clients.

# Testing curls during processing

Optimum curl development occurs only once during the processing time. The ability to read a test curl 'S' formation and recognise proper wave development will help you avoid over-processing and under-processing. Three test curls should be taken: in the nape, on top of the head and on the side of the head. These three locations will allow you to judge the progress of curl development on the most resistant and the least resistant areas of the head. Follow the procedure for unwinding the curler and checking the 'S' pattern formation described in the preliminary (pre-perm) test curl section on page 192 (see Figure 8.40).

# Water rinsing

Rinsing the waving lotion from the hair is extremely important. Any lotion left in the hair can cause poor perm results. When your test curl indicates that the optimum curl has been achieved, remove the cotton wool from around the hairline. Rinse the hair thoroughly with a moderate force of warm water. The manufacturer's perm directions will indicate for how long you should rinse – usually 3–5 minutes. Always set your timer for the exact time. Remember, you are rinsing the lotion out of the internal hair structure, not merely off the surface. Make sure that all curlers

■ Figure 8.40 A properly processed strand opens up into an 'S' formation

are thoroughly rinsed. Pay particular attention to the curlers at the nape of the neck. They are a little difficult to reach, but they must be rinsed as well as all the other curlers. Long hair and thick hair usually require the maximum rinsing time (5 minutes) to make sure that all lotion has been removed from all hair wrapped around the curlers. Indicator papers are available which, when pressed to the hair, will indicate if any perm lotion remains in the hair.

Undesirable effects of improper or incomplete rinsing include the following.

- **Early curl relaxation.** Even if the perm has been processed correctly, any waving lotion left in the hair can interfere with the action of the neutraliser. If the neutraliser is not able to properly rebond the hair, the curl will be weak or will not last very long.

- **Lightening of hair colour (natural or tint).** Rinsing helps reduce the pH of the hair and helps to close the cuticle layer. If the hair is not rinsed properly, the hydrogen peroxide in the neutraliser can react with waving lotion left in the hair and cause the hair colour to lighten. This lightening effect is usually seen on the hair ends.

- **Residual perm odour.** If any waving lotion is left in the hair, it will become trapped inside the hair when the neutraliser is applied. This is especially true of acid-balanced perms. Unpleasant odours may be evident each time the hair gets wet or damp.

# Blotting after water rinsing

Careful blotting ensures that the neutraliser will penetrate the hair immediately and completely: do not omit this important step. To obtain the best results from towel blotting, carefully press a towel between each curler, using your fingers. Do not rock or roll the rods while blotting. When the hair is in a softened state, any such movement can cause hair breakage. Change to dry towels frequently in order to remove as much excess water as possible. Excess water left in the hair can dilute or weaken the action of the neutraliser. If this happens the curl can be either weakened or relaxed.

After rinsing and blotting has been completed, place a fresh, clean band of moistened cotton wool around the hairline before applying neutraliser.

## Neutralising/normalising

Neutralising procedures can vary according to the perm product you are using. Again, follow the manufacturer's directions exactly.

In general, the following procedure is the accepted method of neutralising.

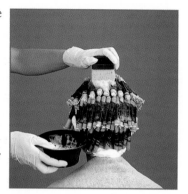

1    Apply neutraliser to the top and underside of the rods: apply to the top of the rod, then gently turn the rod up and apply to the underside of the rod in the same manner you applied the waving lotion. When using foam neutraliser, apply the neutraliser to the curlers and foam up (see Figure 8.41).

2    Repeat the entire application a second time, to ensure complete coverage.

3    Wait 5 minutes to allow for optimum rebonding. Set a timer for accuracy.

4    Remove the curlers carefully and gently, unwinding without tension as this may straighten the hair.

5    Work remaining neutraliser on to the ends of the hair, pushing the neutraliser on to the hair so as not to drag the curl.

■ Figure 8.41 Applying foam neutraliser

6    Rinse the hair thoroughly with warm water and apply an after-perm treatment if required.

7    Towel blot the hair and, using a wide-tooth comb, gently comb the hair into place.

If you are uncertain of the procedure, or whether an after-perm treatment should be applied, consult with your supervisor or stylist.

 *REMEMBER!*
*Promptly update your client's records to reflect the perm treatment provided.*

## Post-perm precautions

After blotting, the new perm is ready for final shaping and styling. It is important to avoid shampooing, conditioning, stretching or excessive manipulation of freshly permed hair. When styling, do not pull on the hair or use intense heat that could result in curl relaxation. Generally, hair should not be shampooed, conditioned, or treated harshly for 48 hours after perming. This special care will help to ensure that the perm does not relax.

## Cleaning up

1   Discard all used materials.

2   Clean up the work area.

3   Thoroughly clean and sterilise the curlers and other tools used.

4   Wash and dry your hands.

5   Complete your client's record card.

## Ten pointers for a perfect perm

1   Consult with your client.

2   Analyse the hair and scalp carefully.

3   Select the correct curler size for the desired style.

4   Choose the appropriate perm product for the hair type and final design. Follow the manufacturer's directions carefully.

5   Section and make accurate partings for each curler. Wrap specifically for the style chosen.

6   Apply waving lotion to the top and underside of all wound curlers, one at a time. Ensure each curler is thoroughly wet with lotion.

7   If the perm product requires a test curl, be sure the result is a firmly formed 'S' shape.

8   Water rinse for at least 3–5 minutes and carefully towel blot each curler.

*continued over*

## KEY SKILL TASK

*This task could produce evidence that supports C1.1, C1.2, C1.3, N1.1, N1.2 & N1.3*

*Discuss with your assessor or supervisor how you plan to undertake a perm on your client that s/he can observe and produce a record of observation or a witness testimony.*

◆   *Undertake a consultation and record your findings and agreements. It is likely you will use a consultation sheet and record card.*

◆   *Forecast the size, type and number of perm rods you will use, the winding technique you will use and any factors likely to influence your choices. Use the manufacturer's instructions, and visual aids to support your descriptions.*

◆   *Using the salon record card, record the products and quantities used, the perm rods used and the proportions of each size.*

◆   *Calculate your client's bill, the % commission you will earn and the VAT content of the bill. Present your findings and the records of the process, being prepared to explain your choices and justify your decisions.*

9   Apply neutraliser to the top and underside of all curlers. Saturate thoroughly. Wait 5 minutes; remove the curlers carefully, without pulling. Apply remaining neutraliser and gently work through the hair. Rinse with warm water.

10  Educate your client in how to care for their new look. Recommend haircare and styling products which are suitable. Instruct in how best to style the hair at home and remind your client not to shampoo the hair for at least 24 hours and to avoid getting the hair wet during that period.

# Chemical relaxing

Relaxing services are regular ongoing processes that form a large proportion of the chemical work carried out on clients with over-curly and/or African-Caribbean style hair. It is the essential skill of the hairstylist who wants to work on this type of hair.

Due to the high alkalinity of the chemicals used in the process it is essential that the hairstylist is fully conversant with the process and observes the safety precautions.

Chemical relaxing is the process of permanently rearranging the basic structure of very curly hair into a straight form, and relaxing perms to reshape overly curly hair into a more clearly defined open curl shape. When done professionally, it leaves the hair straight and in a satisfactory condition, ready to be set or dried into almost any style. Due to the nature of the chemicals used for permanently straightening hair, it is essential that you have a thorough understanding of their correct use.

## Chemical hair relaxing products

The basic products that are used in chemical hair relaxing are a chemical hair relaxer, a neutraliser and a petroleum cream, which is used as a protective base to protect your client's scalp during the sodium hydroxide chemical straightening process.

### Chemical hair relaxers

Two general types of hair relaxer are:

1   hydroxide, which does not require pre-shampooing

2   ammonium thioglycolate, which may require pre-shampooing.

The hydroxide relaxers are divided into two groups: sodium hydroxide and calcium hydroxide.

● Sodium hydroxide relaxers, sometimes called *lye* or *caustic soda*, generally have fast processing times and produce straightness that has a reduced likeliness to revert following shampooing. This caustic relaxer is often called a hair straightener; it both softens and swells hair fibres. As the solution penetrates into the cortex, the sulphur and hydrogen cross-bonds are broken. The action of the comb, the brush or the hands in smoothing the hair and distributing the chemical straightens the softened hair. Manufacturers vary the sodium hydroxide content of the solution from 5%–10% and the pH factor from 10–14. In general, the more sodium hydroxide used the higher the pH, the quicker the chemical reaction will take place on the hair, and the greater the danger will be of hair damage.

● Calcium hydroxide relaxers are sometimes called *no-lye*. These are not caustic soda based.

*HEALTH & SAFETY*

Due to the high alkaline content of sodium hydroxide, great care must be taken in its use: always wear protective gloves when handling and applying these products.

Although ammonium thioglycolate (a thio-type relaxer often called a *relaxer*) is less drastic in its action than sodium hydroxide, it softens and relaxes overly curly hair in much the same manner. You may recall that this is the same solution used in permanent waving.

## Neutraliser

The neutraliser is also called a *stabiliser* or *fixative*. The neutraliser stops the action of any chemical relaxer that may remain in the hair after rinsing. The neutraliser for a thio-type relaxer reforms the cysteine (sulphur) cross-bonds in their new position and rehardens the hair.

## Base and no-base formulas

Sodium hydroxide relaxers have two types of formula: base and no-base. The base formula requires the use of a petroleum cream that is designed to protect the client's skin and scalp during the sodium hydroxide chemical straightening process. This protective base is also important during a chemical straightening retouch. It is applied to protect hair that has been straightened previously, and to prevent over-processing and hair breakage.

Petroleum cream has a lighter consistency than petroleum jelly, and is formulated to melt at body temperature. The melting process ensures complete protective coverage of the scalp and other areas with a thin, oily coating. This helps to prevent burning and/or irritation of the scalp and skin. Previously treated hair should be protected with cream conditioner during the straightening process.

*No-base* relaxers are also available. These relaxers have the same chemical reaction on the hair, although usually the reaction is milder. The procedure for the application of a no-base relaxer is the same as for a normal relaxer except that the base cream is not applied. It is advisable to use a protective cream around the hairline and over the ears.

# Steps in chemical hair relaxing

All chemical hair relaxing involves three basic steps: processing, neutralising and conditioning.

## Processing

As soon as the chemical relaxer is applied, the hair begins to soften so that the chemical can penetrate to loosen and relax the natural curl.

## Neutralising

As soon as the hair has been sufficiently processed, the chemical relaxer is thoroughly rinsed out with warm water, followed by either a built-in shampoo neutraliser or a prescribed shampoo and neutraliser.

## Conditioning

Depending on your client's needs, the conditioner may be part of a series of hair treatments, or it may be applied to the hair before or after the relaxing treatment.

Hair treated with lighteners or metallic dyes must not be given a chemical hair relaxer, because it might suffer excessive damage or breakage.

## REMEMBER!

*Overly curly hair that has been damaged from heat appliances or other chemicals must be reconditioned before a relaxer service is performed.*

# Recommended strength of relaxer

The strength of relaxer used is determined by a strand test. The following guidelines can help in determining which strength relaxer to use for the test:

◆ fine, tinted or lightened hair – use mild relaxer

◆ normal, medium-textured virgin hair – use regular relaxer

◆ coarse virgin hair – use strong or super relaxer.

# Analysis of your client's hair

It is essential that you have a working knowledge of human hair, particularly when giving a relaxing treatment. You will learn to recognise the qualities of hair by visual inspection, feel and special tests. Before attempting to give a relaxing treatment to overly curly hair, you must judge its texture, porosity, elasticity and the extent, if any, of damage to the hair.

---

**RELAXER RECORD**

Name.................................................................Tel..............................................

Address ........................................................................................................

...............................................................................................................

**DESCRIPTION OF HAIR**

| Form | Length | Texture | | Porosity | |
|------|--------|---------|---|----------|---|
| ☐ wavy | ☐ short | ☐ coarse | ☐ soft | ☐ very porous | ☐ less porous |
| ☐ curly | ☐ medium | ☐ medium | ☐ silky | ☐ moderately | ☐ least |
| ☐ extra-curly | ☐ long | ☐ fine | ☐ wiry | porous | porous |
| | | | | ☐ normal | ☐ resistant |

**Condition**

☐ virgin          ☐ retouched          ☐ dry          ☐ oily          ☐ lightened

Tinted with ................................................................................................

Previously relaxed with (name of relaxer).................................................................

☐ Original sample of hair enclosed          ☐ not enclosed

**TYPE OF RELAXER OR STRAIGHTENER**

☐ whole head                              ☐ retouch

☐ retouch ............... strength...............          ☐ straightener............. strength...............

**Results**

☐ good          ☐ poor          ☐ sample of relaxed hair enclosed          ☐ not enclosed

Date                          Operator     Date                          Operator

.................................................          .................................................

.................................................          .................................................

---

■ Figure 8.42 Relaxer record

## Your client's hair history

To help ensure consistent, satisfactory results, records should be kept of each chemical hair-relaxing treatment. These records should include the client's hair history and all products and conditioners used (see sample form in Figure 8.42). You should be sure to find out if your client has ever had hair-relaxing treatment before. If so, was there any adverse reaction? You must not chemically relax hair that has been treated with a metallic dye. To do so will damage and destroy the hair. In addition, it is not advisable to use chemical relaxers on hair that has been bleached lighter.

Before starting to process the hair, you must know how the client will react to the relaxer. Therefore, the client must receive:

◆ a thorough scalp and hair examination

◆ a hair strand test.

## Scalp examination

Inspect the scalp carefully for eruptions, scratches or abrasions. To obtain a clearer view of the scalp, part the hair into 1cm-deep sections. Hair parting may be done with the first and second fingers or with the handle of a tail comb. In either case, you must exercise great care not to scratch the scalp. Such scratches may become seriously infected when aggravated by the chemicals in the relaxer (see Figure 8.43).

If your client has scalp eruptions or abrasions, do not apply the chemical hair relaxer until the scalp is healthy. If the hair is not in a healthy condition, prescribe a series of conditioning treatments to return it to a more normal condition. Then you may give a strand test.

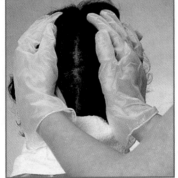
■ Figure 8.43 Examining the scalp

## Strand tests

To help you estimate the results you may expect to get from chemical relaxing, it is advisable to test the hair for porosity and elasticity. This can be done using one of the following strand tests.

### Finger test

A finger test determines the degree of porosity of the hair. Grasp a strand of hair and run it between the thumb and first finger of the right hand, from the end towards the scalp. If it ruffles or feels bumpy, the hair is porous and can absorb moisture.

### Pull test

This test determines the degree of elasticity in the hair. Normally, dry curly hair will stretch by about 20% of its normal length without breaking. Grasp half a dozen strands from the crown area and pull them gently. If the hair appears to stretch, it has elasticity and can withstand the relaxer. If not, conditioning treatments are recommended prior to a chemical relaxing treatment.

### Relaxer test

Application of the relaxer to a hair strand will indicate the reaction of the relaxer on the hair. Take a small section of hair from the crown or another area where the hair is wiry and resistant. Pull it through a slit in a piece of aluminium foil placed as close to the scalp as possible. Apply relaxer to the strand in the same manner as you would apply it to the entire head. Process the strand until it is sufficiently relaxed, checking the strand every 3–5 minutes. Make careful notes of timing, the smoothing required and the hair strength. Shampoo the relaxer from the strand only, towel dry and cover with protective cream to avoid damage during the relaxing service. If breakage has occurred, you should do another strand test using a milder solution (see Figure 8.44).

# Chemical hair relaxing process (with sodium hydroxide)

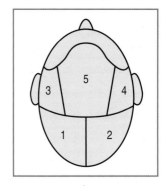

Figure 8.44 Relaxer strand test

The procedure outlined below is based primarily on products containing sodium hydroxide. For this or any other kind of product, follow the manufacturer's directions.

## Preparation

1    Select and arrange the required equipment, implements and materials.

2    Wash and dry your hands.

3    Seat your client comfortably. Remove earrings and neck jewellery; adjust towel and shampoo cape.

4    Examine and evaluate the scalp and hair.

5    Give a strand test and check results.

6    Do not shampoo hair. (Hair ends may be trimmed after application of hair relaxer.)

7    Check the client's record card.

## Procedure

1    Part hair into four or five sections (see Figures 8.45 and 8.46).

2    Dry the hair. If moisture or perspiration is present on the scalp because of excessive heat or humidity, place your client under a cool dryer for several minutes.

3    Apply protective base. Manufacturers recommend the use of a protective base to protect the scalp from the strong chemicals in the relaxer. To apply it properly, subdivide each of the four or five major sections into 1 to 2cm partings to permit thorough scalp coverage (see Figure 8.47).

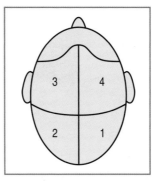

Figure 8.45 Part hair into four sections

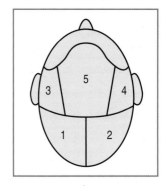

Figure 8.46 Part hair into five sections; three sections in front area, two sections in back area

Apply the base freely to the entire scalp with your fingers. The hairline around the forehead, nape of the neck, and area over and around the ears must be completely covered. Complete coverage is important to protect the scalp and hairline from irritation.

## Applying the conditioner-filler

In many cases a conditioner-filler is required before the chemical relaxer can be used. The conditioner-filler, usually a protein polymer product, is applied to the entire head of hair when dry. It protects over-porous or slightly damaged hair from being over-processed on any part of the hair shaft. It evens out the porosity of the hair shaft, and permits uniform distribution and action of the chemical relaxer.

To give the full benefit of the conditioner-filler, rub it gently on to the hair from the scalp to the hair ends, using either the hands or a comb. Then towel dry the hair or use a cool dryer to completely dry the hair.

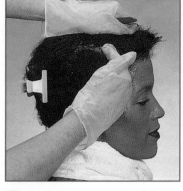

■ Figure 8.47 Applying protective base

## Applying the relaxer

Divide the head into four or five sections, in the same manner as for the application of the protective base.

The processing cream is applied last to the scalp area and hair ends. Body heat will speed up the processing action at the scalp. The hair is more porous at the ends and may be damaged. In both these areas, less processing time is required and, therefore, the relaxer is applied last to these parts.

 # REMEMBER!

*When using a no-base relaxer, a protective base is not necessary. It is recommended that a protective cream be used on the hairline and around the ears.*

There are three methods in general use for the application of the chemical hair relaxer: the comb method, the brush method and the finger method.

### Comb method

Remove a quantity of relaxing cream from the tub, using a spatula. Beginning at the back-right section of the head, carefully part off 0.5–1 cm of hair, depending on its thickness and curliness. Apply the relaxer with the back of the comb, starting 0.5–1 cm from the scalp, and spread to within 1 cm of the hair ends. First apply the relaxer to the top side of the strand (see Figure 8.48). Then raise the subsection and apply the relaxer underneath. Gently lay the completed strand up, out of the way (see Figure 8.49).

■ Figure 8.48 Applying relaxer on top of strand

■ Figure 8.49 Applying relaxer underneath strand

Complete the right-back area and, moving in a clockwise direction, cover each section of the head in the same manner. Then, go back over the head in the same order, applying additional relaxing cream if necessary, and spreading the relaxer close to the scalp and up to the hair ends. Avoid excessive pressure or stretching of the hair.

Smoothing the cream through the hair not only spreads the cream, but also stretches the hair gently into a straight position.

An alternative technique is to begin application at the nape, approximately 2 cm from the hairline, and continue towards the crown. The last place to apply relaxer is at the hairline. Be guided by the manufacturer's instructions.

### Brush or finger method

The brush or finger method of applying the relaxer to the hair is the same as the comb method, except that the brush or fingers and palms are used instead of the back of the comb.

## Periodic strand testing

While spreading the relaxer, inspect its action by stretching the strands to see how fast the natural curls are being removed. Another method of testing is to press the strand to the scalp using the back of the comb or your finger. Examine the strand after your finger is removed. If it lies smoothly, the strand is sufficiently relaxed; if the strand revert or *beads* back away from the scalp, continue processing.

## Rinsing out the relaxer

When the hair has been sufficiently straightened, rinse the relaxer out rapidly and thoroughly. The water must be warm, not hot (see Figure 8.50). If the water is too hot, it may burn the client and cause discomfort because of the very sensitive condition of the scalp. If the water is too cold, it will not stop the processing action. The direct force of the rinse water should be used to remove the relaxer and avoid tangling the hair. Part hair with fingers to make sure no traces of the relaxer remain. Unless the relaxer is completely removed, its chemical action will continue on the hair. The stream of water should be directed from the scalp to the hair ends.

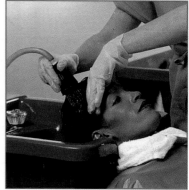

■ Figure 8.50 Rinsing out relaxer

## Shampooing/neutralising

When the hair is thoroughly rinsed, neutralise the hair as directed by the manufacturer's directions. Most manufacturers provide a neutralising shampoo that is applied to the hair after rinsing. Others prescribe the use of a non-alkaline or cream shampoo followed by a neutraliser.

Gently work the shampoo into the hair. Take care to avoid tangling the hair or breaking any fragile ends. Manipulate the shampoo by working with the fingers underneath the hair, not on top. Rinse with warm water, making sure to keep the hair straight. Repeat the shampoo until the hair lathers well and all the relaxer is removed (see Figure 8.51).

After shampooing, completely saturate the hair with the neutraliser if it is required by the manufacturer. Begin at the nape, and comb carefully with a wide-toothed comb, working upwards towards the forehead. Use the comb to:

■ Figure 8.51 Shampooing the hair

- ◆ keep the hair straight
- ◆ ensure complete saturation with the neutraliser
- ◆ remove any tangles without pulling.

■ Figure 8.52 Straightened hair

Time the neutraliser as directed and rinse thoroughly. Towel blot gently.
Condition hair as necessary and proceed with styling (see Figure 8.52). Discard used materials. Clean and sterilise equipment. Wash and dry your hands. Complete the record of all timings and treatments during the service, and file the record card.

## Applying the conditioner

Many manufacturers recommend that you apply a conditioner before setting the hair, to offset the harshness of the sodium hydroxide in the relaxer and to help preserve some of the natural oils of the scalp and hair.

Two types of conditioner are available: cream-type and protein-type.

### Cream-type conditioners

These are applied to the scalp and hair, and then rinsed out carefully. The hair is then towel dried. Apply setting lotion, set the hair on rollers, dry and style the hair in the usual manner.

 REMEMBER!

*Because of the fragile condition of the hair, it is advisable to wind the hair on the roller without great tension.*

### Protein-type (liquid) conditioners

These are applied to the scalp and hair prior to hair setting and allowed to remain in the hair to serve as a setting lotion. Set the hair on rollers, dry and style in the usual manner.

# Sodium hydroxide retouch

Hair grows about 0.5–1.25cm per month. A retouch should probably be done every 6 weeks to 2 months, depending on how quickly your client's hair grows.

Follow all the steps for a chemical hair relaxing treatment, with one exception: apply the relaxer only to the new growth. In order to prevent previously treated hair from breaking, apply a cream conditioner over the hair that received the earlier treatment, thus avoiding overlap and damage.

# Two-step perming

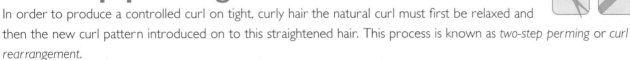

In order to produce a controlled curl on tight, curly hair the natural curl must first be relaxed and then the new curl pattern introduced on to this straightened hair. This process is known as *two-step perming* or *curl rearrangement*.

A solution (curl rearranger) containing ammonium thioglycolate is applied to the tight curly hair. The hair is relaxed to a straight curl pattern. This solution is then rinsed from the hair.

A milder solution of ammonium thioglycolate is applied and the hair is wound on to large perm rods and processed, often under a pre-heated dryer. Once processed, the hair is rinsed with water.

A neutraliser, usually containing sodium bromate (which will not lighten the hair in the way that a hydrogen peroxide-based neutraliser can) is applied, processed and then the curlers are removed and the hair conditioned.

---

## REMEMBER!

*Always read and follow the manufacturer's directions. These may vary slightly between different manufacturers.*

---

# The method of perming

1   Only shampoo the hair if it is heavily oiled, as oil may create a barrier. If shampooing is required, do not use hot water or stimulate the scalp by rubbing. It is better if the hair is shampooed a few days earlier. Remove any tangles from the hair (see Figure 8.53).

2   Hair that is fragile due to heat or chemical treatment should be treated with a protective polymer pre-treatment (conditioner/filler). This provides a protective coating of polymer to the hair This is usually dried on to the hair.

3   Apply protective cream to the complete hairline and divide the hair into four. Apply the rearranger to small sections, to within 0.5cm of the scalp, starting at the most resistant areas of the head (see Figure 8.54).

4   Once the application is complete, cover with a plastic cap and a towel.

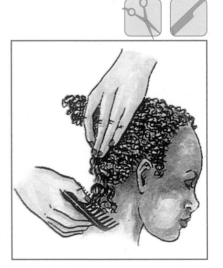

■ Figure 8.53 Remove tangles from hair

Do not allow the product to dry out. Follow the manufacturer's guidance for timing. Process until the hair is straight, and take care not to over-process as this may result in hair breakage.

5   The rearranger is then rinsed from the hair, taking care not to tangle the hair.

6   Section the hair, taking care as the hair will be fragile. The hair may be wound following the orthodox nine-section pattern or by brick winding.

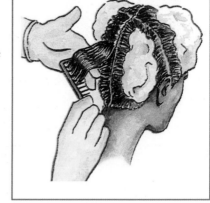

■ Figure 8.54 Part hair into sections and coat with thiogel

 REMEMBER!

*Hair that has already been relaxed should not be given a curly perm.*

7   Perm curler sections should be half the depth of the perm rods. The sections of hair should be over-directed, that is combed up and away from the direction of the wind. This will ensure controlled curl as close to the scalp as possible.

8   Wind evenly, without tension, using the width of the curler. The ends are protected using end tissues; fragile hair should be protected.

9   Protect your client by placing barrier cream around the hairline followed with a moist cotton wool strip. Then, using the applicator, apply the curl booster, ensuring complete coverage of the wound hair (see Figures 8.55 and 8.56).

10  Cover the head with a plastic cap and process under a pre-heated dryer, following the manufacturer's guidance for timing (see Figure 8.57).

11  Check the processing, taking samples from various areas of the head. Gently unwind a curler for

■ Figure 8.55 Protect client's skin with cotton wool around hairline

■ Figure 8.56 Apply the gel to curls

■ Figure 8.57 Process under pre-heated drier

■ Figure 8.58 Test a curl

half of its length and gently push the hair towards the scalp. A full 'S' shape indicates full development (see Figure 8.58).

12    Once the hair is fully processed, rinse the wound curlers with tepid water to remove the curl booster from the hair (see Figure 8.59).

13    Blot the wound curlers thoroughly.

14    Re-apply barrier cream and moist cotton wool to the client's hairline and then apply the neutraliser (see Figures 8.60 and Figure 8.61).

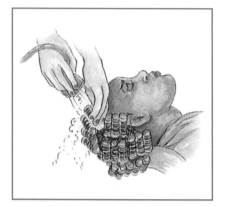

■ Figure 8.59 Rinse the hair

■ Figure 8.60 Apply neutraliser

■ Figure 8.61 Work neutraliser through hair

15    Rinse the neutraliser thoroughly from the hair, blot dry and then remove the perm rods, gently and without any tension.

16    Condition the hair thoroughly. This should be followed by the application of a scalp conditioner to compensate for the drying effect.

17    The hair may now be styled (see Figures 8.62 and 8.63).

■ Figure 8.62 Style hair

■ Figure 8.63 Finished

# Two-step perm retouch

The main difference between the two-step perm and the two-step perm retouch is that the curl rearranger is applied only to the regrowth area. The protective polymer lotion will protect the previously treated hair when the curl booster is applied.

# After-care

It should be remembered that the chemical processes described within this chapter cause damage to the hair, making it become dry and brittle. Excessive or incorrect use of strong chemicals on the hair can result in severe hair breakage.

Following straightening processes clients should be informed of how best to care for their hair. This is an opportunity to guide your client in the selection and purchase of suitable products to moisturise their hair. There are shampoos that will replace the oils lost and moisturise the hair, preventing further damage from atmospheric conditions. Deep-penetrating conditioners, usually containing protein, should be recommended for use.

Styling lotions should be suggested to suit the method of styling, as well as setting lotions which contain protein and will strengthen the hair. For curly looks, curl activators may be used to maintain the level of moisture and oil in the hair.

# KEY SKILL TASK

*This task could produce evidence that supports CI.I, CI.2, CI.3, NI.I, NI.2 & NI.3.*

*Discuss with your assessor or supervisor how you plan to undertake a two-step perm that s/he can observe and produce a record of observation or a witness testimony.*

1. *Undertake a consultation and record your findings and agreements. It is likely you will use a consultation sheet and record card.*
2. *Forecast the size, type and number of perm rods you will use, the winding technique you will use and any factors likely to influence your choices. Use the manufacturer's instructions, and visual aids to support your descriptions.*
3. *Using the salon record card, record the products and quantities used, the perm rods used and the proportions of each size.*
4. *Calculate your client's bill, the % commission you will earn and the VAT content of the bill. Present your findings and the records of the process, being prepared to explain your choices and justify your decisions.*

## Useful Task

By undertaking this task you will demonstrate that you know what products and equipment are required to carry out either a perm or relaxer in your salon. You can use this to refer to or as a guide for colleagues undertaking your role in your absence.

Prepare a checklist of materials needed when undertaking a perm or relaxer in your salon. Include in your list the equipment (including numbers) that are required, as well as the products needed to prepare the client and provide the service. Produce a diagram to indicate how these items should be set out ready for the task.

## Self review

1. What does the pH scale indicate?

2. What is the pH range for acid-balanced permanent waves?

3. Name the main active ingredient in acid-balanced waving lotions.

4. List the seven stages of perming.

5. What does porosity refer to in connection with hair and perming?

6. What type of shampoo should be used on hair when preparing it for perming?

7. At what angle to the head should the hair mesh normally be held when perm winding?

8. What impact does heat have on the processing of a perm?

9. Why is it important to thoroughly blot hair dry following water rinsing before neutralising?

10. How should perm curlers be unwound from the hair following the application of neutraliser?

11. Name two chemicals often used in chemical hair relaxing products.

12. What does the term *base* mean in relation to hair relaxation processes?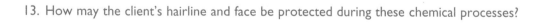

13. How may the client's hairline and face be protected during these chemical processes?

14. What are the three main stages of the chemical hair relaxation process?

15. What is a strand test used for?

16. How should hairdressers protect themselves when working with relaxing/straightening substances?

17. How close to the scalp should straightening products be applied?

18. What are the main stages of a two-step perm?

19. What is meant by over-directing when curler winding?

20. What tension should be used when winding hair during a two-step perm?

# Useful contacts

| | |
|---|---|
| Afro products websites: | www.afroshack.co.uk |
| | www.blacklikeme.co.uk |
| | www.streetsaheadbrixton.co.uk |
| Clynol | www.clynol.com |
| Goldwell | www.goldwell.com |
| HABIA | www.habia.org.uk |
| L'Oréal | www.loreal.co.uk |
| Wella (GB) | www.wella.co.uk |

## CHAPTER 9

# Massaging the scalp

## CHAPTER CONTENTS

**Unit H18** Provide scalp massage services

## WHAT THIS CHAPTER WILL PROVIDE

This chapter provides you with guidance in a range of scalp massage techniques. You will be able to select appropriate methods for your client's particular needs and be aware of those occasions when scalp massage is contra-indicated.

## Scalp massage

Massage has a beneficial impact on the scalp. These benefits include:

◆ increased capillary blood flow (*erythema*); blood brings nourishment to the papilla of the hair root

◆ improved removal of waste products; the lymphatic flow removes waste products produced from metabolism

◆ stimulated sebaceous glands that produce the hair and skin's natural oil

◆ soothing and relaxing the client.

Scalp massage can be provided by hand and/or mechanically. In most cases it is undertaken when the hair and scalp are lubricated with an oil or cream. This enables the massage to be given without causing discomfort to the client.

## KEY WORDS

**Erythema** – *increased capillary blood flow*

In most cases it is unwise to undertake scalp massage when the following are present:

◆ open sores or cuts on the scalp

◆ contagious disorders

◆ fresh scar tissue.

## Massage media

In most cases when undertaking scalp massage the hair and scalp should be lubricated. This allows the hands and other massage tools to move without causing discomfort to the client. Most massage media also have additional benefits in conditioning either the hair or scalp. One notable exception to the requirement for lubrication is high frequency, when the hair must be completely dry when undertaking the treatment (see page 218).

## Vegetable oils

Most vegetable oils can be used beneficially on the hair. They are used to treat dry and brittle hair. The oil should be applied to dry hair, usually before shampooing. If external heat is applied to the oil it will become more liquid and can run on to the client's neck and face. Vegetable oil can be difficult to remove from the hair following the treatment. To remove add shampoo to the oiled hair and massage into a lather before adding any water and shampooing in the normal way. Sulphonated oil will emulsify with water and is therefore more easily removed following treatment.

**KEY WORDS**

**Sulphonated vegetable oil** – *usually castor oil that has been treated to be soluble in water*

---

**REMEMBER!**

*Always read manufacturer's guidelines in safe working practices and use of personal protective clothing.*

---

## Treatment conditioners

These creams have additives that can penetrate the scalp and hair. Always follow manufacturer's guidelines when selecting the product to use and when using it.

## Treatment shampoos

Some shampoos from treatment ranges remain on the hair and scalp before finally being rinsed away. During this time their action can sometimes be enhanced by massage.

# Massage techniques

## Hand massage techniques

### Effleurage

Effleurage is a soothing stroking movement using the pads of the fingers and the palms of the hands. It is used to aid the distribution of the increased capillary blood flow (see Figure 9.1).

## Petrissage

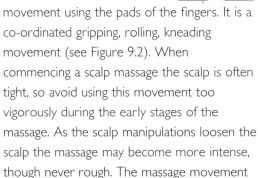

Petrissage is a deep movement using the pads of the fingers. It is a co-ordinated gripping, rolling, kneading movement (see Figure 9.2). When commencing a scalp massage the scalp is often tight, so avoid using this movement too vigorously during the early stages of the massage. As the scalp manipulations loosen the scalp the massage may become more intense, though never rough. The massage movement should follow an organised pattern over the

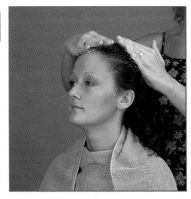

■ Figure 9.1 Effleurage massage movement

■ Figure 9.2 Petrissage massage movement

scalp with both hands using an even pressure. Take care not to exert too much pressure on the sensitive areas of the scalp: the temporal and mastoid areas.

> REMEMBER!
> Massage should be soothing and should not cause your client pain.

## Tapotement

This is a percussive tapping movement. This should be undertaken gently on the scalp as there is little tissue on this area of the body.

## Vibrations

A light trembling movement performed by placing the flat of the palms on the scalp and vibrating the forearm.

## Friction

These are brisk tweaking movements on the scalp. This movement is often used with a stimulating perfumed spirit that is called *friction lotion*. This product is often used to combat greasy scalp conditions.

# Mechanical massage

## Vibro massage: direct

You may provide scalp massage using vibro massage. The hair and scalp should be lubricated with a suitable massage oil or cream. The vibro massager is a gun-like apparatus with a spike applicator. Ensure that the applicator is attached firmly to the vibro massager. Gently press the applicator on to the scalp and move it in small circular movements in an organised pattern over the scalp (see Figure 9.3). Lift the applicator away from the hair and scalp occasionally to prevent tangling the hair. This must be done more frequently if you are massaging the scalp of a client with long hair.

When using the vibro massage on your client for the first time, allow the client to become accustomed to its sensation by applying it for a few moments to the back of their hand. The direction of the treatment may be extended gradually, at each application, to a maximum of ten minutes.

The applicator should be washed, dried and sterilised after each use.

## Vibro massage: indirect

In indirect massage your hands become the applicators that make contact with your client's scalp. A specialised vibro massager is attached to the back of the hands, causing them to vibrate. The hands then perform the petrissage and effleurage movements on the client's scalp. The hair and scalp should be lubricated with a suitable massage oil or cream.

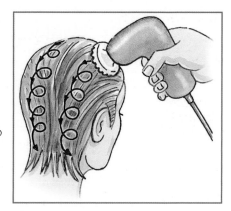

■ Figure 9.3 Using a vibro massager on the scalp

# REMEMBER!

*Your salon may have procedures for visually checking electrical appliances and reporting faults. Find out what your salon's procedures are for this.*

## High frequency

High frequency is an electrical form of massage that may be used on the scalp. It is used to stimulate blood flow in the capillaries in the treatment of hair loss. The apparatus produces small electrical sparks between its electrodes and the client's scalp.

This massage is usually provided through a programme of regular treatments. While it increases blood flow that can aid hair growth, the hairdresser would be unwise to undertake any form of guarantee to that effect.

The apparatus consists of a case containing a vulcanite handle connected to the high frequency machine which has a range of controls and dials. The exact layout will vary between manufacturers. There are three electrodes that fit snugly into the holder; these are:

1   bulb

2   rake or comb

3   saturator.

Each electrode has a specific use.

### Bulb

This is a glass electrode with a bulb shape at the end and filled with an inert gas. This is used around the hairline and on bald patches. Work the bulb in small circular movements around the area of hair loss.

### Rake or comb

This is a glass electrode with prongs similar to a rake or comb and filled with an inert gas. This is pushed through areas of thinning hair.

> REMEMBER!
>
> *Always follow the manufacturer's guidelines when using the high frequency apparatus.*

### Saturator

This metal tube is held by the client, and the hairdresser's hands, acting as the electrodes, massage the scalp.

The treatment is carried out on hair when it is dry. Seat your client and gown them to protect their clothing. Gently brush the hair to remove any tangles that may otherwise snag the electrodes. The hairdresser should remove any jewellery on the hands and the client should remove jewellery from the head and scalp area. With the machine switched off, gently but firmly locate the electrode in the holder. Turn the machine on, select the setting required and gradually raise the frequency until the electrode shows a purple light and a crackling sound is heard. With one finger touching the electrode, locate it on to the client's scalp and move it on the scalp. Ensure the electrode maintains contact with the scalp. Lifting the electrode from the scalp will cause sparks to occur. The finger may be removed while the electrode is in contact with the scalp. The finger contact prevents the sparking occurring as the electrode nears the scalp. Remake the finger contact to the electrode just prior to its removal from the scalp.

When using the saturator the client holds the electrode with one hand and has the other on the holder. The hairdresser places one hand on the client's scalp and uses the other to switch the machine on, select the setting and gradually increase the frequency. The hairdresser's hands, in effect, become the electrode with small sparks occurring between the client's scalp and the hairdresser's fingers. The client will not experience any sensation between their hands and the electrode itself.

> REMEMBER!
>
> *When used on clients for the first time, the treatment can be quite imposing so explain fully to your clients what to expect and allow them to feel the effect on the back of their hand.*

The duration of the treatment can be extended as the client becomes used to the sensation. It should be discontinued if the client experiences any pain. The client's scalp will colour as capillary blood flow is increased (erythema).

When the treatment is completed the electrodes should be cleaned and sterilised. The glass electrodes are most easily cleaned using denatured alcohol.

### Contra-indications

Do not use on clients:

◆ of a nervous disposition

◆ with scalp cuts or abrasions

◆ who are pregnant

◆ whose hair is wet, very greasy or contains excessive hairspray or dressings.

Do not use:

◆ with wet hands

◆ near concentrations of metal.

# Anatomy

Massage has a penetrating effect on the body. More information about the hair and scalp is given in Chapter 13. Figures 9.4 and 9.5 indicate the skeletal and muscular structures beneath the skin of the head and neck.

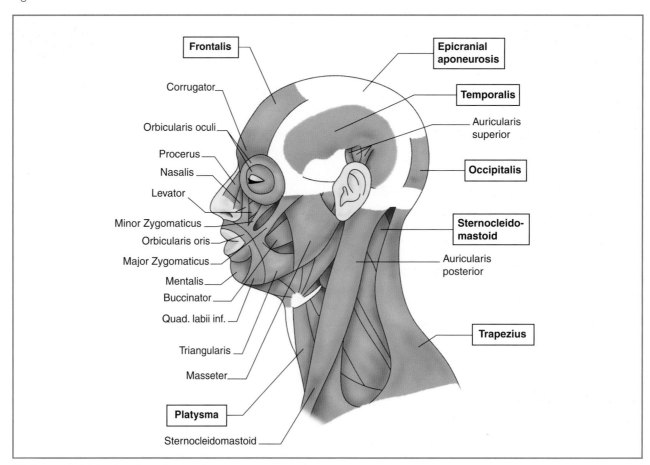

■ Figure 9.4 Head and neck muscles

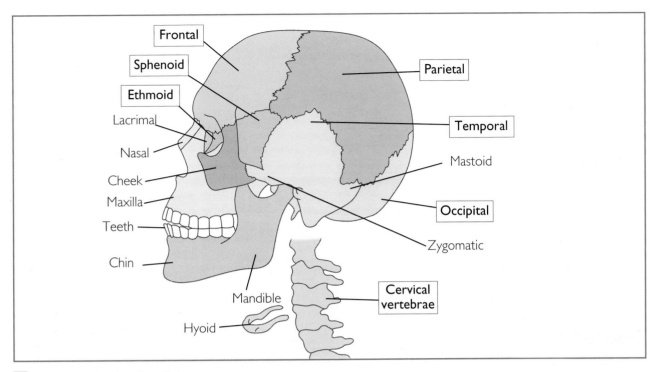

■ Figure 9.5 Head and neck bones

## Self review

1. What is erythema?

2. State one contra-indication to scalp massage.

3. What type of vegetable oil will emulsify with water?

4. Describe the effleurage massage movement.

5. Describe the petrissage massage movement.

6. Describe the friction massage movement.

7. What type of applicator is used with the vibro massager?

8. In what state should hair be during high frequency?

9. Which high frequency electrode is used on areas of thinning hair?

10. What does the lymphatic system do?

## Useful contacts

HABIA                    www.habia.org.uk

Institute of Trichologists    www.trichologists.org.uk

# Receiving clients

## CHAPTER CONTENTS

## WHAT THIS CHAPTER WILL PROVIDE

This chapter provides guidance in the practical and essential knowledge you need to understand for effective client reception and the phasing of client appointments. This includes welcoming and receiving people entering the salon, responding to enquiries, making appointments, and maintaining a tidy and effective reception.

## Your client's first impressions

The salon reception area is usually one of the first points of contact that your client has with the salon. This contact may be either by their visit to the salon or by the telephone contact made when your client calls to make an appointment. It is therefore at this stage that the initial image of the salon and its customer orientation is perceived by your client.

When your client first visits the salon, their first impression will be of the facade of the salon and the display provided in the salon window. New clients must make the conscious decision to enter the salon, and the way they are greeted and their enquiry is handled will shape the view that they have of the salon. Receptionists have a crucial role in this, putting the client at ease and ensuring their needs are identified and fulfilled.

When a new client makes contact by telephone, the response received will be all that influences the client and is therefore a crucial part of the process.

# REMEMBER!

*When clients visit the salon for the first time, they may feel vulnerable. Ensure that you guide these clients in the procedures of the salon and the location of cloakrooms, toilets and other client facilities. A client who is made aware of what to expect will feel more relaxed and more likely to enjoy their visit (see Figure 10.1).*

## The role of the receptionist

The reception function may vary from salon to salon. In some salons the role is carried out by a dedicated receptionist (someone whose job is solely to be the receptionist), in others it is carried out by the hairstylists as part of their overall duties. Whoever carries out the function and in whatever way this is done, their objective is the same throughout: to attend to enquiries and to phase appointments effectively, to manage the allocation of work and satisfy the client's expectations. This contributes to the success of the salon.

Figure 10.1 Hairdressing reception area

## The receptionist's duties

◆ Responding to clients' enquiries, either by telephone or when they visit.

◆ Scheduling appointments to ensure allocation of work in a way that is manageable by the hairstylist.

◆ Informing hairstylists of their clients' arrival.

◆ Ensuring the comfort of clients while they wait.

◆ Referring clients to the relevant person to fulfil their needs.

◆ Calculating client bills, recording and collecting payments.

◆ Receiving sales representatives and other visitors, and directing them to appropriate person.

◆ A point of sale for retail goods (see Figure 10.2).

Figure 10.2 The hairdresser as sales person

## Qualities of a receptionist

This person should be organised, as they will be organising others and their workloads. They will project the salon's image and will therefore be expected to have an appropriate appearance. Clear speech, together with the ability to communicate effectively, are essential features of a good receptionist.

## Maintaining the reception area

The reception area is usually the first area inside the salon the client sees (see Figure 10.3). Often they will spend a little time in this area, time enough to form opinions about the salon. At the beginning of the working day ensure:

◆ the area is clean and tidy, bins should be empty, floor surfaces clean and chairs, etc. tidy; the reception desk should be free of scraps of paper from the previous day and if an appointment book is used this should be open to that day's page; any magazines and style books should be tidied; damaged magazines should be removed from the reception

◆ there are adequate supplies of appointment cards, bill books (if used), pencils, message pads and other relevant stationery

◆ retail product displays are clean and filled to the correct level – clients will not wish to purchase products that are dusty or appear to be the last of the line

◆ supplies of refreshments for clients are adequate – this may include water and cups in a water cooler, coffee and tea supplies in the refreshment preparation area.

■ Figure 10.3 Clean and tidy reception area

At set times and whenever required throughout the day you should check to ensure that the area is clean and tidy and that levels of supplies are maintained. It is good practice to:

◆ become accustomed to reviewing the condition of the reception area throughout the day and respond to any requirements throughout the salon's opening times

◆ when levels of stationery or stock are low report this to your supervisor so that more can be supplied

◆ if you notice any faulty products remove these from the display and report them to your supervisor.

 *REMEMBER!*

*The client who arrives at the end of the day will have the same expectations and requirements for an effective and pleasant reception experience as the one that arrives in the morning.*

## KEY SKILL TASK

*This task could produce evidence that supports C1.2 & C1.3.*

*Create a checklist for all of the things that require checking each day in the reception area. Within this list include indicators of how many of consumable items are required. Items to be checked may include:*

- *empty and clean bins*
- *tidy the reception desk*
- *dust display stock and top up display.*

*Consumable items may include:*

- *appointment cards*
- *bill books*
- *magazines*
- *cups.*

# Attending to visitors to the salon

## Clients

All clients who step over the threshold of the salon should be greeted promptly and courteously, with a smile and with body language which reflects pleasure in helping them. Greet clients, introducing yourself and asking how you may help them (see Figure 10.4). If you are already attending to a client and another enters the salon make eye contact and acknowledge their presence. This will assure the client of your awareness of their presence. If a colleague is available ask them to respond to the client; if this is not an option ensure that you deal with their needs as soon as you have satisfied the needs of the person you are currently dealing with. You will require patience, as clients may be uncertain of their needs. They may require guidance and advice. Establish the client's requirements, which may range from purchasing retail products to seeking advice on their haircare, making an appointment for a hairdressing service to keeping an appointment or even to meeting a business associate in the salon. The receptionist may be able to handle many enquiries, but the client who requires advice and guidance over and above the scope of the receptionist should be invited to wait while a suitable person is promptly informed or a consultation is arranged.

When a client arrives to keep an appointment s/he should, if possible, be greeted by name, the appointment details should be checked and the relevant member of staff informed of their arrival.

**Figure 10.4 Receptionist greeting client**

Advice given to clients, about suitable services or retail products should be accurate and given in a clear manner. If in any doubt the receptionist should seek advice from a specialist within the salon. Knowledge of the features and benefits of services as well as of retail products is an essential aspect of the receptionist's skill. The cost of these should also be readily available.

Some clients may wish to make a complaint. If this occurs remain calm and objective. A complaint should not be viewed as criticism of your work. If uncertain of how to proceed, or if you do not have the authority to deal with a complaint politely, ask the client to take a seat and promptly refer them to the person with authority. You may say you are sorry that they have a complaint but, at this stage, do not admit to being at fault. Those clients who appear angry are best responded to by remaining calm and seating the client in a quiet part of the salon where the matter can be dealt with in confidence. Identify the cause of their anger and then undertake to address the issues one at a time. Big issues when handled in small stages can often appear quite minor. The following are points of good practice.

◆ Discussions are best undertaken when both people are seated. Make eye contact and avoid confrontational body language. This may include crossing the arms as a barrier, pointing fingers at people while you talk and talking into people's faces.

◆ When listening to the client, nod your head or comment to show you are listening.

◆ Recap your perceptions of a problem to the client to check your correct understanding.

◆ Ask closed questions – requiring yes or no for an answer – to gain agreement.

◆ Use open-ended questions – why, what, when, how, who – to gain information.

◆ Listen to your client but should the client become emotional step in and summarise.

◆ Check client records to determine recorded actions.

◆ Do not apportion guilt or blame before you have all of the information.

◆ You may need to speak with more than one person to verify the accuracy and authenticity of a complaint.

◆ Remain calm and objective; use language that does not infer prior judgement and ensure the client understands what is being said.

◆ Do not make decisions if you need more information but defer to a later date.

 # REMEMBER!

*If you feel you are unable to handle a client's problems refer to your supervisor.*

## Things to avoid

Do not …

◆ … keep clients waiting for service while you carry on a conversation about a non-work-related issue with colleagues; always acknowledge the client's presence even if you are unable to attend to them straight away due to a prior commitment

◆ … allow any displeasure or harassment to show in your greeting to the client; your client should be the centre of your attention

◆ ... keep clients waiting without informing them of possible delays and the reasons for these; in the case of lengthy delays, consider options which the client may prefer, a revised appointment or alternative stylist; this is usually avoided through effective phasing of appointments

◆ ... discuss client's issues or disclose client details with others; there is more information about data protection in Chapter 1

◆ ... eat, drink or smoke at reception; responding to a client while you are eating or drinking is not a pleasant experience for them; smoking can be anti-social and its smell can be unpleasant for your clients.

## Useful Task

Practise how to respond to a client who has a complaint and is angry. This will better equip you to respond calmly should this occur on a busy day in the salon. With a colleague, practise how to speak slowly, showing empathy with the client, not admitting liability but calmly questioning to determine the true nature of the problem and possible causes. Swap around to experience the client's point of view. Rehearse responding to these situations:

◆ a client whose perm has dropped

◆ a client who has purchased an aerosol spray that does not work

◆ a client who has been kept waiting a long time for their appointment.

## Sales representatives

The receptionist will be the first point of contact for visiting sales representatives. Clients of the salon must take precedence over the representative. Check the credentials of the representative; most will carry a business card, which will confirm her or his name and the company that they represent. Having established her or his identity, ask them to take a seat in the waiting area and then inform the person with the responsibility for liaising with them. Some salons have a policy that sales representatives may only be seen by appointment with the relevant person and others will meet representatives if they are available. The receptionist must ensure that they are aware of the salon's policy in these matters.

 # REMEMBER!

*Deliveries of goods are usually made to the reception area of the salon. Salons may have policies regarding where goods should be delivered and who is eligible to sign the carrier's dockets, confirming receipt of goods in good order, and the procedure to be adopted. If you are in doubt about your salon's procedures ask your supervisor or manager.*

## Other visitors

Any visitor to the salon should report to the reception. Your salon may have policies on how visitors other than clients should be greeted. If in doubt, you should check the visitor's identity and, having seated her or him in the waiting area, seek advice from your supervisor or manager.

Visitors may include local authority representatives, training advisers and awarding body verifiers, business consultants, personal friends and acquaintances. The salon may have a policy about members of staff receiving unofficial visits from friends and relatives, except in emergencies.

## REMEMBER!

*Details about the level of salon business should be considered as confidential to the business and should not be discussed with others either within or outside of the business, without approval from the salon management.*

If messages are taken for members of staff or management these should be recorded and promptly passed to the relevant person or placed in the correct location for collection. Some salons have noticeboards or pigeonholes for messages to be posted. When taking messages, the salon may have its own procedures or pro-forma message pads. The detail usually required includes the name of the intended recipient, the name of the message leaver, the date and time of the message, the actual detail of the message, and any action or response that is required. Your salon may have a procedure for passing messages to ensure that they are passed promptly and that follow-up action is taken.

**KEY SKILLS**

## Use of the telephone

The telephone forms a link between your salon and its clientele, enabling them to make contact without the need to actually visit the salon. With this in mind it is important that this service is available for as much time throughout the working day as possible. Personal telephone calls should be avoided, and in many cases are prohibited, except in an emergency. Conversations with clients should be clear and effective but at the same time as brief as possible without making the client feel rushed. When the telephone is in use other clients cannot make contact with you.

**KEY SKILLS**

## REMEMBER!

*When taking messages for others, make a written note of the caller's name, date and time of call, the nature of the message and a contact telephone/fax number, email address or postal address if a response is required. This should be passed promptly to the person concerned. Remember messages taken that are not passed on may result in ineffective service to your clients.*

The telephone may also be used in a proactive manner to promote business: as a method of checking on clients who have perhaps not visited the salon for some time and a way of reminding them of the services that you offer.

In cases of emergency, perhaps due to a member of staff's unplanned absence due to ill-health, the telephone provides a method of contacting clients and rescheduling appointments.

## Responding to a call

The telephone should be answered promptly. Many salons have a policy of always responding to the telephone within three rings. This should be considered good practice (see Figure 10.5). Callers should be informed of the name of the salon, who is responding to the call, and an invitation or offer of

**KEY SKILLS**

service, for example: 'This is Salon Hair, Paula speaking, how may I help you?'
Speak clearly to the caller. When making an appointment using the telephone
repeat back to the client these details:

- date

- time

- service to be offered

- if relevant, the name of the stylist who will be undertaking the task

- approximate costs, if this was discussed during the conversation.

Figure 10.5 The telephone is
an important part of the salon
business

# REMEMBER!

*When dealing with a telephone request for an appointment which cannot be met, do not
say 'no'. Always offer alternatives. 'No' can terminate the conversation leaving no room for
negotiation.*

If in doubt about the spelling of a client's name ask the client to spell this out for you. This is not usually considered
impolite. When you book clients who are visiting the salon for the first time, check that they are aware of the
average cost of treatments. Your salon may have specific requirements when making appointments, particularly if a
computerised appointment system is used, as details of the client will be called up for checking when the
appointment is entered.

# REMEMBER!

*At the end of the conversation, thank the caller for calling.*

*The telephone can easily reflect, to the listener, the attitude of the speaker. Take care
always to speak cheerfully and not to reflect annoyance or irritation.*

## Good practice points

- When taking a message, read this back to the caller to check the accuracy of the message taken.

- When speaking, remember that background noise from the reception area may be heard. Confidential
  conversations may be overheard. If you must keep the client waiting while you source information use the
  *mute* button on the telephone.

- Should the telephone ring while you are busy dealing with another client, answer the telephone and ask the
  caller if they can hold on while the current client's transaction is dealt with. If the client states that they cannot
  hold, then ask for a return telephone number with an undertaking to return the call at the earliest opportunity.
  It is important that this undertaking is not subsequently neglected.

## REMEMBER!

*Information about clients is confidential. Receptionists should not release any information about a client to anyone not normally authorised without first consulting the salon management.*

# Appointment systems

Every salon needs a record of planned appointments for its clients. The record not only serves to ensure that the salon has a planned schedule of clients assisting the stylist planning their working day, it also serves as a reconciliation document: a check of takings by the stylist against the anticipated income from a number of clients.

# The manual appointment book

The appointment schedule usually takes the form of a written appointment book, with a page per day, containing columns allocated to particular hairstylists and specialists which is divided into time slots, usually in 15-minute intervals. The client's name, contact telephone number and the nature of the service required are then entered in the relevant stylist's column at the appropriate time of the day.

The receptionist must be aware of the stylist's competencies and the length of time that they require to complete services. This will enable them to phase clients realistically to ensure maximum efficiency without delay to the client.

# The computerised appointment system

More and more hairdressing salons are using computerised systems to retain their customer information and to phase their appointments. In most systems the computer software will have built-in the range of services available from the salon and the timings which are required for each stylist to undertake these tasks. This is usually linked to an automatic billing system that not only calculates the client's bill but is also often capable of re-booking appointments and generating reminders of these appointments.

# General guidance

Communicate effectively, ensuring that your client is aware of the:

◆ time

◆ date of the next appointment

◆ details of the service to be provided and approximate time taken

◆ stylist who will provide the service.

Always confirm the appointment by completing an appointment card. This card will remind the client of the date and time of their next appointment as well as being a reminder to your client of the business, enabling them to recommend and direct new clients to you easily.

Should someone request an appointment with a particular hairstylist for a particular day and time when that stylist is not available, there are several ways to handle the situation, as described opposite.

◆ If the client regularly uses that one hairstylist, suggest other times when the stylist is available.

◆ If the client cannot come in at any of those times, suggest an alternative stylist.

◆ If the client is unwilling to try another hairstylist, offer to call the client if there is a cancellation at or near the desired time.

◆ If a client requests an appointment outside of your authority refer this to your supervisor. These appointment requests may include demands for unusual appointment times, specialist treatments, practices not normally undertaken by the salon (for example, no skin test before a tint), and unusual cost variations.

◆ When clients pay their bill at the end of the service, always offer and encourage them to make further appointments. This will help to ensure repeat visits by clients and maintains the relationship between the salon and client.

# Receiving client payments

An important part of the receptionist's role is handling client payments. This requires numerical skills and tact.

Following the treatment the client's total bill must be calculated. Salons have differing ways of doing this. In some, the hairstylist informs the receptionist of the services and items that are to be added to the bill. In other salons each individual who contributes to the client's treatments reports this to the receptionist who then maintains a record of the service given and subsequently calculates the bill based upon this information.

Provided that all details of all services are keyed in correctly, a computerised client reservation and recording system will then calculate the client's bill and will record all treatments. Many electronic tills will calculate the amount of change to be given to the client, if required. Some may also record the stylist's name so that commissions and performance figures can be established.

Each day a cash *float* is required so that change may be given to clients. This consists of an agreed amount of cash in small denominations. The receptionist should check the level of the float and record it, so that it may be accurately deducted when the takings are reconciled (when actual takings are compared to recorded takings). The receptionist should operate the cash flow to avoid running out of a range of cash for change. A reserve may be kept in a safe and the receptionist should be aware of how to obtain this easily and should forecast when it may be required so as to save shortages at crucial times.

 REMEMBER!

*Avoid holding large amounts of money in the till, as this can be a security risk.*

Unless otherwise stated on the price list, prices charged are assumed, if appropriate, to include Value Added Tax (VAT) at the current rate.

# KEY SKILL TASK

*Calculate a client's total bill for the following groups of services in your salon.*

| Client 1 | Client 2 | Client 3 |
|---|---|---|
| Haircut – restyle | Shampoo | Haircut |
| Shampoo | Blow-dry | Permanent wave |
| Highlights – tin foil | Semi-permanent colour | Conditioner |
| Blow-dry | | Set |

*Calculate upwards the amount of money the client would hand you in notes to meet each of these clients' payments. For each how much change would you give them?*

People who may be required to undertake reception duties must make themselves aware of acceptable forms of payment within the salon. These may include:

◆ cash

◆ cheques

◆ cards

◆ cash equivalents

◆ vouchers.

# Cash payments

The most frequently used form of payment for services, cash is accepted in all salons. When receiving cash as payment note the following.

◆ Always count and agree the actual payment before placing the cash in the cash drawer.

◆ When change is required, retain the original payment outside the cash drawer while change is calculated. This can help to avoid disagreements about the amount of the initial payment.

◆ Always follow the salon's policy in checking the validity of bank notes used for payments.

◆ It is not usual to open a cash drawer just to obtain change for a client; the opening of the till should normally coincide with a transaction.

Always check bank notes for authenticity. Some salons use special marker pens or ultra-violet lights to confirm if notes are authentic. Currently authentic bank notes from the United Kingdom have a metal strip through the note and an embossed hologram. Forged currency should be declined and reported to your supervisor.

Some salons accept cash payment in euros. Before accepting payment in this currency check with your supervisor if this is acceptable and the current exchange rates.

# Payment by cheque

Most salons accept payment from clients by cheque. Some do, however, set a minimum level above which the cheque payment should be, usually to offset the bank charges levied against the business for handling the cheque. When receiving a cheque, note the following procedures.

◆ The cheque should be signed in the presence of the receiver. The remainder of the detail may have been printed for the client by a computerised till or may have been written by the client.

◆ Check that the day's date is correct, with the correct year, that it is made payable to the correct company name and that the amount payable is correct both in writing and in figures.

◆ Most businesses require that a cheque payment be supported by a cheque guarantee card. If this is the case write the card number on the reverse side of the cheque. The receptionist should check the card will guarantee the cheque to the required level – this amount (usually £50 or £100) is indicated on the card – that the signature on the cheque is the same as that on the card, and that it is tendered within the card's start and expiry dates (you may be required to note this detail on the reverse of the cheque).

◆ If there is doubt about the validity of the card it should be retained by the receptionist while checks are made. If you are in any doubt about the salon procedures for doing this consult with your line manager.

> ## REMEMBER!
>
> *The checking of the validity of a cheque guarantee card or credit card can cause some clients embarrassment; therefore this process should be carried out with discretion and the utmost courtesy to the client.*

It is not normal practice to cash cheques for clients or to give cash change for cheques made out to greater amounts than that of the bill without the agreement of the salon management. It is unwise to accept cheques that are not made payable to a specific name, or where any detail is incomplete.

# Card payments

Payment by this method is accepted by many, but not all, businesses. Agreement between the business and the particular card company is required. The business pays a percentage of each card transaction to the card company. Always follow your salon's policy in receiving these cards. These transactions may be completed via an electronic point of sale, which links direct with the card company and validates and records the transaction direct. The use of sales vouchers, either printed via a computerised till or by hand, may also be used. Some general notes of guidance are as follows.

◆ Always check that the card is valid and within the start and expiry dates.

◆ If completing a sales voucher by hand, use a ballpoint pen, ensuring that the writing can be seen on all copies. The details from the card may be transferred to the sales voucher using an imprinter. Pass the top copy of the voucher to the client, for their records. All others to be placed in the cash drawer.

◆ Check that the card is not the subject of a warning notice. From time to time card companies will circulate a listing of card numbers that should not be accepted, and if used should be retained by the salon, which should inform the card company.

◆ Do not accept damaged or torn cards, particularly if the signature strip has been partially or completely removed.

◆ Each business will have been set a level of payment above which authorisation must be obtained from the card company if the payment is to be guaranteed. This may be done by a simple telephone call and a transaction number recorded on the sales voucher; you will need to have your merchant number at hand when making this call.

On some occasions a card payment may generate a request from the card company for them to be contacted to verify payment. This is sometimes prompted by the card company's security system checking on unusual payment patterns.

Cards are currently being introduced that contain a microchip containing the holder's personal information (chip and pin). Your salon may have a specialist machine for processing these where the client is required to enter a confidential pin number to verify the transaction.

If you are in doubt whether a particular card is accepted by your salon, consult with your manager. Do not accept payment via this method if you are not fully aware of the process, as errors may invalidate payment. If in doubt seek advice and help.

## Cash equivalents

Some clients may offer payment via traveller's cheques, either in sterling or in a foreign currency. Sterling cheques may be received very much like an ordinary cheque. Ensure that the customer signs the traveller's cheque in your presence and that this signature is the same as that on the traveller's cheque folder or passport. If accepting traveller's cheques in non-sterling currency the bank will give a valuation for the exchange.

If you are in any doubt about the procedures for receiving traveller's cheques then consult your manager.

 *REMEMBER!*

*A client may request to make payment using traveller's cheques. Consult with a responsible person before undertaking this.*

## Vouchers

Your salon may offer vouchers for sale, which may be used as gifts that are in turn used to purchase goods or services from the salon. These may be used to the equivalent value of the stated cash figure. Salons' policies with regard to giving cash as change on these occasions may differ – if in doubt, consult with your manager.

 *REMEMBER!*

*Always follow your salon's policy in receiving payments from clients.*

# Key points to note

- If you are in doubt about the validity of the payment being made, follow salon procedure or consult with your manager.

- A receipt for payment should be given. This is your client's proof of payment, particularly for unrecorded treatments or retail sales, and will be required should a refund be necessary.

- Do not give refunds to clients unless you have the authority to do so, or you have consulted with and have permission from the authorised person.

- Do not leave the cash drawer open when not in use. When the reception is unattended the cash drawer should be locked.

- Large amounts of cash or notes of high denomination should be removed from the cash drawer and placed in a safe. This will help to reduce any security risk.

## Useful Task

Ensure that you know whom to go to for advice when making appointments for clients and when receiving payments. Familiarise yourself with the range of services offered within your salon, their duration and cost. Find out if your salon has a policy for:

- the manner in which the telephone is answered

- who makes client appointments

- how the client's bill is calculated and who gives information on the services provided

- who is empowered to receive payments or to authorise particular methods of payment

- the process of making refunds.

## Self review

1. May information about clients be given to whoever asks?

2. How should the client be greeted when they visit the salon?

3. List three functions of the salon's receptionist.

4. When booking a client what detail is normally required to be listed in the salon's appointment book?

5. How should a telephone appointment booking be confirmed with a client?

6. What is meant by phasing of appointments?

7. What action should be taken following receipt of a message for someone within the salon?

8. What detail must be checked when receiving a cheque guarantee card in support of a cheque payment?

9. What is the purpose of a cash float?

10. What is the level of payment above which authorisation must be obtained in relation to credit card usage?

# Useful contacts

| | |
|---|---|
| Computill | www.computill.com |
| HABIA | www.habia.org.uk |
| Institute of Customer Service | www.instituteofcustomerservice.com |

# CHAPTER 11

# Promoting products and services

## WHAT THIS CHAPTER WILL PROVIDE

This chapter provides guidance in the practical skills and essential knowledge you need to understand in order to promote additional products and services to your clients as well as ways of keeping up to date and obtaining further information about the products and services your salon provides. You will be provided with the opportunity to further develop your knowledge about products and services your salon provides, how they interrelate, and their suitability for particular clients.

## The psychology of selling

Each person who enters a salon is an individual with specific needs. No matter how good a hairdressing service or product may be you will find it difficult to make a sale if the client has no need for it. Your first task is to determine whether the client needs or is interested in a service or product. As more products are added to salon operations, selling is becoming an increasingly important responsibility of the hairdresser and an important income generator. The hairdresser who is equally proficient as a hairstylist and a sales person is most likely to be the one to succeed in business. Advising clients about the appropriate products to use in their haircare programme will not only add to your income, but will better enable your clients to maintain the look you worked so hard to achieve. The sale of suitable home haircare products should be considered an integral part of the hairdressing process and all part of the need to satisfy the client's expectations, the one service supporting the good work of the other. Figure 11.1 shows a typical retail display of hairdressing products.

Figure 11.1 A hairdressing product display stand

The largest percentage of home haircare products are sold in high-street retail shops, where advice in appropriate selection and correct use is given usually by non-hairdressers. You are at an advantage for the following reasons.

◆ You are a well-informed professional.

◆ Your client is able to purchase products that complement those you have used on their hair.

◆ Your client has indicated their willingness to purchase, by coming to you for advice and a professional service.

◆ The ambience of haircare and beauty will set the mood for considering the purchase of products related to this.

## REMEMBER!

*Do not be embarrassed about suggesting a treatment or product that will enhance your client's hair. They will appreciate your professional interest in their hair and the way they look.*

# Promotional opportunities

Within your hairdressing salon there will be opportunities to promote:

◆ additional services

◆ haircare products

◆ haircare equipment.

To be able to guide your clients towards appropriate products and services you need to keep up to date with what is available. Often information about products and services is shared within salon staff meetings. If the service is specialist, for example hair extensions, speak to the relevant salon specialist to gain information about the service:

◆ the effect the service gives and the type of hair and client it suits

◆ how long it takes

◆ how long it lasts

◆ costs.

■ Figure 11.2 A retail display

Some salons use staff meetings for team members to introduce their colleagues to products (see Figure 11.2), each member of the team researching a product and presenting it to the rest of the team.

When a new product is introduced to your salon's range find out:

◆ about the product, its features, benefits and suitability for differing hair types

◆ in what form it is available – aerosols, jars, tubs, tubes, etc.

◆ sizes of unit available

◆ price

◆ complementary products.

This information may be obtained from your supervisor, your colleagues, sales representatives and technical demonstrators, and product fact sheets. It will enable you to guide your client in appropriate purchases.

## REMEMBER!

*Always seek advice from a colleague or supervisor before recommending to clients products that you are unfamiliar with. Your client will value your opinion even more if they recognise that you are honest and will seek advice before advising them about products with which you are unfamiliar. Be honest: if you do not know the answer to a client's questions, undertake to find out the correct information. This is more effective than backtracking over previously provided incorrect information.*

## Additional services

Your client wants to look her or his very best when leaving the salon so be prepared to recommend services that will enhance the hairstyle and the way s/he looks. Most salons use accessible display areas near the reception area to remind clients of the availability of retail products from the salon (see Figure 11.1). Consider whether your client's hair would benefit from conditioning, hair colour or style support. Comments from your client about how the previous styling has lasted, and the ease of its care and maintenance may lead you to make suggestions about additional services. You are the knowledgeable professional – offer advice to your client about what will suit her or his hair and enhance it. Be prepared to justify your suggestions and to explain, in simple terms, how the process works, how long it will take, the costs, how long the effect will last and whether the process must be repeated at set intervals. You must be fully aware of the features and benefits of these services if you are to be able to speak with conviction. Be honest: if you guarantee an outcome the client will be dissatisfied if this is not achieved. If asked whether you would use a particular treatment it is OK to say no, but justify why it is not suitable for you but why it *is* appropriate for her or him.

## REMEMBER!

*Often you can speak with more conviction about treatments you have experienced personally. You can also use experiences that your colleagues have had.*

Look for signs that your client has understood what you have told them. These may be continued interest in the conversation or further questioning about the service. Encourage your client to ask questions, and ask for her or his opinions about potential services. You may do this by asking open-ended questions:

- 'What do you think?'

- 'How do you currently cope with …?'

- 'How would you feel?'

- 'When have you tried …?'

Don't be afraid to express your views, saying:

- 'I feel this will …'

- 'I like this …'

- 'I have used this and it was …'.

If your client indicates that s/he is not interested then do not linger on the subject, thank her or him for listening and move on. Figure 11.3 indicates a typical client consultation opportunity when products and services can be introduced.

**Figure 11.3 Client consultation**

 ## REMEMBER!

*Do not be embarrassed by the cost of a salon service. If the price is appropriate for the service it should not be a barrier to the sale. There is often a perceived value in a service according to the price that is paid.*

There will be services you promote that do not directly link to the current hairstyling you are providing, for example manicures and facials. Remember to follow this up and make appointments for them in the future.

Some suggestions you make will not be accepted until a later date – this may be due to cost, available time, or that the client wishes to discuss the matter with someone else first.

 ## REMEMBER!

*Your client may not be aware of the full range of services your salon can offer and you will need to inform her or him of what is available.*

# Selling principles

KEY SKILLS

To become a proficient sales person you must understand and be able to apply the following selling principles.

- Be familiar with the features and benefits of each service and product.

- Adapt your approach and technique to meet the needs of each client.

- Be self-confident but not arrogant.

- Generate interest and desire, which may lead to a sale.

- Look for indications of interest in products and services. Clients may be nervous about declaring interest, but they may look at the product or linger by the merchandising stand, asking questions about the product or service.

- Never misrepresent your service or product.

- Use tact when selling to a client.

- Don't underestimate the client or the client's intelligence.

- To sell a product or service, deliver a sales talk in a relaxed, friendly manner and, if possible, demonstrate its use.

- If selling a product, allow your client to handle the item.

- Recognise the right psychological moment to close (complete) any sale. Once the client has offered to buy, stop selling – don't over-sell, except to praise the client for the purchase and assure them that they will be happy with it.

- Do not be embarrassed when informing the client of the cost of the purchase: the product does have a value.

## Four-step approach

1   Create the interest – attract your client to the product through display, and talk about the products you retail.

2   Generate the need – show your client how they may benefit from the use of the product.

3   Overcome objections – deal with resistance to the sale, questions, suitability and competitors' products.

4   Close the sale – confirm the purchase.

## Successful sales

To be successful in sales you need ambition, determination and a good personality. The first step in selling is to sell yourself. Clients must like and trust you before they will purchase haircare services, products or other merchandise. Every client who enters the salon is a prospective purchaser of additional services and merchandise. The manner in which you treat that person lays the foundation for suggestive selling. Recognising the needs and preferences of clients makes the intelligent use of suggestive selling possible.

Do not ignore the buying signals that your client gives. Clients who display interest in a product will often respond positively if provided with honest, professional guidance on their suitability. Part of your role, as a hairdresser, is to support your client in caring for their hair effectively.

The promotion and sales process can occur at any time during the client's visit. An early opportunity during an initial consultation, particularly if the service promoted, is one that is relevant to that salon visit.

## REMEMBER!

*Some salons use a consultation checklist to prompt the stylist to ask questions and make decisions about appropriate services and additional products. Often this checklist forms a consultation record. All records should be treated as confidential and their content should not be disclosed to other clients. Information held about clients is subject to the Data Protection Act. See Chapter 1 for more information.*

Be prepared to respond to signs the client gives that they are interested in additional products or services. These signs can include:

◆   asking for your opinion about a product or service

◆   looking at themselves and a style book

◆   showing an interest in something else happening in the salon

◆   handling products or equipment, reading labels and instructions.

## REMEMBER!

*Always be prepared to up-sell – that is, recommend a product from a higher price range if appropriate, if available. Never assume your client cannot afford or does not regard themselves highly enough to make the investment.*

# Questions and suggestions

Effective communication is essential. In order to satisfy a need you need to find out what the need is. To find out your client's wishes you will need to use questioning. Use open-ended questions that enable you to gain information, for example:

◆   'Why do you shampoo your hair so frequently?'

◆   'Which colour do you prefer?'

◆   'Which of these have you used previously? Which did you prefer? Why was that?'

You must know what your client is looking for in order to advise her or him.

Find out what products your client currently uses. This can provide guidance in their normal level of spending and quality of product used.

Never assume, always ask and confirm. If your client selects a product to purchase always check to determine if any complementary products are required. Should your client's selection be from a product range, indicate what additional options are available. If your salon has any promotional offers that may suit your client's requirements, introduce these.

When providing suggestions about the suitability of particular goods take care not to overstate what the product can achieve. The Trade Descriptions Act 1968 prohibits false claims being made about products (more information is provided later in this chapter).

## REMEMBER!

*The features of a product are what it does and how it does it. A product may have features that are unique and make it different from others. Benefits are the advantages obtained by the client in a product's use.*

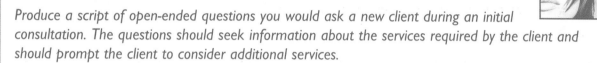

## KEY SKILL TASK

*This task could produce evidence that supports C1.1 & C1.2.*

*Produce a script of open-ended questions you would ask a new client during an initial consultation. The questions should seek information about the services required by the client and should prompt the client to consider additional services.*

*Test the questions with a colleague to see if the information gained from their responses would enable you to have a clear picture of the services they require and to check that you could describe any products and services they currently use on their hair.*

*When you are satisfied you have a script of useful questions that generate the information you require, rehearse these and use them in your client consultations. Remember to evaluate how effective your questioning is and make improvements where you think appropriate.*

## Overcoming objections

If your client demonstrates resistance to a sale, find out what the problem is by questioning. Break down problems into small parts and deal with each in turn. Large problems can appear insurmountable but when broken down appear a lot less of a problem. They can appear quite trivial and more easily responded to in a positive manner. Remember, do not be critical of a client who displays resistance; respect their point of view.

Advise your client about the product and which of the range will suit and support their requirements. Be prepared to explain the features and benefits more fully and to relate them to the specific needs of your client. Ultimately your client will make the decision whether or not to purchase and it is your role to ensure products are presented and explained appropriately and their positive aspects highlighted.

Never be afraid of an objection as this can provide you with an opportunity to promote and confirm the product's features and benefits.

## Closing the sale

When promoting after-care products encourage your client to handle the product; holding the product and reading the label are strong signs that your client is accepting the sale. Check, by questioning, which products your client wishes to purchase. Inform her or him of any available choices, including size of additional products from the range. Package the products and confirm with your client her or his total spend (see Figure 11.4).

When promoting a salon service summarise the agreed actions with your client, confirm with her or him that it is acceptable and s/he wishes to proceed.

## Types of client

The hairdresser who is most likely to be successful in selling additional services or merchandise to clients is one who can recognise the many different types of people and who knows how to deal with each type.

The following are four of the most usual types you are likely to meet. Each person type might be treated in the way suggested.

■ Figure 11.4 Client buying products at the till

1　Shy, timid type. Make this client feel at ease. Lead the conversation. Don't force the conversation. Be cheerful.

2　Talkative type. Be a good listener. Tactfully switch the conversation to haircare product need.

3　Nervous, irritable type. Does not want much conversation. Wants simple, practical hairstyle and a fast worker. Get started and finished as quickly as possible.

4　Inquisitive, over-cautious type. Explain everything in detail. Show her or him facts – information leaflets, brand names. Ask for the client's opinion.

## Haircare equipment

New looks in hair fashion sometime require specialist haircare equipment with which to maintain them. The salon is the place most suited to provide these for your clients. When you provide a new look for your client which requires unfamiliar equipment, spend time to provide practical guidance in its safe and correct use. A client who is able to maintain their new look effectively will be an advertisement for your work as well as being very satisfied with your professional competence.

# Consumer legislation (law)

## Consumer Protection Act 1987

This Act is about the liability for damage caused by defective products. Product liability provides for the producer of a product, and any salon putting their name to the product, and any person importing a product, to be liable for any damage caused by that product.

The Act makes it an offence to give a misleading indication of the price of goods and/or services. Products used by or sold to clients, if proven to have caused damage, whether faulty or not, may result in compensation being sought as well as possible criminal prosecution.

# Sale of Goods Act 1979

This Act provides the consumer with the right to expect a product to be of *merchantable quality* – that is, fit for the purpose for which it was sold. It provides the consumer with the right to seek a refund or replacement for the product should it be shown not to be of appropriate quality or as described. The refund or replacement should be provided by the salon, which subsequently may take a similar action with its supplier. Proof of purchase may be required and a credit note need not be accepted by the client, though it may be offered by the salon.

# Supply of Goods and Services Act 1982

This Act requires a person providing a service to do so with reasonable care and skill; for example, a technician undertaking a perm must do so with a proper standard of workmanship. Unless otherwise agreed, the treatment should be provided in a reasonable time and for a reasonable charge. The term *reasonable* is decided by comparing this with the normal standard for supplying the service. The latter two areas apply only when nothing is previously stated about the time scale or price.

# Trade Descriptions Act 1968

This Act prohibits any false claims about goods, including:

◆ quantity and size

◆ method of manufacture

◆ composition

◆ fitness for the purpose, strength, performance and behaviour

◆ physical characteristics

◆ testing and/or approval by any personality

◆ place, dates and person who undertook manufacture

◆ any other history.

The Act prohibits false trade descriptions claimed about services. In a hairdressing context this may affect claims about products and treatments, their effects, contents, production history, etc.

It is illegal to sell something as being a *sale item* or *reduced price* unless it was sold at the original higher price for a period of 28 days prior to being reduced. If the goods were not sold at the higher price, then the salon must display a sign stating that it has never sold the goods at the higher price.

# KEY SKILL TASK

*This task could produce evidence that supports C1.1, C1.2, C1.3, N1.1 & N1.2.*

*Produce an information folder for clients. The folder will list and describe the range of services provided by your salon, their features, benefits, the duration of the service, how long the effect will last, and the costs. Indicate the suitability of each service for client types and how the services relate to each other. Use non-technical language that your clients will understand.*

*Consult with colleagues, read manufacturer's information leaflets and speak to manufacturer's representatives to gather the required information.*

*Remember, before introducing the folder to clients consult and gain the agreement of your supervisor.*

## Self review

1. What are open-ended questions?

2. Which Act prohibits any false claims about goods?

3. Which Act provides the client with the right to expect a product to be of merchantable quality?

4. Within the hairdressing salon what three aspects are available to promote?

5. What are the four steps to selling?

6. What does the term up-sell mean?

7. How should you deal with problems that form objections to a sale?

8. What is meant by the expression feature of a product?

9. What is meant by the expression benefit of a product?

10. State one buying signal that a client may exhibit.

## Useful contacts

Institute of Customer Service    www.instituteofcustomerservice.com
Trading Standards Department    www.tradingstandards.gov.uk
Her Majesty's Stationery Office    www.hmso.gov.uk

## CHAPTER 12

# Working effectively

## CHAPTER CONTENTS

**Unit G3** Contribute to the development of effective working relationships

**Unit G8** Develop and maintain your effectiveness at work

## WHAT THIS CHAPTER WILL PROVIDE

This chapter provides the essential knowledge to help you understand the principles and practices involved in working as a hairdresser. The information in this chapter will affect all other areas in the book.

# Introduction

As a professional hairdresser you will project an image, both as a professional hair artist and  as a socially conscious person; aware of current fashion trends that may be both caring and objective when advising clients (see Figure 12.1). Your development as a hairdresser is integral with all of the other tasks that you carry out. It is impossible to separate your development from the day-to-day work that you perform. As a novice hairdresser you will always be learning, either from formal training sessions or by watching and being involved with the effective running of the business. Every experience that you have in this profession must be viewed as a learning process that enables you to develop your skills further.

Take every opportunity to reflect upon your performance of a task. Consider what you did well and build on this; for those areas where you feel that you did not perform so well, be objective and consider what changes you should make in your future actions which will improve your performance. Be aware of whom you may approach for advice and guidance in these matters, and when this may be most appropriate.

As a hairstylist the learning and development process never ends. In the early stages it may be that you have basic skills to acquire and you must

■ Figure 12.1 Be caring and objective

develop a work ethos that ensures that you approach your work with enthusiasm, remembering that in a service industry your performance with your client is what ensures their return and therefore your ongoing success. Not only will you be developing your practical skills but also your social skills. Very rarely will you work in isolation. At all levels you will need to be able to interact with colleagues, supporting each other in your workplace, and this will be seen by your clientele. You must therefore develop skills of working together as part of a team, as well as relating to your client on a one-to-one basis.

Fashion does not stand still, so neither do the requirements of your clients or your employer. As a commercial hairstylist you must keep abreast of both current and emerging fashion trends. This may be achieved in a variety of ways that are mentioned elsewhere in this book. Your role within the hairdressing salon will also develop. You will be expected, at certain stages, to accept responsibilities. These may appear quite minor – preparing workstations, for example – or they may take the form of supervisory skills, allocation and checking of work being carried out by others, or making judgements on other people's performance. All are important and may be essential to the running of the business. They all require different skills, which must be developed and do not normally happen without a level of planning.

As an employee in a business, you will interact with your line manager. You must take on the skills of negotiation and interaction not only with your colleagues, but also with those for whom you have responsibility and with your line managers.

# People you work with

By its nature hairdressing involves offering a service to others, our clients, so interaction with others is an essential aspect of this profession.

There are four categories of people with whom we interact:

◆ our clients

◆ those from whom we purchase goods and services which enable us to carry out the hairdressing process

◆ those with whom we work

◆ those who employ or manage us in our role.

In order to be effective in our work we must work effectively with all these categories.

## Clients

As the hairdresser, you will control the relationship that develops between yourself and your client. You will be in the position of the expert in your field, whom the client has visited to receive a service. You will set the scene. You will be responsible for providing your client with a service delivered in a style that will satisfy their expectations. You will be judged not only on your level of hairdressing skill but also on the efficiency and ambience of delivery of that skill, and what you do will determine the level of customer satisfaction.

When communicating with clients remember that information about the salon's clients is confidential and should not be discussed or disclosed to others. Clients expect a standard of care: if you agree or commit to undertake a task you should deliver this or, if not possible, you should inform your client of why this cannot be done. Do not leave clients expecting a service which cannot be delivered.

Your salon may have guidelines in handling clients' belongings. If you are uncertain about your salon's procedures consult with your supervisor. Do not accept responsibility for clients' belongings outside of the policies of your salon.

If you observe that your client has concerns or questions that are beyond your responsibility, promptly but discreetly refer this to your supervisor. Avoid discussing client concerns in front of the client or others.

■ Figure 12.2 Reception is often the initial point of contact

For guidance in standards of behaviour, personal appearance, client care and communication refer to Chapter 2. Everyone within the salon influences clients' perceptions and experience from the initial point of contact – often at reception (see Figure 12.2) – through the entire team to the last point of contact.

## Providers of goods and services

These people provide a support service. Effective communication with this group is essential to ensure that the correct level of support is provided. This support will include the provision of both products and equipment at the appropriate level at the appropriate time, and the provision of guidance and training in the correct and effective use of products. They may also keep you informed of emerging product developments.

## Co-workers/colleagues

Most of us work with others at a variety of levels within a team. The team has a common goal, which must be the success of the team. Everyone within the team has a role to play and you can be more effective as a team than by working independently. In working as a team, members must respect each other. There are skills which must be developed by all members of the team. These include skills of working together and acknowledging each other's worth. People have different characters and work within a team in different ways, so the successful team will evolve by using each member's attributes most effectively. This can happen purely by chance, but it usually requires an expert in group dynamics to maximise the team's potential. Team meetings are often a good opportunity to share experiences and feedback to each other (see Figure 12.3).

■ Figure 12.3 Staff meeting

## Employers/management

Employees interact with management and employers. To be successful the hairdresser must develop skills of negotiation and interaction with his or her managers. The hairdresser will negotiate terms and conditions of employment, scales and rates of pay, holiday periods and potential improvements in services offered within the salon. Due to the varied sizes of hairdressing businesses, the relationships that develop between management and workers will differ considerably between salons. However, the communication role between the hairdresser and the manager is two-way, and the hairdresser must be aware of appropriate opportunities. A successful management will ensure that its staff is fully aware of this and that easy access to management is made available.

# Working as part of a team

Within the salon you are part of a team with one common objective: the success of the salon. You will often work closely with a colleague and at other times work independently but within the team framework. Examples of working closely include:

◆ receiving a colleague's client

◆ shampooing a client for a stylist

◆ preparing the workstation for a perm or hair colour, and passing equipment to the stylist as they work.

Examples of working independently within the team framework include:

◆ preparing the shampoo area at the beginning of the working day

◆ maintaining the client reception area

◆ keeping the floor swept of hair cuttings

◆ blow-drying your client's hair.

The key aspects of working as part of a team are: communication, integrity, honesty and competence.

## Communication

Within the team there needs to be effective communication. This starts with a common objective: what you as a team are striving to achieve, how you will accomplish this and what you will see as a result. It is essential that as part of the team you understand what is expected of you and what you can expect from others. Do not assume that others are aware of your needs – it is best to explain to colleagues what you want.

Features to be communicated include:

◆ your responsibilities – these may be stated in your job description, through a work rota, or agreed through discussion

◆ standards of work – the quality of work and service the team aims to provide

◆ how people will work together – who works with whom, and who reports to whom

◆ targets to be achieved – the volume of work to be undertaken, levels of activity, success measures, time scales.

# Integrity

Team members need to feel they can depend on their colleagues and that undertakings made will be fulfilled. No matter the inner workings of the team, outwardly to clients it must appear as a cohesive group working together for a common goal.

Aspects of integrity include:

◆ being aware of the limits of your own authority and that of others in the team; if you are in doubt about your own authority discuss this with your supervisor; exceeding your own authority may result in disciplinary procedures being implemented

◆ being aware of the standards of acceptable behaviour within the team

◆ being supportive to colleagues

◆ fulfilling the undertakings and guarantees made to colleagues

◆ fulfilling the expectations of your job role.

# Honesty

Team members need to feel they can trust each other and that any statements made are truly the opinions and views of the individual. This can be achieved by:

◆ providing honest and objective feedback to colleagues in a supportive manner

◆ ensuring that any undertakings made will be fulfilled.

# Competence

Each team member should have the competence to undertake their role effectively. This includes:

◆ undertaking work within commercially acceptable times

◆ meeting your own work targets

◆ working to an agreed minimum standard.

When a team has effective communication, all its members have integrity, there is trust between all and each person has the competence to undertake the role, the team will become high performing.

## Useful Task

Create a chart of services provided in your salon and how much time is allowed for each to be completed. Time yourself next time you undertake one of these tasks and compare your own times to the salon average. The findings will inform you of those areas where further experience is required to improve your service delivery to fit with those of the team.

# Guidance for less experienced members of the team

As a less experienced member of the team you may require more guidance from colleagues. Do not be afraid to ask for help or clarification. Remember, it is better to check than to proceed blindly, which could cause damage to clients' hair. When seeking guidance avoid discussing problems and concerns about a particular client in front of them or other clients. If a question is not urgent, avoid distracting a colleague from their work.

Within your support role you will be asked by others to provide support and assistance. This assistance is part of the team's approach to meeting its aims and objectives. Support should always be provided in a polite and courteous manner. If asked to provide support while already undertaking a task, explain this and either offer to provide the support once your current task is completed or explain the nature of your current task and ask for guidance in which should have precedence.

Try to develop a proactive approach to your support role. As you become accustomed to the salon's procedures and differing stylists' ways of working you will be able to forecast when your support will be required. Plan your work so that you are available to support at the appropriate times. Part of this approach includes identifying how differing stylists need support. From your observations you will soon note how differing stylists prefer perm rods to be passed, hair sections to be held and their preferred side of the client to work from. Supporting the stylist in this is part of supporting the achievements of the team.

If you note any problems likely to affect the salon's services report these to the relevant person as soon as possible. For areas of your own responsibility try to establish a pattern of predicting shortages of stock, etc. This could include levels of consumables and linen at the shampoo area. Do not allow levels to become critical before raising concerns, particularly if you are aware of forthcoming high levels of activity. When reporting problems be discreet. Do not discuss salon problems in front of clients.

# Human relationships

The following are guidelines for good human relations that will help you to gain confidence and perform successfully with your colleagues.

◆   As a member of a team, you should make yourself aware of the structure of the team, who your line manager is, who is the overall team leader/manager and what are the responsibilities of the individual team members. There will be those who are responsible for particular tasks or functions within the salon.

◆   Find out precisely what is expected of you as a member of the team. What are your duties? To whom are you accountable? Whom do you approach for advice and guidance? Be prepared to respond to requests for guidance if this is within your capability and authority.

◆   As a team member, you will interact with others. As a junior member of a team, your role will be more responsive rather than initiating, but you will have a role with defined parameters of personal responsibility. As a more established member of a team, your role will evolve into a more responsible one and gradually may take on supervisory functions at various levels.

◆   In the supervisory function, the needs of others should be anticipated and if possible advice and guidance given, or, if necessary, arrangements made for others to do this.

◆ Requests for assistance by colleagues should be viewed positively. Take care to ensure that your own duties are not neglected in your attempts to assist others. If you are in doubt consult with your line manager about which tasks should be given priority. In an emergency, all possible help should be given, particularly when people may be at risk. Do not undertake tasks for which you are not trained, or use equipment with which you are unfamiliar.

◆ When you are not actively busy as a member of a team you should be prepared to offer help and assistance in tasks that you can undertake for colleagues.

◆ Deal with all disputes and differences in private. Take care of all problems promptly. If problems cannot be resolved your line manager should be informed.

 REMEMBER!

*As an effective team you will achieve more than by working in isolation.*

Remember that the team is only as strong as its weakest member. Every member of a team is important to ensure success. Responsibilities, no matter how unimportant they may appear, should be taken seriously. As a team member, ensure that you are fully aware of what is expected of you by the rest of the team. Should you be unable to undertake certain tasks, you should discuss this with your manager, to gain suitable training/instruction.

Team meetings are ideal occasions to raise issues that are relevant to the team. Be prepared to listen to others as well as putting forward your own thoughts. As a team member you must be prepared to accept justified constructive feedback, as well as being able to give it. When giving comment it can help to consider how you might best prefer to receive such comment and use this as guidance in how to undertake this.

# Career development

For successful career progression you should have a planned route (Professional Development Plan). Consider what you wish to achieve within your career, and when determining this consider your strengths and weaknesses. Chart how you might achieve these goals. Consider what experiences and training you need to achieve these expectations, being realistic in considering a time scale. As you progress within your career, review your development plan. Be prepared to amend the plan in the light of your experience. It may turn out that you achieve milestones within your plan sooner than expected.

 REMEMBER!

*If you have a vision of what you want to achieve, work backwards from this point to identify the stepping stones you must reach for success. When you know what you want to achieve and the route to achievement, your journey to success is more likely to be the outcome.*

This will necessitate a change in part of the plan. The reverse may also apply. In the experience of work you may decide that your original goals no longer apply and you wish to amend them. The Professional Development Plan is a dynamic document, always prepared to respond to change. In the light of changed expectations the route to achieve this will need to be mapped out. The entire process may be done either formally as part of a work review and appraisal process, or very informally as a personal thought process.

## REMEMBER!

*It is always wise to safeguard your future. As a hairdresser, illness or accident can result in disability that could prevent you from continuing your job or role. You may be able to insure against loss of use of certain parts of your body – your hands, for example – which may prevent you from carrying out your hairdressing role.*

Without a Professional Development Plan, achievement will occur more by accident than by design, and time and experience may be wasted.

As part of your career development consider the following points.

◆ **Review your performance objectively.** Take time to reflect on the work that you do. Consider what went well and why. What did you do that made it a success? When you are aware of what you did that caused the success you will be able to do it again. Consider what did not go well and why. Consider how you should avoid that or what you should do differently next time. If you always model your actions on the greatest successes you will constantly improve.

Your supervisor or trainer will be able to help you to review your work and achievements, and guide you in appropriate actions.

◆ **Identify your strengths and weaknesses.** Awareness of these can help you to capitalise on the former and address the latter. Be honest and objective with yourself. Often we enjoy doing the things we do well and avoid doing the things we do not do well. Review yourself; if your weaknesses are things that have to be done as part of your job consider ways of practising and improving.

Your supervisor or trainer will be able to help you to review your strengths and weaknesses, and guide you in appropriate actions.

◆ **Make the most of feedback.** Your colleagues, as well as your supervisor and trainer, can provide you with objective feedback. This can take the form of an opinion from someone looking in on your work activity providing comment on what you have done well, less well and making suggestions for development.

◆ **Make the most of opportunities to learn and develop skills.** Within hairdressing there are many opportunities to learn and develop skills. These include:

➤ learning from colleagues, either by watching their work, helping them in their work or asking for advice and guidance; if your salon runs training sessions participate fully in these; if you are asked to show a colleague how to undertake a task this can be developmental for you as you will have to break down the task into each of its stages, making you reflect on how well you actually do the task

- experimenting and practising on training heads

- consumer fashion magazine articles

- trade magazine articles and training sections

- hairdressing textbooks

- watching video tapes that demonstrate hairdressing skills

- watching demonstrations provided by colleagues, visiting trainers and technicians – many hairdressing manufacturers have their own technical demonstrator whose role is to train you in how best to use their products and to achieve the best results from them

- visiting hairdressing and fashion exhibitions – these events usually include product and technique demonstrations

- attending training programmes at academies, colleges and training centres.

## REMEMBER!

*You can develop skills not only by attending formal training courses but also by participation in salon activity and practice.*

◆ **Keep yourself aware of developments in hairdressing**. Do this by reading the trade press, reviewing consumer fashion magazines and attending hairdressing events.

## REMEMBER!

*If you are to effectively carry out your role within the salon, you must be aware of what is expected of you.*

## Useful Task

Produce your own professional development plan. An example is provided below; you may wish to use a similar format.

| **Professional Development Plan for** Rosemary Higgins | | | | |
|---|---|---|---|---|
| **Describe your ultimate career goal here** Have my own high-street hairdressing salon by 2010 | | **Action** | **Date** | **Outcome** |
| | | Gain work experience in a high-street hairdressing salon | 2003 | I have a Saturday and school holiday job in a central hairdressing salon |
| | | Attend City Hair Academy to learn and become qualified as a hairdresser | 2004/5 | Achieve NVQ Level 2 Hairdressing award |
| | | Work in a hairdressing salon | 2004/10 | 2004 work as a junior  2005 work as a graduate hairstylist  2007 work as a senior hairstylist |
| | | Attend City Hair Academy to learn more advanced hairdressing skills | 2007 | Achieve NVQ Level 3 Hairdressing award |
| | | Undertake a management course | 2009 | By 2011 achieve NVQ Level 4 Management award |
| | | Locate suitable premises to lease for a salon  Produce a business plan | 2010 | I have a business plan that demonstrates that what I want to achieve can be done  Salon premises are located and a lease secured |

| Describe additional supportive career goals here<br><br>To be recognised as a long hair specialist | | Attend salon internal each year and watch any available long hair demonstrations | 2004 onwards | I can describe currently fashionable long hairstyles and how they are achieved |
| --- | --- | --- | --- | --- |
| | | Obtain a long hair tuition head and practise dressing the long hair styles I have seen for two hours each week | 2005 | I am able to dress the styles I have seen |
| | | Attend the City Hair Academy for long hair work | 2007 | I complete the course and gain a diploma. I can produce the styles that I am shown at the Academy on my clients in the salon |

# Performance review

As part of your employment you may be involved in the process of performance review. This is a quality opportunity, with your manager, supervisor or training manager, to regularly review your work performance and plan future work. This process may focus on evaluating your performance to date and/or your career action plan and/or planning/responding to your training and development requirements. This becomes your opportunity to review your performance and to highlight those achievements that you consider noteworthy, gain advice on areas of possible improvement, and to negotiate and agree further training.

The key aspects of performance review are:

◆ agree targets for achievement, these may include

➤ volumes of clients to be worked with

➤ volumes of clients receiving certain services (for example, perms or colours)

➤ levels of takings

➤ ability to undertake new tasks or improvements in existing skills

➤ achievements

◆ reviewing progress towards previously agreed targets

◆ identifying any training or development needs in order for agreed targets to be achieved.

The hairdressing industry involves constant evolution of fashion, techniques and equipment. The experienced hairdresser must learn continuously if s/he is to maintain the currency of their skills.

# REMEMBER!

*When setting your targets, make them SMARTER:*
<u>S</u>pecific/<u>S</u>tretching
<u>M</u>easurable
<u>A</u>chievable
<u>R</u>elevant
<u>T</u>ime bound
<u>E</u>valuated
<u>R</u>esourced

# Discipline and grievance procedures

Most salons have procedures to follow in cases of disciplinary issues and grievances. You will normally be informed of these when you join the salon and will be reminded of them should the need arise for them to be implemented.

## Discipline procedures

These procedures would only normally be implemented as a last resort or when all else has failed. They are used for issues of conduct or capability, for example:

◆ consistently arriving late for work

◆ refusing to undertake reasonable requests by the salon

◆ failure to dress according to agreed standards

◆ misuse of salon property.

In most cases the salon will provide verbal feedback, coaching and counselling to guide you in acceptable and appropriate behaviour. Failure to comply with reasonable requests will result in a process that includes verbal warnings, written warnings and could ultimately result in dismissal. The process usually focuses on the nature of the offence, corrective actions or required level of performance, time scales for these actions and the potential implications of failure to meet these requirements.

## Gross misconduct

In some circumstances employees may be dismissed without notice. These include:

◆ theft of property belonging to the employer, an employee or a client

◆ deliberate damage to, or unauthorised use of, the employer's property

◆ a serious breach of salon rules, including those for health and safety

◆ violent, abusive, dangerous, bullying or intimidating conduct

◆ serious sexual, racial or other harassment.

# Grievance procedures

A grievance is likely to be a problem or concern that someone has about work, the salon environment or working relationships that an individual wants to raise and have addressed. These could include:

◆ a change in terms and conditions of work

◆ introduction of new salon opening times or days

◆ changes in staff structure and supervisory lines

◆ concerns about health and safety

◆ discrimination

◆ bullying or harassment.

A grievance procedure is a step-by-step procedure allowing a member of the team to raise an issue with the salon manager in a formal way. Grievance procedures are beneficial both for salon owners and team members as they provide a structured way for concerns to be raised and give salon owners the opportunity to deal with issues before they develop into major problems.

## Self review

1. What is the ideal situation within which to raise team issues?

2. How should confidential information about clients be treated?

3. Give two guidelines in handling a dispute between yourself and a colleague.

4. Suggest five ways of learning about and developing new skills in hairdressing.

5. What does a Professional Development Plan indicate?

6. Who would you usually undertake your performance review with?

7. What are the three key stages of a performance review?

8. What does SMARTER stand for?

9. What is gross misconduct and what can it lead to?

10. What is a grievance?

# Useful contacts

Advisory, Conciliation and Arbitration Service (ACAS)    www.acas.org.uk
Department for Trade and Industry    www.dti.gov.uk
Health & Safety Executive    www.hse.gov.uk
Her Majesty's Stationery Office    www.hmso.gov.uk

## CHAPTER 13

# The hair and scalp

## WHAT THIS CHAPTER WILL PROVIDE

This chapter gives you essential knowledge about the structure and properties of the hair, scalp and skin. It also helps you to identify hair, scalp and skin disorders and to be aware of those that may preclude hairdressing processes and those that do not.

# Introduction

As a hairstylist, it is important to have a good technical knowledge of the hair and scalp. This knowledge will be an asset to you as a professional hairdresser.

Hair comes in a variety of colours, shapes and sizes. To keep hair healthy and attractive, proper attention must be given to its care and treatment. Applying a harsh cosmetic, such as one that contains a lot of alcohol, or providing improper hairdressing services, can cause the hair structure to become weakened or damaged. Knowledge and analysis of the client's hair, tactful suggestions for its improvement and a sincere interest in maintaining its health and beauty should be primary concerns of every hairstylist.

# Hair

The study of the hair, technically called *trichology*, is important because stylists deal with hair on a daily basis. The chief purposes of hair are adornment, and protection of the head from heat, cold and injury.

Hair is an appendage of the skin, a slender, threadlike outgrowth of the skin and scalp (see Figure 13.1). There is no sense of feeling in hair, due to the absence of nerves.

## KEY WORDS

**Trichology** – *the study of the structures, functions and diseases of hair*

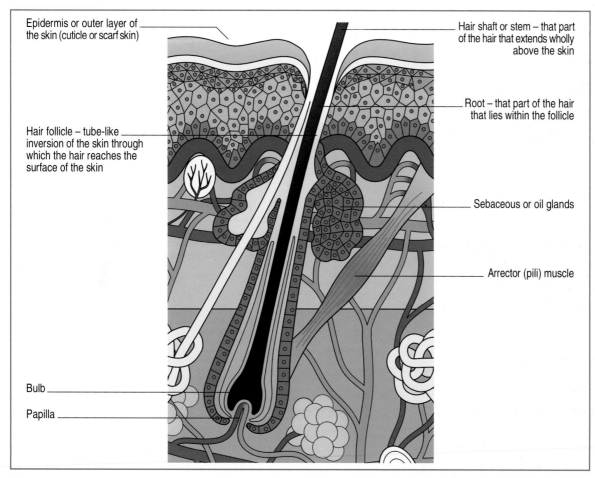

Epidermis or outer layer of the skin (cuticle or scarf skin)

Hair follicle – tube-like inversion of the skin through which the hair reaches the surface of the skin

Bulb

Papilla

Hair shaft or stem – that part of the hair that extends wholly above the skin

Root – that part of the hair that lies within the follicle

Sebaceous or oil glands

Arrector (pili) muscle

■ Figure 13.1 The hair follicle and its appendages

# Composition of the hair

Hair is composed chiefly of the protein *keratin*, which is found in all horny growths, including the nails and skin. The chemical composition of hair varies with its colour. Darker hair has more carbon and less oxygen; the reverse is true for lighter hair. Average hair is composed of 50.65% carbon, 6.36% hydrogen, 17.14% nitrogen, 5.0% sulphur and 20.85% oxygen.

# Divisions of the hair

Full-grown human hair is divided into two principal parts: the *root* and the *shaft*.

1    The hair root is that portion of the hair structure located beneath the skin's surface. This is the portion enclosed within the follicle.

2    The hair shaft is that portion of the hair structure extending above the skin's surface.

## Structures associated with the hair root

The three main structures associated with the hair root are the *follicle*, *bulb* and *papilla*. The follicle is a tube-like depression or pocket in the skin or scalp that encases the hair root (see Figure 13.1). Each hair has its own follicle, which varies in depth depending on its thickness and the location of the skin. One or more oil glands (*sebaceous glands*) are attached to each hair follicle (see Figures 13.2 and 13.3).

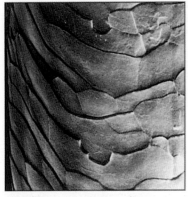

Figure 13.2 Magnified view of hair cuticle, which is composed of keratin

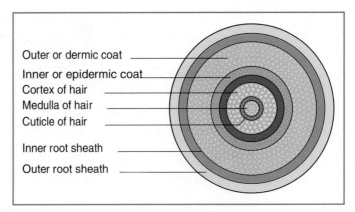

Outer or dermic coat
Inner or epidermic coat
Cortex of hair
Medulla of hair
Cuticle of hair

Inner root sheath
Outer root sheath

Figure 13.3 Cross-section of the hair and follicle

The follicle does not run straight down into the skin or scalp, but is set at an angle so that the hair above the surface flows naturally to one side (see Direction of hair growth opposite).

The bulb is a thickened, club-shaped structure that forms the lower part of the hair root. The lower part of the hair bulb is hollowed out to fit over and cover the hair papilla.

The papilla is a small, cone-shaped elevation located at the bottom of the hair follicle. It fits into the hair bulb. There is a rich blood and nerve supply in the hair papilla that contributes to the growth and regeneration of the hair. It is through the papilla that nourishment reaches the hair bulb. As long as the papilla is healthy and well nourished, it produces hair cells that enable new hair to grow.

## Structures associated with hair follicles

### Arrector pili muscle

The *arrector pili* muscle is a small involuntary muscle attached to the underside of a hair follicle. Fear or cold causes it to contract and the hair to stand up straight, giving the skin the appearance of gooseflesh. Eyelash and eyebrow hair do not have arrector pili muscles.

### Sebaceous (or oil) glands

These glands consist of little sac-like structures in the dermis (see Figure 13.1). The ducts are connected to and open into the hair follicle. Sebaceous glands frequently become troublesome by over-producing oil and bringing on a common form of oily dandruff. Normal secretion from these glands of an oily substance called *sebum* gives lustre and pliability to the hair, and keeps the skin surface soft and supple. The production of sebum is influenced by diet, blood circulation, emotional disturbances, stimulation of endocrine glands, and medication, as described below.

## KEY WORDS

**Epidermis** – *outermost layer of the skin, a thin protective covering over the body*
**Dermis** – *underlying layer of the skin containing blood vessels, lymph, vessels, nerves, hair follicles*
**Subcutaneous tissue** – *fatty layer found below the dermis*

◆ **Diet.** Food influences the general health of the hair. Eating too much sweet, starchy and fatty food can cause the sebaceous glands to become overactive and to secrete too much sebum.

◆ **Blood circulation.** The hair obtains its nourishment from the blood supply, which in turn depends on the foods we eat for certain elements. In the absence of necessary foods, the health of the hair can be affected.

◆ **Emotional disturbances.** Well-being is linked with the health of the hair through the nervous system. Unhealthy hair can be an indication of an unhealthy emotional state.

◆ **Endocrine glands.** The secretions of the endocrine glands influence the health of the body. Any disturbance of these glands can affect the health of the body and, ultimately, the health of the hair.

◆ **Medication.** Drugs, such as hormone replacement medication, can adversely affect the hair's ability to receive permanent waving and other chemical services.

# Hair shapes

Hair usually has one of three general shapes (see Figure 13.4). As it is pushed out and hardens, hair assumes the shape, size and curve of the follicle. A cross-sectional view of the hair under the microscope reveals that:

◆ straight hair is usually round in section

◆ wavy hair is usually oval in section

◆ curly or kinky hair is almost flat in section.

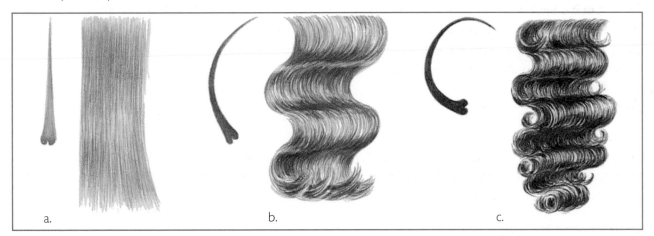

Figure 13.4 Straight hair (a), wavy hair (b), curly hair (c)

There is no strict rule regarding the cross-sectional shapes of hair. Oval, straight and curly hair has been found in all shapes.

# Direction of hair growth

Hair flowing in the same direction is known as *hair stream* or *hair fall*. It is the result of the follicles sloping in the same direction. Two such streams, sloping in opposite directions, form a natural parting of the hair.

◆ **Crown.** Hair that forms a circular pattern, as at the top, is called a crown. Having two *whorls* at either side of the crown is known as a *double crown* (see Figure 13.5). Whorls are often located at the nape; these *nape whorls* require special consideration when styling (see Figure 13.6).

◆ **Cowlick.** A tuft of hair standing up is known as a cowlick. Cowlicks are more noticeable at the front hairline. However, they may be located on other areas of the scalp. When shaping or styling the hair, it is important to consider the direction and lift caused by a cowlick (see Figure 13.7 below).

◆ **Widow's peak.** This is a strong pointed shape of the front hairline, forming a bold 'V' shape.

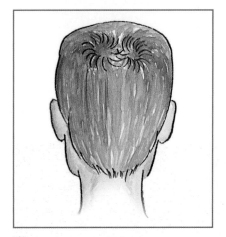

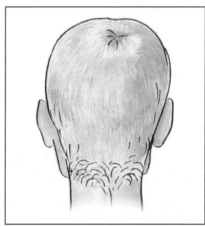

 Figure 13.5 Double crown    ■ Figure 13.6 Nape whorls    ■ Figure 13.7 Cowlick

# Layers of the hair

The structure of the hair is composed of cells arranged in three layers (see Figure 13.3).

◆ **Cuticle.** The outside horny layer is composed of transparent, protective scale-like cells, pointing or overlapping away from the scalp towards the hair ends. Chemicals raise these scales so that solutions such as chemical relaxers, permanent hair colour or wave solutions can enter the cortex. The cuticle protects the inner structure of the hair (see Figure 13.2).

◆ **Cortex.** The middle or inner layer, which gives strength and elasticity to the hair, is made up of a fibrous substance formed by intertwined elongated cells. This layer contains the natural pigment that gives the hair its colour.

◆ **Medulla.** The innermost layer is referred to as the *pith,* or *marrow,* of the hair shaft and is composed of a honeycomb structure of moisture and air pockets. The medulla may be absent in fine and very fine hair and in other textures of hair may be variable in thickness.

# Hair distribution

Hair is distributed all over the body, except on the palms of the hands, soles of the feet, lips, eyelids and the terminal joints of the fingers and toes. There are three types of hair on the body, as described below.

◆ **Terminal hair.** This protects the scalp against the sun's rays and injury, and adorns the head. This hair also grows in the armpits and pubic areas of both sexes, and on the faces of men. Male hormones, however, make a man's facial hair coarser than a woman's.

◆ **Vellus hair.** This is fine, soft, downy hair on the cheeks, forehead and nearly all other areas of the body. It helps in the efficient evaporation of perspiration.

◆ **Lanugo hair.** This grows on the body of the human foetus, being shed at about one month before birth when vellus hair starts to grow.

## Hair on the head and face

The different types of hair on the head and face are referred to by the following terms:

◆ *barba* – the face

◆ *capilli* – the head

◆ *cilia* – the eyelashes

◆ *supercilia* – the eyebrows

## KEY WORDS

**Barba** – *the face*
**Capilli** – *the head*
**Cilia** – *the eyelashes*
**Supercilia** – *the eyebrows*

## Hair growth

If the hair is normal and healthy, each individual hair goes through a steady cycle of events: *growth*, *fall* and *replacement*. You will notice that the average growth of healthy hair on the scalp is about 1.25cm per month. The rate of growth of human hair differs on specific parts of the body, between sexes, among ethnic groups and with age. Scalp hair also differs among individuals in strength, elasticity and degree of wave/curl.

The growth of scalp hair occurs rapidly between the ages of 15–30, but declines sharply between 50 and 60. Scalp hair grows faster on women than on men. Hair growth is also influenced by seasons of the year, nutrition, health and hormones.

Climatic conditions and seasonal changes affect hair in the following ways:

◆ humidity and moisture encourage wavy hair to curl

◆ cold air causes hair to contract

◆ heat causes hair to swell or expand and absorb moisture.

Here are some myths about hair growth:

◆ close clipping, shaving, trimming, cutting or singeing have an effect on the rate of hair growth; this is not true

◆ the application of ointments and oils increases hair growth; this is not true; ointments and oils lubricate the hair shaft, but they do not feed the hair

■ Figure 13.8 Modern head and facial hair looks

◆    hair grows after death; this is not true; the flesh and skin contract, and there is the *appearance* of hair growth

◆    singeing the hair seals in the natural oil; this is not true.

## Normal hair loss

A certain amount of hair is shed daily. This is nature's method of making way for new hair. This average daily shedding is estimated at 50–100 hairs. Hair loss beyond this estimated average indicates some scalp or hair abnormality.

## Life and density of the hair

The average life of hair ranges from 4–7 years, the *anagen* period of hair growth. Factors such as sex, age, type of hair, heredity and health have a bearing on the duration of hair life.

The area of an average head is about 780 cm². There is an average of 1000 hairs to the square inch (645 mm²). The average number of hairs on the head varies with the colour of the hair: blonde, 140,000; brown, 110,000; black, 108,000; red, 90,000.

## The growth cycle of hair

Hair depends on the papilla for its growth. As long as the papilla is not destroyed, the hair will grow. If the hair is pulled out from the roots, it will grow again. But should the papilla be destroyed, the hair will never grow again. In humans, new hair replaces old hair in the following manner.

I    The bulb loosens and separates from the papilla, *catagen* (see Figure 13.9).

2    The bulb moves upwards in the follicle, *telogen.*

3    The hair moves slowly to the surface, where it is shed.

4    The new hair is formed by cell division, which takes place at the root of the hair around the papilla, *anagen*, the growth period of hair (see Figure 13.10).

Eyebrows and eyelashes are replaced every four to five months.

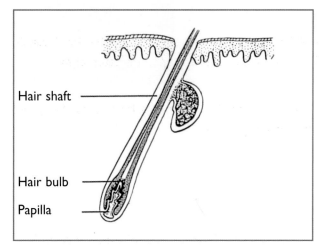

■ Figure 13.9 At an early stage of shedding, the hair shows its separation from the papilla, catagen

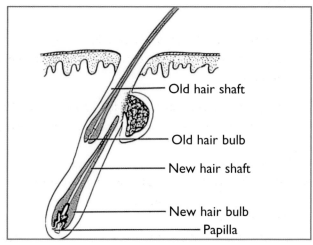

■ Figure 13.10 At a later stage of the hair shedding, you will note a new hair growing from the same papilla, anagen

# Colour of hair

The natural colour of hair, its strength and its texture depend mainly on genetics. The cortex contains colouring matter, minute grains of melanin or pigment. Although there is no definite scientific proof, it appears that pigment is derived from the colour-forming substances in the blood, as is all pigment of the human body. The colour of a person's hair, how light or dark it is, depends on the number of grains of pigment in each strand.

An albino is a person born with white hair, the result of an absence of colouring matter in the hair shaft, accompanied by no marked pigment colouring in the skin or irises of the eyes.

To give successful hair lightening and tinting services, you need to know about natural hair colour and distribution of hair pigment.

## Greying of hair

Grey hair is caused by a mixture of hair without pigment in the cortex (white hair) and naturally coloured hair. The more grey in the overall appearance of the head of hair, the greater percentage of white hair in the mix.

In most cases, the greying of hair is a result of the natural ageing process in humans, although greying can also occur as a result of a serious illnesses or nervous shock. An early diminishing of pigment brought on by emotional tensions can also cause the hair to turn grey.

Premature greying of hair in a young person is usually the result of a defect in pigment formation occurring at birth. Often it will be found that several members of a family are affected with premature greyness.

# Disorders of the hair

None of the following conditions is contagious.

## Canities

Canities is the technical term for grey hair. Its immediate cause is the loss of natural pigment in the hair. There are two types.

1    Congenital canities exists at or before birth. It occurs in albinos and occasionally in persons with normal hair. A patchy type of congenital canities may develop either slowly or rapidly depending upon the cause of the condition.

2    Acquired canities may be due to old age, or onset may occur prematurely in early adult life. Causes of acquired canities may be worry, anxiety, nervous strain, prolonged illness or genetics.

## Ringed hair

Ringed hair has alternate bands of white and dark hair.

## Hypertrichosis

*Hypertrichosis* or *hirsuties* means superfluous hair, an abnormal development of hair on areas of the body normally bearing only downy hair.

Treatment: tweeze or remove by depilatories, electrolysis, shaving or epilation.

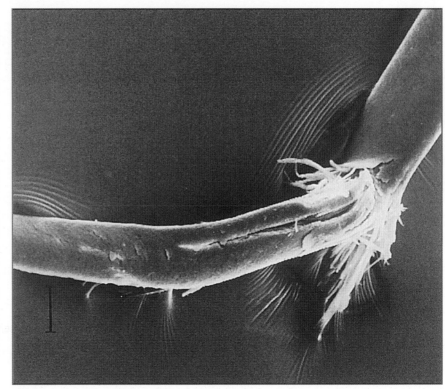

■ Figure 13.11 Split ends    ■ Figure 13.12 Knotted hair

# Trichoptilosis

*Trichoptilosis* is the technical term for *split ends* (see Figure 13.11).

Treatment: the hair should be well oiled to soften and lubricate the dry ends. The splits must be removed by cutting. Split ends may be treated temporarily by proprietary brands of split-end treatment, but these are purely temporary.

# Trichorrexis nodosa

*Trichorrexis nodosa,* or *knotted hair,* is a dry, brittle condition including the formation of nodular swellings along the hair shaft (see Figure 13.12). The hair breaks easily and there is a brush-like spreading out of the fibres of the broken-off hair along the hair shaft.

Treatment: softening the hair with conditioners may prove beneficial.

# Monilethrix

*Monilethrix* is the technical term for *beaded hair* (see Figure 13.13). The hair breaks between the beads or nodes.

Treatment: scalp and hair treatments may improve the hair condition.

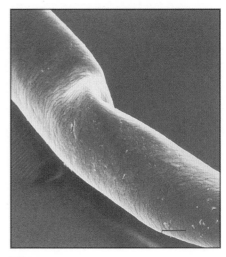

■ Figure 13.13 Beaded hair

## Fragilitas crinium

*Fragilitas crinium* is the technical term for *brittle hair,* or split ends. The hairs may split at any part of their length.

Treatment: conditioning hair treatment may be recommended; the most effective is to cut and remove the split.

# Disorders of the scalp

Just as the skin is continually being shed and replaced, the uppermost layer of the scalp is also being cast off all the time. Ordinarily, these horny scales loosen and fall off freely. The natural shedding of these horny scales should not be mistaken for dandruff.

## Dandruff

Dandruff consists of small, white scales that usually appear on the scalp and hair. The medical term for dandruff is *pityriasis.* Long neglected, excessive dandruff can lead to baldness. The nature of dandruff is not clearly defined by medical authorities although it is generally believed to be of infectious origin. Some authorities hold that it is due to a specific microbe.

A direct cause of dandruff is the excessive shedding of the *epithelial* or surface cells. Instead of growing to the surface and falling off, these horny scales accumulate on the scalp.

Indirect or associated causes of dandruff are a sluggish condition of the scalp, possibly due to poor circulation, infection, injury, lack of nerve stimulation, improper diet and uncleanness. Contributing causes are the use of strong shampoos and insufficient rinsing of the hair after shampooing. There are two principal types of dandruff.

Figure 13.14. Pityriasis capitis simplex

1   **Pityriasis capitis simplex** (dry dandruff) is characterised by an itchy scalp and small white scales, which are usually attached to the scalp in masses, or scattered loosely in the hair. Occasionally, they are so profuse that they fall to the shoulders. Dry dandruff is often the result of a sluggish scalp caused by poor circulation, lack of nerve stimulation, improper diet, emotional and glandular disturbances, or uncleanness (see Figure 13.14).

Treatment: frequent scalp treatments, use of mild shampoos, regular scalp massage, daily use of antiseptic scalp lotions, and applications of scalp ointments.

Figure 13.15. Pityriasis steatoides

2   **Pityriasis steatoides** (greasy or waxy dandruff) is a scaly condition of the epidermis (surface skin). The scales become mixed with sebum, causing them to stick to the scalp in patches. There may be itchiness, causing the person to scratch the scalp. If the greasy scales are torn off, bleeding or oozing of sebum may follow. Both forms of dandruff are considered to be contagious and can be spread by the common use of brushes, combs and

other articles. Therefore, the hairdresser must take the necessary precautions to sterilise everything that comes into contact with the client (see Figure 13.15).

Treatment: medical treatment is advisable.

# Alopecia

This is the technical term for any abnormal hair loss. The natural falling-out of the hair should not be confused with alopecia. As we learned earlier, when hair has gone through its growing stage (anagen), it falls out and is replaced by a new hair. The natural shedding of hair occurs most frequently in spring and autumn. Hair loss due to alopecia is not replaced unless special treatments are given to encourage hair growth. Hairstyles such as ponytails and tight braids cause tension on the hair and can contribute to constant hair loss or baldness.

◆ **Alopecia senilis.** This form of baldness occurs in old age. This loss of hair is permanent. It is not contagious.

◆ **Alopecia premature.** This form of baldness begins any time before middle age with a slow, thinning process. This condition is caused when hairs fall out and are replaced by weaker ones. It is not contagious.

◆ **Alopecia areata.** This is a sudden falling-out of hair in round patches, or baldness in spots, sometimes caused by anaemia, scarlet fever, typhoid fever or syphilis. Patches are round or irregular in shape and can vary in size from 1.25–5 or 7.5cm in diameter. Affected areas are slightly depressed, smooth and very pale due to a decreased blood supply. In most conditions of alopecia areata, the nervous system has been subjected to some injury. Since the flow of blood is influenced by the nervous system, the affected area also is poorly nourished (see Figure 13.16).

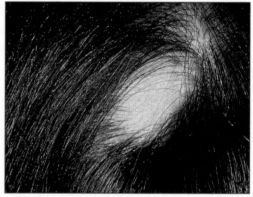

Treatment: alopecia appears in a variety of different forms, caused by many abnormal conditions. Sometimes an alopecia condition can be improved by scalp treatments.

Figure 13.16 Alopecia areata

# Infections

All the infections covered below are contagious.

### Fungal infections

◆ **Tinea.** This is the medical term for ringworm. Ringworm is caused by a fungus. All forms are contagious and can be transmitted from one person to another. The disease is commonly carried by scales or hairs containing fungi. Bathtubs, swimming pools and unsterilised articles are also sources of transmission.

Ringworm starts with a small, reddened patch of little blisters. Several such patches may be present.

Treatment: any ringworm condition should be referred to a medical practitioner.

◆ **Tinea capitis.** Also known as ringworm of the scalp, is characterised by red papules, or spots, at the opening of the hair follicles (see Figure 13.17). The patches spread and the hair becomes brittle and lifeless. It breaks off, leaving a stump, or falls from the enlarged open follicles.

Treatment: as a ringworm condition, it should be referred to a medical practitioner.

◆ **Tinea favosa.** Also known as favus or honeycomb ringworm is characterised by dry sulphur yellow cuplike crusts on the scalp, called scutula, which have a peculiar odour (see Figure 13.18). Scars from favus are bald patches that may be pink or white and shiny. It is very contagious.

Treatment: as a ringworm condition, it should be referred to a medical practitioner.

## Animal parasitic infections

◆ **Scabies.** *Itch* is a highly contagious, animal parasitic skin disease, caused by the itch mite. Vesicles and pustules can form from the irritation of the parasites or from scratching the affected areas.

Treatment: proprietary brands of treatment may be purchased. The lotion is applied to almost the entire body and remains for a set period of time (hours) and then removed. It is generally wise to treat the whole family as well.

◆ **Pediculosis capitis.** This is a contagious condition caused by the *head louse* (animal parasite) infesting the hair of the scalp (see Figure 13.19). The adult female is 3–4mm long, the male slightly smaller. The female adult, during its life span of approximately one month, lays seven to ten eggs per day. The eggs hatch in about eight days and the louse becomes sexually mature within a further eight days. As the parasites feed on blood at the scalp, itching occurs and the resultant scratching can cause infection. The head louse may be transmitted from one person to another by contact with infested hats, combs, brushes or other personal articles.

Treatment: to kill head lice advise the client to apply a proprietary brand of treatment, following the manufacturer's instructions. Proprietary brands of treatment shampoo may be used to remove the infestation. However, to prevent re-infestation the application of a treatment lotion is usually required. The duration of an infestation may be calculated by the position of the egg along the hair's length. The female adult lays its egg on the hair next to the scalp, therefore eggs located 1.25cm from the scalp will have been produced one month before. The unsightly husks of the *nit*, or egg, may be removed using a fine-toothed comb.

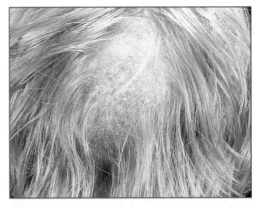

■ Figure 13.17 Tinea capitis

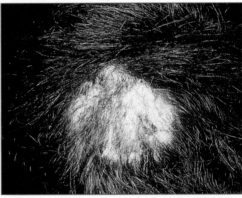

■ Figure 13.18 Tinea favosa (honeycomb ringworm)

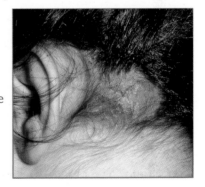

■ Figure 13.19 Pediculosis capitis

### Staphylococci infections

◆ **Furuncle.** Also known as a *boil*, this is an acute staphylococci infection of a hair follicle that produces constant pain (see Figure 13.20). It is limited to a specific area and produces a pustule perforated by hair.

Treatment: minor boils will often disappear themselves without treatment. Their presence can be indicative of other medical problems. The continuous presence of furuncles should be referred to a medical practitioner.

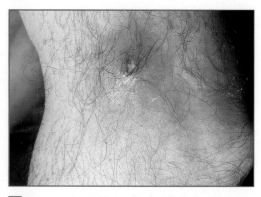

■ Figure 13.20 Furuncle or boil

◆ **Carbuncle.** This is the result of an acute staphylococci infection and is larger than a furuncle. Treatment: refer the client to a medical practitioner.

# Skin

The skin is the largest and one of the most important organs of the body. The scientific study of the skin and scalp is important to the hairdresser and beautician because it forms the basis for an effective programme of skincare, beauty services and scalp treatments. A hairdresser who has a thorough understanding of skin, its structure and functions is in a better position to give clients professional advice on scalp, facial and hand care (see Figure 13.21).

A healthy skin is slightly moist, soft and flexible, possesses a slightly acid reaction, and is free from any disease or disorder. The skin also has immunity responses to organisms that touch or try to enter it. Its texture (feel and appearance) ideally is smooth and fine grained. A person with a good complexion has fine skin texture and healthy skin colour. Appendages of the skin are hair, nails, and sweat and oil glands.

Skin varies in thickness. It is thinnest on the eyelids and thickest on the palms and soles. Continued pressure on any part of the skin can cause it to thicken and develop a callus.

■ Figure 13.21 Microscopic section of skin

The skin of the scalp is constructed similarly to the skin elsewhere on the human body. However, the scalp has larger and deeper hair follicles to accommodate the longer hair of the head.

# Histology of the skin

The skin contains two main divisions: the epidermis and the dermis (see Figure 13.22).

## Epidermis

The outermost layer of the skin, it is the thinnest layer and forms a protective covering for the body. It contains no blood vessels, but it has many small nerve endings. The epidermis is made up of the following layers.

◆ **Stratum corneum.** The *horny* layer, is the outer layer of the skin. Its scale-like cells are continually being shed and replaced by underneath cells coming to the surface. These cells contain the protein keratin, and combined with a thin covering layer of oil help make the *stratum corneum* almost waterproof.

◆ **Stratum lucidum.** The clear layer, consists of small, transparent cells through which light can pass.

◆ **Stratum granulosu.** The granular layer, consists of cells that look like distinct granules. These cells are almost dead and are pushed to the surface to replace cells that are shed from the *stratum corneum.*

◆ **Stratum germinativum.** This was formerly known as the *stratum mucosum* and is also referred to as the *basal* or *Malpighian layer.* It is composed of several layers of different-shaped cells. The deepest layer is responsible for the growth of the epidermis. It also contains a dark skin pigment, called *melanin,* which determines skin colour and protects the sensitive cells below from the destructive effects of excessive ultra-violet rays of the sun or of an ultra-violet lamp. These special cells are called *melanocytes.*

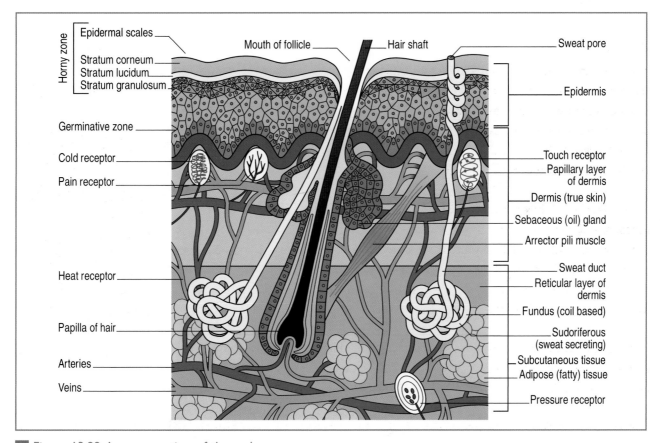

■ Figure 13.22 A cross-section of the scalp

# Dermis

The *dermis* is the underlying, or inner, layer of the skin. It is also called the *derma, corium, cutis* or *true skin.* It is about 25 times thicker than the epidermis. It is a highly sensitive and vascular layer of connective tissue. Within its structure there are numerous blood vessels, lymph vessels, nerves, sweat glands, oil glands, hair follicles, arrector pili muscles and papillae. The dermis is made up of two layers: the *papillary* or superficial layer, and the *reticular* or deeper layer.

- **The papillary layer.** This layer lies directly beneath the epidermis. It contains small cone-shaped projections of elastic tissue that point upwards into the epidermis. These projections are called *papillae*. Some of these papillae contain looped *capillaries*; others contain nerve fibre endings, called *tactile corpuscles*, which are nerve endings for the sense of touch. This layer also contains some of the melanin skin pigment.

- **The reticular layer.** This contains the following structures within its network: fat cells, blood vessels, lymph vessels, oils glands, sweat glands, hair follicles, arrector pili muscles. This layer also supplies the skin with oxygen and nutrients.

- **Subcutaneous tissue.** This fatty layer is found below the dermis. Some histologists consider this tissue as a continuation of the dermis. This tissue is also called *adipose* or *subcutis* tissue, and varies in thickness according to the age, sex and general health of the individual. It gives smoothness and contour to the body, contains fats for use as energy and also acts as a protective cushion for the outer skin. Circulation is maintained by a network of *arteries* and *lymphatics*.

## How the skin is nourished

Blood and lymph supply nourishment to the skin. As they circulate through the skin, the blood and lymph contribute essential materials for growth, nourishment and repair of the skin, hair and nails. (Note: hair and nails are not able to repair themselves as they are dead materials.) In the subcutaneous tissue are found networks of arteries and lymphatics that send their smaller branches to hair papillae, hair follicles and skin glands.

## Nerves of the skin

The skin contains the surface endings of many nerve fibres, as described below.

- **Motor nerve fibres.** These are distributed to the arrector pili muscles attached to the hair follicles. This muscle can cause 'gooseflesh' when you are frightened or cold.

- **Sensory nerve fibres.** These react to heat, cold, touch, pressure and pain. These sensory receptors send messages to the brain (see Figure 13.23).

- **Secretory nerve fibres.** These are distributed to the sweat and oil glands of the skin. These nerves regulate the excretion of perspiration from the sweat glands and control the flow of sebum to the surface of the skin.

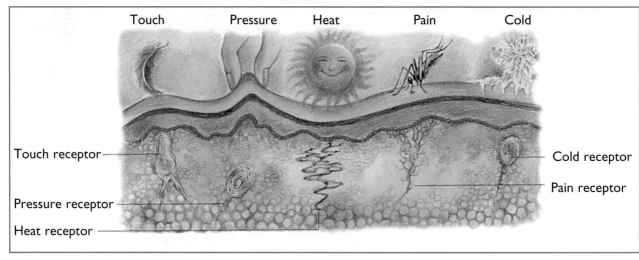

Figure 13.23 Sensory nerves of the skin

## Sense of touch

The papillary layer of the dermis houses the nerve endings that provide the body with the sense of touch. These nerve endings register basic sensations: touch, pain, heat, cold, pressure or deep touch. Nerve endings are most abundant in the fingertips. Complex sensations, such as vibrations, seem to depend on the sensitivity of a combination of these nerve endings.

## Skin elasticity

The pliability of the skin depends on the elasticity of the dermis. For example, healthy skin regains its former shape almost immediately after being expanded.

## Ageing skin

The ageing process of the skin is a subject of vital importance to many people. Perhaps the most outstanding characteristic of the aged skin is its loss of elasticity. One factor that contributes to the loss of elasticity is that, as we age, subcutaneous tissue shrinks and is not as effective a support system in preventing the skin from wrinkling.

## Skin colour

The colour of the skin, whether fair, medium or dark, depends, in part, on the blood supply to the skin and primarily on melanin, the colouring matter that is deposited in the *stratum germinativum* and the papillary layers of the dermis. The colour of pigment varies from person to person. The distinctive colour of the skin is a hereditary trait and varies among ethnic origins and races. Melanin protects sensitive cells from sunburn and tanning beds with ultra-violet rays. A sun protection factor (SPF) should be used to help the melanin in the skin and protect it from burning.

## Glands of the skin

The skin contains two types of duct gland that extract materials from the blood to form new substances: the *sudoriferous* or *sweat glands,* and the *sebaceous* or *oil glands* (see Figure 13.24).

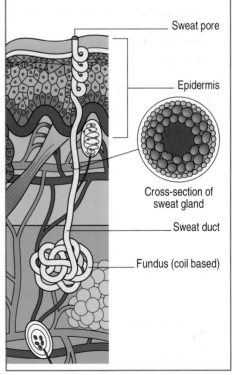

- ◆ **Sweat glands.** The sweat glands (tubular type), which excrete sweat, consist of a coiled base, or *fundus*, and a tube-like duct that terminates at the skin surface to form the sweat pore (see Figure 13.25). Practically all parts of the body are supplied with sweat glands, which are more numerous on the palms, soles, forehead and in the armpits.

The sweat glands regulate body temperature and help to eliminate waste products from the body. Their activity is greatly increased by heat, exercise, emotions and certain drugs.

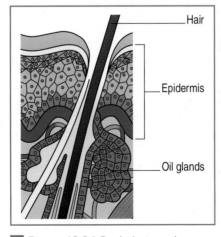

■ Figure 13.24 Body hair and follicle, showing oil glands

■ Figure 13.25 Sweat gland

The excretion of sweat is controlled by the nervous system. Normally, one to two pints of liquids containing salts are eliminated daily through sweat pores in the skin.

◆ **Oil glands.** The oil glands (saccular type) consist of little sacs whose ducts open into the hair follicles. They secrete sebum, which lubricates the skin and preserves the softness of the hair. With the exception of the palms and soles, these glands are found in all parts of the body, particularly in the face and scalp where they are larger.

Sebum is an oily substance produced by the oil glands. Ordinarily, it flows through the oil ducts leading to the mouths of the hair follicles. However, when the sebum becomes hardened and the duct becomes clogged, a *blackhead* is formed.

# Functions of the skin

The principal functions of the skin are protection, sensation, heat regulation, excretion, secretion and absorption.

◆ **Protection.** The skin protects the body from injury and bacterial invasion. The outermost layer of the epidermis is covered with a thin layer of sebum, thus rendering it waterproof. It is resistant to wide variations in temperature, minor injuries, chemically active substances and many forms of bacteria.

◆ **Sensation.** By stimulating sensory nerve endings, the skin responds to heat, cold, touch, pressure and pain. When the nerve endings are stimulated, a message is sent to the brain. You respond by saying 'ouch' if you feel pain, by scratching an itch, or pulling away when you touch something hot. Sensory nerve endings, responsive to touch and pressure, are located near hair follicles.

◆ **Heat regulation.** This means that the skin protects the body from the environment. A healthy body maintains a constant internal temperature of about 98.6° Fahrenheit (37° Celsius). As changes occur in the outside temperature, the blood and sweat glands of the skin make necessary adjustments and the body is cooled by the evaporation of sweat.

◆ **Excretion.** Perspiration from the sweat glands is excreted through the skin. Water lost through perspiration takes salt and other chemicals with it.

◆ **Secretion.** Sebum, or oil, is secreted by the sebaceous glands. This oil lubricates the skin, keeping it soft and pliable. Oil also keeps hair soft. Emotional stress can increase the flow of sebum.

◆ **Absorption.** This is limited, but it does occur. Female hormones, when an ingredient of a face cream, can enter the body through the skin and influence it to a minor degree. Fatty materials, such as lanolin creams, are absorbed largely through hair follicles and sebaceous gland openings. Some hairdressing products, for example oxidation tints, are detectable in the blood stream following application to the scalp.

# Disorders of the skin

In your work as a hairdresser in a salon you will come into contact with skin and scalp disorders. You must be prepared to recognise certain common skin conditions and know what you can and cannot do with them. If a client has a skin condition that the hairdresser does not recognise as a simple disorder, the person should be referred to a medical practitioner.

It is extremely important that a client who has an inflamed skin disorder, infectious or not, should not be treated in the salon. The hairdresser should be able to recognise these conditions and suggest that appropriate measures be taken to prevent more serious consequences. Thus the health of the hairdresser as well as the health of the public is safeguarded.

# Definitions of disease

Before describing the diseases of the skin and scalp so that they will be recognisable to the hairdresser, it is necessary to understand what is meant by disease.

- **Acute disease.** One with symptoms of a more or less violent character, such as fever, and usually of short duration.

- **Allergy.** A sensitivity that some people develop to normally harmless substances. Skin allergies are quite common. Contact with certain types of cosmetics, medicines and tints, or eating certain foods can all cause an itching eruption, accompanied by redness, swelling, blisters, oozing and scaling.

- **Chronic disease.** One of long duration, usually mild but recurring.

- **Congenital disease.** One that is present in the infant at birth.

- **Contagious disease.** One that is communicable by contact.

- **Disease.** Any departure from a normal state of health.

- **Epidemic.** The appearance of a disease that simultaneously attacks a large number of persons living in a particular locality. Infantile paralysis, influenza and smallpox are examples of epidemic-causing diseases.

- **Infectious disease.** One due to germs (bacterial or viral) taken into the body as a result of contact with a contaminated object or lesion.

- **Inflammation.** A skin disorder characterised by redness, pain, swelling and heat.

- **Occupational disease** (such as dermatitis). One that is due to certain kinds of employment, such as coming in contact with cosmetics, chemicals or metals (e.g. nickel).

- **Parasitic disease.** One that is caused by vegetable or animal parasites, such as pediculosis and ringworm.

- **Pathogenic disease.** One produced by disease-causing bacteria, such as staphylococcus and streptococcus (pus-forming bacteria), or viruses.

- **Seasonal disease.** One that is influenced by the weather, such as prickly heat in the summer, and forms of eczema, which is more prevalent in cold weather.

- **Skin disease.** Any infection of the skin characterised by an objective lesion (one that can be seen), which may consist of scales, pimples or pustules.

- **Systemic disease.** Due to under- or over-functioning of internal glands. It can be caused by faulty diet.

- **Venereal disease.** A contagious disease commonly acquired by contact with an infected person during sexual intercourse.

# Disorders of the sebaceous (oil) glands

There are several common disorders of the sebaceous (oil) glands that the hairdresser should be aware of.

◆ **Comedones** or **blackheads.** Worm-like masses of hardened sebum, appearing most frequently on the face, especially the forehead and nose.

Blackheads accompanied by pimples often occur in youths between the ages of 13 and 20. During this adolescent period, the activity of the sebaceous glands is stimulated, thereby contributing to the formation of blackheads and pimples (see Figure 13.26).

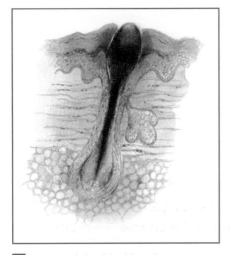

■ Figure 13.26 Blackheads

When the hair follicle is filled with an excess of oil from the sebaceous gland, a blackhead forms and creates a blockage at the mouth of the follicle. Should this condition become severe, medical attention is necessary.

To treat blackheads, the skin's oiliness must be reduced by local applications of cleansers and the blackheads removed under sterile conditions. Thorough skin cleansing each night is a very important factor. Cleansing creams and lotions often achieve better results than common soap and water.

◆ **Milia or whiteheads.** A disorder of the sebaceous (oil) glands caused by the accumulation of sebaceous matter beneath the skin. This can occur on any part of the face, neck and, occasionally, on the chest and shoulders. Whiteheads are associated with fine-textured, dry types of skin.

◆ **Acne.** A chronic inflammatory disorder of the sebaceous glands, occurring most frequently on the face, back and chest. The cause of acne is generally believed to be microbic, but predisposing factors are adolescence and perhaps certain foods in the diet. Acne, or common pimples, is also known as *acne simplex* or *acne vulgaris* (see Figure 13.27).

Acne appears in a variety of different types, ranging from the simple (non-contagious) pimple, to serious, deep-seated skin conditions. It is always advisable to have the condition examined and diagnosed by a medical practitioner before any service is given in a salon.

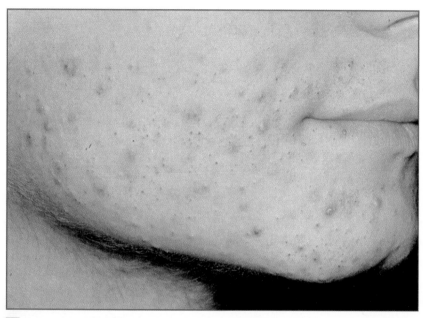

Figure 13.27 Acne simplex, or acne vulgaris

- **Seborrhoea.** A skin condition caused by an excessive secretion of the sebaceous glands. An oily or shiny condition of the nose, forehead or scalp indicates the presence of seborrhoea. On the scalp, it is readily detected by an unusual amount of oil on the hair.

- **Asteatosis.** A condition of dry, scaly skin characterised by absolute or partial deficiency of sebum, due to senile changes (old age) or some bodily disorders. It can be caused by alkalis, such as those found in soaps and washing powders.

- **Rosacea.** Formerly called *acne rosacea*, a chronic inflammatory congestion of the cheeks and nose. It is characterised by redness, dilation of the blood vessels and the formation of papules and pustules. The cause of rosacea is unknown. Certain things are known to aggravate it in some individuals, including consumption of hot liquids, spicy food or alcohol, being exposed to extremes of heat and cold, exposure to sunlight, and stress.

- **Steatoma, or sebaceous cyst.** A subcutaneous tumour of the sebaceous gland. It is filled with sebum and ranges in size from a pea to an orange. It usually appears on the scalp, neck and back.

## Definitions of inflammation

◆ **Dermatitis.** A term used to indicate an inflammatory condition of the skin. The lesions come in various forms, such as vesicles or papules.

◆ **Eczema.** An inflammation of the skin, of acute or chronic nature, presenting many forms of dry or moist lesions. It is frequently accompanied by itching or a burning sensation. All cases of eczema should be referred to a medical practitioner for treatment. Its cause is unknown.

◆ **Psoriasis.** A common, chronic, inflammatory skin disease of which the cause is unknown. It is usually found on the scalp, elbows, knees, chest and lower back, rarely on the face. The lesions are round dry patches covered with coarse silvery scales. If irritated, bleeding points occur. It is not contagious.

◆ **Herpes simplex.** A recurring virus infection, commonly called *fever blisters*. It is characterised by the eruption of a single vesicle or group of vesicles on a red swollen base. The blisters usually appear on the lips, nostrils or other parts of the face and rarely last more than a week. It is contagious (see Figure 13.28).

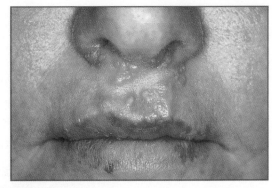

■ Figure 13.28 Herpes simplex, or cold sore

## Occupational disorders in hairdressing

Abnormal conditions resulting from contact with chemicals or tints can occur in the course of performing services in the salon. Some individuals may develop allergies to ingredients in cosmetics, antiseptics, cold waving lotions and aniline derivative tints. These can cause eruptive skin infections known as *dermatitis venenata*. It is important that hairdressers employ protective measures, such as the use of rubber gloves or protective creams, whenever possible.

Research in many countries has shown that between 10 and 50% of hairdressers (male and female) suffer from eczema. Hairdressers' eczema is caused when the skin comes in contact with:

◆ water

◆ chemicals including shampoo, hair bleaches and liquids used with permanent colouring

◆ nickel (in scissors, combs, blow-dryers and money)

◆ airflows (blow-dryers and wind).

Respiratory disorders may be produced by the inhalation of products such as bleach powder, hairsprays and permanent wave treatments.

# Glossary

**Albino.** Lack of colour pigment in skin, hair and irises of the eyes.

**Allergy.** Sensitivity to normally harmless substances.

**Alopecia.** Abnormal hair loss.

**Alopecia areata.** Small patches of hair loss.

**Alopecia premature.** Premature hair loss.

**Alopecia senilis.** Hair loss due to old age.

**Alpha keratin.** Hair in an unstretched state.

**Ammonium thioglycolate.** Active ingredient of many cold wave perms.

**Ampholytic.** Acts as a foam stabiliser and makes shampoo less irritating to the eyes.

**Anagen.** Growth period for hair.

**Anionic.** Lowers the surface tension of water.

**Antioxidant.** Prevents or inhibits oxidation.

**Arrector pili muscle.** Small involuntary muscle attached to the underside of a hair root.

**Asymmetrical.** Uneven but balanced.

**Avant-garde.** Ahead of fashion.

**Bactericides.** Stop the growth of bacteria.

**Barba.** The face.

**Base.** Petroleum cream to protect the scalp during the straightening process.

**Beta keratin.** Hair in a stretched state.

**Body language.** Messages given to others through the way you position your body.

**Calcium hydroxide.** Relaxer, sometimes called *no-lye*.

**Canities.** Grey hair.

**Capilli.** The head.

**Carbuncle.** Acute staphylococci infection.

**Catagen.** Period when hair loosens and separates from the papilla.

**Cationic.** Attracted to the hair, has a positive charge.

**Cilia.** The eyelashes.

**Closed question.** Requires a yes or no answer.

**Contra-indication.** The presence of something that indicates that a service should not be undertaken.

**Cortex.** The middle or inner layer, which gives strength and elasticity to the hair, is made up of a fibrous substance formed by intertwined elongated cells.

**COSHH.** Control of Substances Hazardous to Health.

**Croquignole.** Winding hair on to a curler, starting at the points and winding towards the roots.

**Cuticle.** Outermost layer of the hair. This horny layer is composed of transparent, overlapping, protective scale-like cells, pointing or overlapping away from the scalp towards the hair ends.

**Dermatologist.** Medical skin specialist.

**Dermatology.** Study of skin, its nature, structure, functions, diseases and treatment.

**Dermis.** Inner layer of the skin.

**Detergent.** A cleansing agent.

**Direct hair colours.** Hair coloration applied straight from the bottle to the hair. The colour of the product is the colour imparted to the hair.

**Effleurage.** Stroking massage movement using either the fingers or the palms of the hands.

**Elasticity.** The ability for hair to stretch and return to its original length.

**Endocrine gland.** Secretes directly into the bloodstream.

**Endothermic.** Perming processes using externally provided heat to aid chemical reactions.

**Epidermis.** Outermost layer of the skin.

**Epilation.** Hair removal.

**Erythema.** Increased capillary blood flow.

**Etiology.** Study of the causes of disease.

**Eumelanin.** Black and brown natural hair pigment.

**Exothermic pads.** Pads, often containing calcium oxide, used during perming that are moistened and clamped around wound hair to provide heat to activate curling agents.

**Falling heat.** Applying heat when perming hair using pre-heated clamps that are applied to wound hair and the heat is conducted to the hair. Introduced during the 1930s.

**Favus.** Honeycomb ringworm. Highly contagious.

**Floor limit.** Associated with credit/charge card payments. The maximum amount that a transaction can reach before requiring the card company's authorisation.

**Fragilitas crinium.** Brittle hair – split ends.

**Friction.** A vigorous pinching, rubbing movement usually used when applying astringent lotions.

**Fungicide.** Stops the growth of fungi.

**Furuncle.** A boil – staphylococci infection of a hair follicle.

**Glycerol monothioglycolate.** Main active ingredient of acid-balanced perms.

**Hair bulb.** Thickened, club-shaped structure that forms the lower part of the hair root.

**Hair colour restorers.** Metallic hair coloration.

**Hair follicle.** Tube-like depression or pocket in the skin or scalp that encases the hair root.

**Hair root.** Portion of the hair structure located beneath the skin's surface.

**Hair shaft.** Portion of the hair structure extending above the skin's surface.

**Hazard.** Something with the potential to cause harm.

**Henna.** The dried crushed leaves of the Egyptian privet (*Lawsonia Alba*). Used as a vegetable hair coloration.

**Hirsuties.** Superfluous hair.

**Humectant.** Allows the attraction of water.

**Hydrogen peroxide.** Oxidising agent.

**Hygroscopic.** The ability to absorb moisture from the atmosphere.

**Hypertrichosis.** Superfluous hair.

**Incompatibility test.** A test for the presence of substances on the hair that will react adversely with oxidation processes (usually metallic slats).

**Keratin.** Protein found in hair, nails and skin.

**Lanugo hair.** Hair growth on the human foetus.

**Laurel sulphate.** Detergent base.

**Malpighian layer.** *Stratum germinativum*, the deepest layer of the epidermis. This is the growth layer.

**Medulla.** Central layer of the hair containing air and moisture pockets. May be missing from very fine hair.

**Melanin.** Natural pigment of hair and skin.

**Melanocyte.** Cells that produce melanin.

**Moisturiser.** Allows the attraction of water.

**Monilethrix.** Beaded hair.

**Non-ionic.** Acts as a foam stabiliser.

**Open-ended questions.** Usually include *what, when, who, when* or *how*.

**Papilla.** A cone-shaped elevation located at the bottom of the hair follicle.

**Papillary layer.** First layer of the dermis of the skin, contains nerve endings for the sense of touch.

**Pathology.** Study of disease.

**Pediculosis capitis.** Head lice.

**Penetrating conditioner.** Conditioner that penetrates to the cortex and has a temporary effect on the hair's condition and elasticity.

**Permanent colour.** Hair coloration that makes a permanent change to the hair's colour.

**Petrissage.** A deep kneading massage movement using the pads of the fingers.

**pH.** Potential hydrogen.

**Pheomelanin.** Yellow and red natural hair pigment.

**Pityriasis.** Dandruff.

**Pityriasis capitis simplex.** Dry dandruff.

**Pityriasis simplex.** Dandruff.

**Pityriasis steatoides.** Greasy/waxy dandruff.

**Porosity.** Ability to absorb moisture.

**Postiche.** Added hair.

**Pre-pigmentation.** Adding gold and red tones when recolouring bleached or white hair.

**Progressive hair coloration.** Metallic hair coloration.

**Quasi-permanent colour.** Hair coloration that permanently adds colour to hair, does not lighten hair colour. May cause lightening as colour fades.

**Reticular layer.** Inner layer of the dermis. Contains fat cells, blood vessels, oil glands, sweat glands, hair follicles and arrector pili muscles.

**Ringed hair.** Hair with alternate light/dark colour bands.

**Risk.** The likelihood of a hazard's potential being realised.

**Rotary massage.** Rotating the fingers while rubbing the scalp. Used when shampooing.

**Scabies.** Animal parasite infection caused by the presence of the itch mite.

**Scutula.** Sulphur yellow crusts formed by *tinea favosa*.

**Sebaceous glands.** Sac-like structures in the dermis that produce sebum into the hair follicle.

**Seborrhea.** Greasy scalp.

**Sebum.** Oil secreted by the sebaceous gland; natural oil of the hair and scalp.

**Semi-permanent colour.** Hair colour that last approximately six to ten shampoos.

**Sodium bromate.** Oxidising agent.

**Sodium hydroxide.** Caustic relaxer often called a hair straightener.

**Sodium lauryl ether sulphate.** Detergent base.

**SPF.** Sun protection factor.

**Stratum corneum.** Horny outer layer of the epidermis.

**Stratum germinativum.** Deepest layer of the epidermis – this is the growth layer.

**Stratum granulosum.** Granular third layer of the epidermis.

**Stratum lucidum.** Clear second layer of the epidermis.

**Subcutaneous tissue.** Fatty layer below the dermis of the skin.

**Sudoriferous glands.** Sweat glands, help to regulate body temperature.

**Sulphonated vegetable oil.** Usually castor oil treated with sulphuric acid. Emulsifies with water.

**Supercilia.** The eyebrows.

**Surface-active conditioner.** Conditioner that acts on the outside of the hair shaft.

**Surfactant.** Detergent – cleansing or surface active.

**Sweat glands.** Help to regulate body temperature.

**Symmetrical.** Evenly balanced.

**Telogen.** Period when hair root is dormant.

**Temporary colour.** Hair coloration that lasts from one shampoo to the next.

**Terminal hair.** Hair growing on the head, armpits, pubic area and faces of men.

**Tinea.** Ringworm, a fungal infection.

**Tinea capitis.** Ringworm of the scalp.

**Tinea favosa.** Honeycomb ringworm. Highly contagious.

**Trichology.** Study of the hair and scalp.

**Trichoptilosis.** Split ends.

**Trichorrexis nodosa.** Knotted hair.

**Triethanolomine lauryl sulphate.** Base for soapless detergent.

**Vellus hair.** Fine soft downy hair growing on all areas of the body other than those covered by terminal hair.

**Vulcanite.** Hardened rubber used in the manufacture of combs.

**Wireless system.** Applying heat when perming, using pre-heated clamps that are applied to wrapped hair. Introduced during the 1930s.

# Model answers

## Chapter 1   Working safely

### Self review – page 3

Figure 1.3:

    i     open razor on shelf

    ii    uncovered waste bin

    iii   water spillage on the floor

    iv   loose floor tile

    v    hairdryer electric cable lying in the basin

    vi   clipper cable lying on the floor

    vii  electrical appliances left plugged in when not in use

    viii electric switch located very close to the basin

    ix   large corrosive liquid containers stored on high shelves

    x    sterilising cabinet without sufficient space for air circulation between itself and the shelves.

### Self review – page 11

1    The steriliser that uses moist heat at high temperatures is an autoclave.

2    Floors should be swept at least daily.

3    Tools should be cleaned and dried before being placed in an ultra-violet sterilising cabinet.

4    The Data Protection Act requires your salon's client records are stored securely and contents communicated only to authorised people.

5    A hazard is something with the potential to cause harm.

6    A risk is the likelihood of a hazard's potential being realised.

7    Yes, they have a responsibility not to put themselves or others at risk due to their actions or omissions.

8    Disposal of any sharp objects that may have had contact with bodily fluids.

9    You can find out about your salon's health and safety procedures by asking your manager or supervisor.

10   Emergencies that can occur in the salon include fire, food, gas leak, bomb alert, and suspicious person or packages.

# Chapter 2   Creating a positive image
## Self review – page 20

1   Two potential barriers to effective communication with your client include hearing or sight disadvantages.

2   Always acknowledge the presence of a client even when busy working with another.

3   Indicators that you are communicating effectively with a client include:

 i     asking further questions

 ii    smiling

 iii   appearing relaxed

 iv    nodding their head.

4   One feature of body language that indicates client discomfort is fidgeting. This may indicate physical discomfort with the service being provided or emotional discomfort being caused through concerns about the service time or the suitability of the product being used or sold.

5   Positive feedback – confirming that the service is meeting the client's expectations.

6   Use feedback to adjust and service delivery to better meet your client's wishes, and confirm what works well.

7   When a complaint exceeds your area of responsibility refer it to your line manager or supervisor.

8   You should never admit liability without guidance from your insurance company.

9   Complaints are best discussed in private, without an audience, either in an office or an area private from other clients.

10   Aspects of service that may be monitored through a client questionnaire include:

 i     why they chose to visit this salon in preference to others

 ii    frequency of their salon visit

 iii   the most enjoyable part of the service

 iv    the least enjoyable part of the service

 v     acceptability of the time taken to provide the service

 vi    value for money

 vii   why they returned to the salon

 viii  additional services they would like the salon to offer.

# Chapter 3 Consulting with your clients

## Self review – page 32

1 Visual aids that can be used to communicate proposed style outcomes include style books, photographs, fashion magazines, computerised style viewers and wigs.

2 Additional services that can often enhance someone's hairstyle include colour and permanent wave.

3 Hair texture refers to the degree of coarseness or fineness of the hair (thick or thin).

4 Hair porosity is the ability of all types of hair to absorb moisture (hygroscopic quality).

5 Hair elasticity is the ability of hair to stretch and return to its original form without breaking.

6 The oval-shaped face is generally recognised as the ideal shape.

7 The main feature of a concave profile is a prominent chin.

8 Hair stretches more easily when wet.

9 Strong hair growth patterns are nape whorls, double crowns and cowlicks.

10 Uneven porosity may cause an uneven result in hair colour or degree of curl. This is due to uneven rates of absorption of the chemicals into the hair.

# Chapter 4 Shampooing and conditioning the hair and scalp

## Self review – page 50

1 This will be determined by your salon's choice.

2 Create a build-up of calcium deposits forming limescale on the rose or shower head.

3 Client is unable to get their hair wet, whether due to illness, a lack of water or when there is insufficient time, so a dry shampoo may be used.

4 Test the temperature of the water by spraying it on the back of your hand or the inside of your wrist.

5 Pads of the fingers and thumbs working in small rotary movements on the scalp.

6 Selenium sulphide and zinc pyrethione.

7 Between 4.5 and 5.5.

8 Coats the hair.

9 During perming and to protect hair from the effects of the sun.

10 Stimulate capillary blood flow and the production of sebum, and relax the client.

# Chapter 5   Cutting hair
## Self review – page 84

1   Factors that may affect the choice of haircut for a client are:

    i    client's requirements, personality and lifestyle

    ii   client's face and head shape

    iii  client's body proportion

    iv  hair type, thickness and length

    v   strong directions of hair growth

    vi  suggested hairstyle

    vii client's ability to manage the hairstyle.

2   The purpose of gowning is to protect the client and their clothes from hair clippings and any product spillage.

3   Haircutting scissors should be held using the thumb and third finger.

4   The name given to the hair cutting technique that reduces length but retains all of the hair's natural volume is club cutting.

5   Taper cutting hair will encourage wavy hair to curl.

6   Scissor-over-comb graduation enables the hairdresser to produces a shorter/closer result.

7   A haircutting razor/shaper can be used on wet hair.

8   The electric clipper can be used inverted to outline a beard.

9   A lightly coloured towel should be used when beard trimming so that the outline shape of the beard can clearly be seen.

10   The essential feature of a graduated neckline is that there is a gradual blend of the hairline from the style to the neck. Often the exact point where the two join is indiscernible.

# Chapter 6   Styling and dressing hair
## Self review – page 115

1   A golf ball-sized sphere of styling mousse is usually used when blow-drying.

2   The fishtail nozzle with the blow-dryer helps to control the airflow and concentrate it in one area.

3   Combs are best made of polished aluminum or bone if they are to used when blow-drying hair.

4   When blow-drying for smooth results the airflow should be directed in the direction that the hair lies.

5   Lift can be obtained when blow-drying by directing the airflow into the root area of upheld meshes of hair.

6   Metal mesh hair rollers can mark bleached or very porous hair.

7    The size of roller determines the strength of curl achieved.

8    The section taken should be the same size as the roller.

9    The term over-directing when setting hair means to comb the hair at over 90° to achieve added volume in the hairstyle.

10   Fine pins should be pointed downwards in a finished hairstyle so that they do not fall out.

# Chapter 7   Changing hair colour
## Self review – page 172

1    Factors about a client that may affect the choice of hair colour include: client's wishes, shape and hairstyle, natural hair colour (level and tone), eye colour, skin colour, hair length, porosity, density and texture, and percentage of white hair.

2    The name of the test used on hair to determine the result of using a particular colour formulation on the hair is a test cutting.

3    A predisposition test should be carried out 24–48 hours before every oxidation tint application.

4    The term that describes hair's ability to absorb moisture is *porosity*.

5    *Level* when hair colouring indicates how light or dark the colour. Level 7 is a medium blonde.

6    Another term to describe a green tone in hair is *matt*.

7    The categories of artificial hair colour are: temporary, semi-permanent, quasi-permanent and permanent.

8    Oxidation tints act on the hair by swelling the hair, artificial pigment combines with oxygen in the cortex to form a coloured molecule too large to wash out, oxidation lightens the hair's natural pigment.

9    A two-step application is required when applying lightening oxidation colour to virgin hair as scalp heat accelerates the lightening action at the root area and if applied in a single application would result in the root area being too light.

10   During hair colouring tint staining may be removed from the skin by massaging with moist tint.

# Chapter 8   Changing hair curl
## Self review – page 213

1    Acidity or alkalinity of a substance.

2    4.5–7.9.

3    Glycerol monothioglycolate.

4    The seven stages of the permanent wave process are: client consultation, selection of equipment and products, preparation of the hair, perm wind/wrap, application of perm lotion, processing, neutralising.

5    The hair's capacity to absorb moisture.

6   A specialist shampoo or plain soapless shampoo.

7   Hair should be held at 90° to the head when normally winding hair while perming.

8   Heat speeds up the processing of perms and cold slows it down.

9   Excess water left in the hair may dilute the neutraliser, making it less effective.

10  Gently, without pulling on the hair.

11  Two chemicals often used in chemical hair relaxing products are *sodium hydroxide* and *ammonium thioglycolate*.

12  The term *base* refers, in relation to the hair relaxation process, to a petroleum cream designed to protect the scalp during the straightening process.

13  The client's hairline and face should be protected during chemical relaxing processes by the application to the complete hairline of barrier cream and moist cotton wool.

14  The three main stages of the chemical hair relaxation process are: processing, neutralising and conditioning.

15  The strand test is used to determine the hair's porosity and elasticity.

16  The hairdresser should wear protective gloves when working with relaxing/straightening chemicals.

17  Straightening products should be applied no closer than 5 cm from the scalp.

18  The main stages of a two-step perm are: rearrange the curl (straighten the hair), wind and curl the hair, neutralise the hair and condition the hair.

19  *Over-directing* when curler winding is to comb the hair upwards and away from the direction of the wind.

20  Little or no tension should be used when winding the hair during a two-step perm.

# Chapter 9   Massaging the scalp
## Self review – page 221

1   Erythema is increased capillary blood flow.

2   Contra-indications to scalp massage include:

    i      open sores or cuts on the scalp

    ii     contagious disorders

    iii    fresh scar tissue.

3   Sulphonated oil will emulsify with water.

4   Effleurage is a soothing stroking movement using the pads of the fingers and the palms of the hands.

5   Petrissage is a deep movement using the pads of the fingers. It is a co-ordinated gripping, rolling, kneading movement.

6   The friction massage movement is a brisk tweaking movement on the scalp.

7   The spiked applicator is used with the vibro massager on the scalp.

8  Hair should be dry during high frequency.

9  The high frequency electrode used on areas of thinning hair is the rake or comb.

10  The lymphatic flow removes waste products produced from metabolism.

# Chapter 10    Receiving clients

## Self review – page 235

1  No, it should only be used in line with the salon's data protection statement.

2  Clients should be greeted promptly, courteously and if possible by name when they visit the salon.

3  Attend to client enquiries, schedule appointments and manage the allocation of work to meet the client's expectation.

4  When booking a client, details of the client's name, service required and contact telephone number is normally required to be listed in the salon's appointment book.

5  When accepting a telephone appointment booking, confirm with the client the date, time, service to be offered and the name of the stylist.

6  *Phasing appointments* is to arrange appointments together to allow several services to be provided in the most efficient manner.

7  The action to be taken following receipt of a message for someone within the salon is to record the message and pass it on promptly to the relevant person, or place in the correct location for collection.

8  When accepting a cheque guarantee card in support of a cheque, check the card number, the start and expiry dates, signature, and level of payment guarantee.

9  The purpose of a cash *float* is to enable the salon to provide a range of cash change for client cash payments.

10  The floor limit is the maximum level that a transaction can reach before requiring card company authorisation.

# Chapter 11    Promoting products and services

## Self review – page 246

1  Questions that incorporate the words, *why, who, what, when* and *how.*

2  Trade Descriptions Act 1968.

3  Sale of Goods Act 1979.

4  Additional services, haircare products, haircare equipment.

5  Create the interest, generate the need, overcome objections, close the sale.

6  Recommend a product from a higher price range if appropriate.

7  Break problems down into small parts and deal with each one in turn.

8  What a product or service does and how it does it.

9   The advantages obtained, by the client, in the product or service used.

10  Asking for an opinion about a product or service, looking at themselves and a style book, showing an interest in something else happening in the salon, handling products or equipment, reading labels and instructions.

# Chapter 12   Working effectively

## Self review – page 259

1   The ideal occasion to raise team issues is within a team meeting.

2   Client information is confidential and should not be discussed or disclosed to others.

3   Deal with disputes and differences between colleagues in private. If they cannot be resolved, refer to the line manager.

4   Ways of learning about and developing new skills in hairdressing include:

    i      experimenting and practising on training heads

    ii     consumer fashion magazine articles

    iii    trade magazine articles and training sections

    iv    hairdressing textbooks

    v      watching video tapes that demonstrate hairdressing skills

    vi    watching demonstrations provided by colleagues, visiting trainers and technicians

    vii   visiting hairdressing and fashion exhibitions

    viii  attending training programmes at academies, colleges and training centres.

5   A Professional Development Plan records what you want to achieve within your career and the key stages in its achievement.

6   You usually undertake your performance review with your manager, supervisor or training manager.

7   The three key stages of a performance review are:

    i      agreeing targets for achievement

    ii     reviewing progress towards previously agreed targets

    iii    identifying training or development needs in order to achieve agreed targets.

8   SMARTER stands for:

Specific/Stretching

Measurable

Achievable

Relevant

Time bound

Evaluated

Resourced.

9   Gross misconduct means circumstances in which employees may be dismissed without notice, including:

   i     theft of property belonging to the employer, an employee or a client

   ii    deliberate damage to, or unauthorised use of, the employer's property

   iii   a serious breach of salon rules, including those for health and safety

   iv   violent, abusive, dangerous, bullying or intimidatory conduct

   v    serious sexual, racial or other harassment.

10  A grievance is likely to be a problem or concern that someone has about work, the salon environment or working relationships that an individual wants to raise and have addressed. These could include:

   i     a change in terms and conditions of work

   ii    introduction of new salon opening times or days

   iii   changes in staff structure and supervisory lines

   iv   concerns about health and safety

   v    discrimination

   vi   bullying or harassment

   vii  discrimination

   viii  bullying or harassment.

# INDEX